Exploiting Small Advantages

Eduard Gufeld

D1470729

B.T. Batsford Ltd, *London*

First published in 2001
© Eduard Gufeld and Oleg Stetsko 2001

ISBN 0 7134 8648 1

British Library Cataloguing-in-Publication Data.
A catalogue record for this book is
available from the British Library.

All rights reserved. No part of this book may be
reproduced, by any means, without prior permission
of the publisher.

Printed in Great Britain by
Creative Print and Design (Wales), Ebbw Vale
for the publishers,
B.T. Batsford Ltd,
9 Blenheim Court,
Brewery Road,
London N7 9NT

A member of the Chrysalis Group plc

A BATSFORD CHESS BOOK

Contents

With acknowledgement

to my co-author

Oleg Stetsko

Introduction

Very often a modern day chess game demands precise mastery in exploiting a small advantage. In a battle between two players who are roughly equal in strength, the accurate and by no means straightforward realisation of a small advantage is practically the only chance to win. It is a long time since the era of dashing attacks, the result of which was often the creation of unsightly pawn islands. The strength of average players has grown considerably, enabling them to compete fairly competently and surely against opponents who are slightly superior to them in practical strength, experience and knowledge. And therefore a mastery of typical methods of exploiting the smallest advantage is necessary for achieving success.

It is well-known that two types of advantage exist in chess—material and positional (later we will touch on another, highly interesting but little studied type of advantage—psychological). The chess classics asserted, not without reason, that to win it is necessary to have a combination of both forms of advantage. But what about those cases where only one is present? Then the way to victory becomes a narrow path, often hard to find, between a practical game and a study.

A classic example of such a way is the following game between two great experts of positional play, Mikhail Botvinnik and Tigran Petrosian, which was played in their World Championship match.

Petrosian - Botvinnik
World Championship match,
Moscow 1963
Grünfeld Defence

1 c4 g6 2 d4 ♘f6 3 ♘c3 d5 4 ♘f3 ♗g7 5 e3 0-0 6 ♗e2 dxc4 7 ♗xc4 c5 8 d5 e6

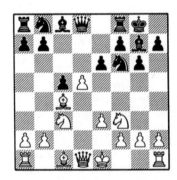

This move deserves separate commentary. We see here a method, characteristic of modern chess. Despite the obvious deterioriation of his pawn structure, Black consents to an early exchange of queens, taking into account that after this he will not really be able to play for a win. In a match situation such an approach is not infrequently linked to a definite strategy: playing for an advantage for White, and a draw with Black. But precisely this concession also represents a basis for handing the opponent an enduring small advantage. We will dwell on this theme in more detail in Chapter 1.

It goes without saying that, by offering an exchange of queens, M.Botvinnik was confident that he would be able to compensate for the, at first sight, small positional concession. Continuations of the type 8...a6, 8...♘bd7, 8...♘e8 would have led to complicated play.

9 dxe6 ♕xd1+ 10 ♔xd1 ♗xe6 11 ♗xe6 fxe6 12 ♔e2

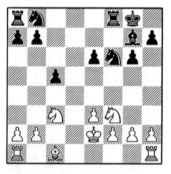

A position has arisen which is characteristic for the theme of our book: White has a small advantage in the endgame, which is determined first and foremost by his better pawn structure—two pawn islands against three for Black. But here is the way T.Petrosian assessed this factor: "White's pawns make a more favourable impression, in the first instance due to Black's e6 pawn being cut off from its colleagues. Of course it is hard to imagine that White can somehow manage to create threats and win it. But the organic defect of the isolated pawn lies not only in the fact that it can become an object of

attack, but to an equal extent that the square or squares in front of it can serve as outposts for the opponent's pieces".

12...♘c6

The first critical moment. There can be no doubt that such a natural developing move would be made by many players. However, further events show that already here Black should seek a plan to neutralise White's possibilities. The most active of these is 12...♘d5 (getting the bishop on g7 into play) 13 ♘e4 ♘d7 14 ♘fg5 ♘c7 15 ♖d1 ♖ad8 16 ♘d6 and, though the assessment of the position has not changed, Black nevertheless has it easier than in the game.

Nevertheless, taking into account the role of the e4 square, G.Kasparov suggested preventing the manoeuvre of the knight to g5 by the radical 12...h6!. Then the way to the e4 square lies through 13 ♘d2 ♘d5 14 ♘de4 ♘xc3+ 15 ♘xc3 ♘c6, but here Black's pieces cooperate more harmoniously and it is harder for White to strengthen his position. We should mention that 13 ♘e5 is harmless after 13...g5 14 ♖d1 ♘d5! 15 ♘xd5 ♗xe5 when Black stands no worse.

13 ♖d1

Stronger is 13 ♘g5!, since Black could now prevent this by 13...h6!.

13...♖ad8?! 14 ♖xd8 ♖xd8 15 ♘g5! ♖e8 16 ♘ge4 ♘xe4

More flexible is 16...b6!? 17 ♘xf6+ ♗xf6 18 ♘e4 ♗e7 19 b3 e5 20 ♗b2 ♖d8 21 f3 ♔f7 and, as the dark-squared bishop is included in the defence, it is not easy for White to find the key to Black's position.

17 ♘xe4 b6 18 ♖b1 ♘b4 19 ♗d2!

Emphasising the illusory nature of the capture 19...♘xa2?, in view of

20 罝a1 ②b4 21 ♗xb4 cxb4 22 罝xa7 with the clearly better endgame. In the event of 19 a3 ②d5 Black would have the time to offer an exchange by ...②d5-f6.

19...②d5 20 a4 罝c8 21 b3 ♗f8

Black threatens to activate his forces by 22...c4 23 罝c1 cxb3 24 罝xc8 b2 25 罝c1 bxc1=♕ 26 ♗xc1 ♗e7 when his chances of a draw are heightened.

22 罝c1 ♗e7 23 b4!

White logically carries out his plan to create a second weakness in Black's position.

23...c4

On the passive 23...♔f7 24 罝c4! h6 25 bxc5 bxc5 26 a5! White increases his advantage (G.Kasparov).

24 b5!

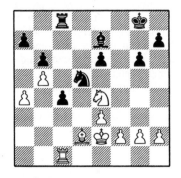

24...♔f7?

The second critical moment. M.Botvinnik remains passive, whereas the only way to obtain counterplay was to 'give up' the c-pawn: 24...♗a3! 25 罝c2 c3 26 ♗xc3 罝c4! 27 ♔d3 罝xa4 and though White, as before, retains a small advantage, both after 28 ♗d2 ♗e7 29 罝c6 罝a3+ 30 ♔c2 ♔f7 31 ②d6+ ♗xd6 32 罝xd6, and also 28 罝a2 罝xe4 29 罝xa3 ②xc3 30 ♔xc3 罝e5 31 罝xa7 罝xb5 32 罝b7 罝c5+ 33 ♔d3 b5, Black retains chances of a draw (G.Kasparov).

25 ♗c3 ♗a3 26 罝c2 ②xc3+ 27 罝xc3 ♗b4 28 罝c2 ♔e7?

This move shows how difficult it is to conduct a defence in such positions, even at the level of reigning world champion. How many times Black has been reduced to passive defence, allowing White step by step to increase his advantage. The last line of defence might be the minor piece endgame after 28...e5 29 ②d2 c3 30 ②e4 ♔e6 31 ♔d3 罝d8+ 32 ♔c4 罝d2 33 ♔b3 罝xc2 34 ♔xc2 ♔d5 35 ②xc3+ ♔c4 36 ②e4 ♗e7 and, though Black is a pawn down, he might find a drawing chance.

29 ②d2! c3

The pawn cannot be saved: 29...♗xd2 30 ♔xd2 ♔d6 31 ♔c3 ♔c5 32 罝d2 etc.

30 ②e4 ♗a5 31 ♔d3 罝d8+ 32 ♔c4 罝d1 33 ②xc3 罝h1?!

More stubborn was 33...♗xc3 34 ♔xc3 罝h1 35 h3 ♔d7.

34 ②e4!

White returns the pawn in order to obtain full domination with his forces. The rest is a matter of technique.

34...罝xh2 35 ♔d4 ♔d7 36 g3 ♗b4 37 ♔e5 罝h5+ 38 ♔f6 ♗e7+ 39 ♔g7 e5 40 罝c6 罝h1 41 ♔f7! 罝a1 42 罝e6 ♗d8 43 罝d6+ ♔c8 44 ♔e8 ♗c7 45 罝c6 罝d1 46 ②g5 罝d8+ 47 ♔f7 罝d7+ 48 ♔g8 Black resigned.

In this game the 9th world champion demonstrated a high level of endgame technique, a characteristic of most outstanding players of the past and present.

For less experienced practical players we would like to add that without the possession of endgame technique it will be difficult to reckon on any high level chess achievements.

By way of an example we recall an episode in which a quite experienced rated player agreed a draw in the following position.

At first sight there was nothing surprising in this, as the position seems quite drawn. Yet all the same White can achieve victory in an original way:

1 c6+! ♔e7 2 ♔c5 ♔d8 3 ♔b4! ♔c8 4 ♔b5 ♔b8 5 ♔c5! ♔a7 6 ♔d4 ♔a6 7 ♔e5 ♔b6 8 ♔d5 ♔a6 9 ♔e6 with a decisive invasion of the king on d7.

This winning method was looked at in the pre-war period by the well-known specialist in pawn endings, N.Grigoriev. We should mention that the work of this most important endgame theoretician is a great help in understanding endgame secrets.

Achieving a necessary standard in this stage of the game is obligatory for any chessplayer in the process of improvement. And yet high endgame technique not infrequently proves impotent when met by powerful resistance.

In this book are gathered interesting examples of complicated endgames, the majority of which have not found their way into endgame manuals. In these endgames, to realise a small advantage, the stronger side has to travel a difficult, and at times also long road. In certain cases even a high level of technique has let down, along this way, even experienced masters. We will come across, dear reader, deep and original ideas, with paradoxical and surprising resources. And so, let us mobilise our attention and imagination. We are about to set off on a fascinating journey along endgame paths.

1 Structural Concessions

As a rule the gaining of a small advantage is the consequence of a measured battle, where the attacking and defending sides are worthy of each another. But not infrequently the prerequisite for such an advantage lies in the choice of an opening variation, anticipating the structures of changing positions, conditioned by the pawn formation. Related to this are positions defined by mutual pawn chains, advanced pawns, cramping of the opponent's pawn complex, characterised by the presence of pawn islands etc. Of course, from the point of view of looking at the themes, an overall examination of opening structures is not possible and therefore our aim is only to draw the reader's attention to critical points in the choice of several opening schemes and their possible consequences.

One example of a structurally changing position appears in the so-called "French endgame", which is often reached from the classical variation of the French Defence: 1 e4 e6 2 d4 d5 3 ②c3 ②f6 4 ♗g5 ♗e7 5 e5 ②fd7 6 ♗xe7 ♕xe7 7 f4 a6 8 ②f3 c5 9 dxc5 ♕xc5 10 ♕d4 ②c6 11 ♕xc5 ②xc5

A characteristic feature of this type of position, with the cramping pawn on e5, is the presence of a solid base on d4 for the knight, from where it controls the most important squares on the board. With queens still on, this is not felt so much since Black has counterattacking resources (therefore it is usual to play the preliminary 9...②c6). In the endgame the influence of the centralised knight is increased and White has a small but enduring advantage. Here is one classical example on this theme.

Konstantinopolsky - Lilienthal
Moscow 1936

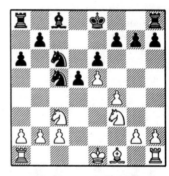

12 ♗d3 ♔e7 13 ♔d2 h6?

"When there is a lack of good moves, a bad one will be made"—was Siegbert Tarrasch's comment on a move like this in one of his own games. Such a prophylactic (but also weakening the position) move should be treated with great respect and made only in case of need. Why is it bad?

The fact is that the only means of freeing himself from the influence of the e5 pawn is to undermine it by ...f7-f6.

However, with the pawn on h6, this leads to an irreparable weakening of the kingside and White obtains the possibility, by means of h2-h4-h5, to completely paralyse the pawn chain e6-f7-g7-h6 and attack the king's flank. Therefore it would be stronger to play 13...f6 at once.

14 ♘e2!

It is important to consolidate the d4 square with the knight.

14...♗d7 15 ♘ed4 ♖ac8 16 ♖ae1 ♖c7

Black develops his pieces on the best squares, but he does not succeed in exploiting the open c-file whereas White can attack on the king's flank.

17 g4 ♘b4

He should hold up White's advance by 17...h5! 18 h3 ♘xd3 19 cxd3 ♘xd4 20 ♘xd4 hxg4 21 hxg4 ♖cc8, though even here White has the advantage.

18 a3 ♘bxd3 19 cxd3 ♖hc8 20 ♖c1

Completely levelling Black's play on the c-file.

20...♔d8 21 h4 ♘a4 22 ♖xc7 ♖xc7 23 b3 ♘b6 24 h5!

A typical position for the start of a kingside pawn storm. The e5 and h5

pawns blockade the king's flank, depriving Black of any sort of activity—all he can do is wait.

24...♔e7 25 g5

The signal for the attack. White prepares a rook invasion.

25...♖c8 26 gxh6 gxh6 27 ♖g1 ♖h8

After 27...♔f8 28 ♘h2 the knight invades on f6.

28 ♘h2 ♗e8

Better was 28...♗c8, providing additional defence to the f5 square, but psychologically it is difficult to "develop" the bishop to its starting square!

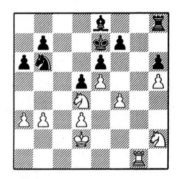

29 ♘g4

An inaccuracy, he should move the king closer to the centre of events—29 ♔e3, since now, as shown by the famous endgame specialist, Moscow master N.Grigoriev, necessary was 29...♖g8!, counting on compensating for the subsequent attack 30 f5! by a win of the h5 pawn: 30...♖g5 31 f6+ ♔d8 32 ♔e3 ♘d7 33 ♘df3 (not 33 ♔f4 because of 33...♘xf6! 34 exf6 e5+) 33...♖xh5. Yet, all the same, White retains an unpleasant initiative by 34 d4, since he can strengthen his position by a transfer of the knight to f4 along the route ♘g4-f2-d3-f4, though to win is not quite so simple: Black's pawn mass is quite compact. However Black cannot feel safe and White will increase his advantage.

29...♘d7? 30 f5 exf5

No help is the counter 30...f6 because of 31 ♘xf6! ♘xf6 32 ♖g7+ ♗f7 (32...♔d8 33 ♘xe6+ ♔c8 34 exf6) 33 fxe6 ♘xh5 34 ♖xf7+ ♔d8 35 ♘f5.

31 ♘xf5+ ♔e6 32 ♘g7+ ♔e7 33 d4

Black's pieces are practically move-bound. The attempt to break free only accelerates the end.

33...f6 34 e6 ♘b6 35 ♖e1 ♖g8 36 ♘f5+ ♔d8

After 36...♔f8 Black is mated in two moves.

37 e7+ ♔c7 38 ♘xf6 ♖g2+ Black resigned.

An analogous pawn structure arises in the so-called Classical system of the Caro-Kann: **1 e4 c6 2 d4 d5 3 ♘c3 dxe4 4 ♘xe4 ♗f5 5 ♘g3 ♗g6 6 h4 h6 7 ♘f3 ♘d7 8 h5 ♗h7 9 ♗d3 ♗xd3 10 ♕xd3 ♕c7 11 ♗d2 e6 12 0-0-0 0-0-0 13 ♕e2 ♘gf6 14 ♘e5 ♘xe5** (the alternative is 14...♘b6) **15 dxe5**

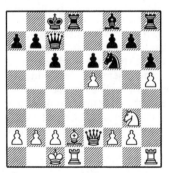

It is worth looking at this position in more detail. The e5 and h5 pawns paralyse the king's flank which secures White a lasting space advan-

tage. Black is restricted in his activity and here it is appropriate to recall the thoughts of Siegbert Tarrasch, that a cramped position bears the germs of defeat.

The attempt to free himself can lead to the creation of new weaknesses. Upon the move ...g7-g6, weak squares appear on f7 and h6. After a prepared undermining by ...f7-f6 White exchanges the e5 pawn in return for new positional concessions. After the recapture on f6 with a pawn, a whole complex of weak pawns, e6, f6, h6, is created. Therefore one usually takes back on f6 with a piece, but then the pawns on e6 and g7 are weak and White has a clear plan to realise his advantage: after the appearance of the bishop on f6, comes the advance g2-g4-g5, while if it is the knight that lands on f6, then the white bishop sets up a blockade on the e5 square.

Let us look at the main knight moves: 15...♘d7 and 15...♘d5.

Spassky - Petrosian
World Championship match
Moscow 1966

15...♘d7

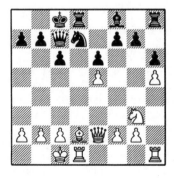

16 f4 ♗e7 17 ♘e4

In the game Suetin-Pachman, Titovo Uzice 1966, followed 17 ♗e3 ♕a5 (after 17...f6 18 exf6 ♘xf6 19 ♗d2 ♖d6 20 ♖de1 ♖hd8 21 ♗c3 ♖6d7 22 ♗e5 ♗d6 23 ♖hf1! the blockade of the e5 square will not be lifted: after an exchange the f-file is opened for the rooks) 18 ♔b1 ♘c5 19 c3 ♖xd1+ 20 ♖xd1 ♖d8 21 ♖d4 ♖xd4 22 ♗xd4 ♕d8 23 ♕c2 a5 24 ♘f1 ♕d5 25 ♘e3 ♕e4 26 ♗xc5 ♕xc2+ 27 ♔xc2 ♗xc5 28 ♘c4 a4 29 ♔d3 ♔d7 30 g4 b5 31 ♘d2 ♗g1 32 ♔e4 c5 33 b3 axb3 34 axb3 ♔e7 35 ♔f3 b4 (White threatened 36 ♘e4) 36 cxb4 cxb4 37 ♔e4 ♗c5 38 ♘f3 ♔d7 39 ♘d4 g6 40 ♔d3 gxh5 41 gxh5 ♔c7 42 ♘c4 ♗b6 43 ♘b5+ ♔d7 44 ♘d4 ♔c7. The b4 pawn is doomed, but Suetin played the inaccurate 45 ♘e2?! ♔c6 46 ♔xb4 ♔d5 and Black obtained counterplay. Stronger was 45 ♘c2! ♔b7 46 ♘xb4! ♗e3 47 f5 exf5 48 ♔d5 ♔c7 49 ♘c2 f4 50 ♘d4 with real winning chances.

· **17...♘c5 18 ♘c3 f6 19 exf6 ♗xf6 20 ♕c4 ♕b6 21 b4! ♘a6**

The transfer to an endgame is unpromising: 21...♕a6 22 ♕xa6 ♘xa6 23 ♘e4 ♗e7 24 a3 ♘c7 25 ♗c3 ♖hg8 26 ♗e5 and after further exchanges the breakthrough with the g-pawn decides.

22 ♘e4 ♘c7 23 ♖he1 ♖d4 24 ♕b3 ♕b5 25 c3 ♖xe4!

The best choice when compared to 25...♖dd8 26 ♘c5.

26 ♖xe4 ♕xh5 27 ♕c4 ♕f5 28 ♕e2 h5 29 ♗e1 ♖e8 30 g3 a5 31 bxa5 ♕xa5 32 ♕c2 ♕f5 33 ♖a4 g5 34 fxg5 ♗xg5+ 35 ♔b1 ♕xc2+ 36 ♔xc2 e5

After the exchange of queens the game passes to the technical stage. As before, White's advantage is small.

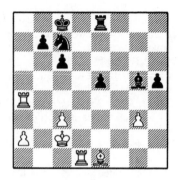

For the exchange, Black has quite good compensation—the more so that Tigran Petrosian is in his element. Not for nothing is he considered one of the great defensive players. Testimony to this is the time that Spassky needed to realise his small material advantage—a whole 55 moves. But let the reader exercise patience, there is much of interest on such a long path. Here we come across one of the most important methods of play in the endgame.

Festina lente—more haste, less speed. This was one of the favourite sayings of the Roman emperor Octavian Augustus. Surprisingly it is applied to the style of playing chess endings. This is what the well-known Soviet master S.Belavenets wrote apropos this: "The rule 'do not rush' to many might seem paradoxical, whereas it shines through in nearly all endings of the great masters of the endgame. Look closely at the endgames of Capablanca and Flohr and you will see how slowly, at times tediously, they realised their advantage. Repeating moves in the endgame plays a great role. Omitting the fact that they gained time for thinking, it is possible to mention that, by repeating moves, the active side obtains a well-known psychological advantage. Defending a position which is worse, frequently untenable, leads to new weaknesses and facilitates the task of the opponent".

For the reader there will be quite a few opportunities in future chapters of the book to convince himself of this approach to playing endings. But here, for a start, let us turn our attention to White's manoeuvre ♖a4-e4-a4-e4 during the course of the next few moves.

37 ♖e4 ♘d5 38 ♗f2 ♘f6 39 ♖a4 ♔c7 40 ♗c5 ♘d5 41 ♖e4 b6 42 ♗g1

After 42 c4 bxc5 43 cxd5 ♔d6 44 ♖a4 ♗e3! 45 ♖a6 ♗d4 46 dxc6 ♖f8 and Black has quite good counterplay.

42...♗d8 43 ♖f1 ♘f6 44 ♖e2 c5 45 ♖f5 ♔d6 46 a4!

A deep understanding of the position. White intends to convert all Black's pawns into potential objects of attack.

46...♔d5 47 ♔d3 ♘g4 48 ♖b2

White will not allow any chances of counterplay after 48 ♖xh5 ♖f8.

48...♖h8

49 a5! c4+

On 49...bxa5 follows 50 ♖b5.

50 ♔e2 ♔e4 51 ♖f7 bxa5 52 ♖b8 a4 53 ♖c8 ♗f6 54 ♖xc4+

A slight inaccuracy. To this pawn might also have been added an

exchange of rooks: 54 ♖xh8 ♗xh8 55 ♖c7, which would increase his advantage.

54...♔f5 55 ♖a7

The more direct 55 ♖xa4 ♖c8! 56 c4 ♖b8 57 ♖a2 ♖b3 would have given Black chances of counterplay.

55...a3

White would have had more worries after 55...♖d8!? 56 ♖cxa4 ♗g5!.

56 ♖xa3 ♖b8 57 ♖b4 ♖c8 58 c4 ♗e7 59 c5 e4 60 ♖a7 ♗f6 61 ♖h7

Stronger is 61 ♖aa4!.

61...♔g6 62 ♖d7 ♔f5 63 ♖d5+ ♗e5 64 ♖b6 e3!

In this game, T.Petrosian, for the umpteenth time, demonstrates his ability to find counterplay. After 64...♖a8 65 ♗d4 ♖a2+ 66 ♗b2! ♖a5 67 ♗xe5 ♘xe5 68 ♖h6! would have extinguished the last centre of resistance. Now, however, after 65 ♗xe3 ♔e4 66 ♖d3 ♖xg3 the outcome of the struggle is unclear.

65 ♔f3 ♘f6 66 ♖d3 ♖xc5 67 ♗xe3 ♖c2 68 ♖d8 ♖c3 69 ♔e2 ♖c2+ 70 ♔d1 ♖c3 71 ♗f2 ♘e4?

Even the greats make their mistakes! Simpler was to stand his ground with 71... ♖a3 or give preference to 71...♘g4.

72 ♖f8+ ♔g5

It is worth going back with 72...♘f6, since no good is 73 ♖fxf6+ ♗xf6 74 ♖xf6+ ♔xf6 75 ♗d4+ ♔g5! 76 ♗xc3 h4 with a draw. Now, however, White forces the exchange of rooks.

73 ♖b5! ♖d3+

73...♘xf2+?! 74 ♖xf2 ♖e3 75 ♖e2 would have led to a simple technical endgame.

74 ♔e2 ♖d5 75 ♖xd5 ♘c3+ 76 ♔f3 ♘xd5 77 ♖a8

Useless is 77 ♔e4 ♘f6+ and 78 ♔xe5? is not possible because of 78...♘d7+.

77...♔f5 78 ♖a5 ♔e6 79 ♗e1 ♘f6 80 ♖b5 ♘d5 81 ♗d2 ♗g7 82 ♗c1 ♗e5 83 ♗b2 ♗c7 84 ♖c5 ♗d6 85 ♖c1 ♘e7 86 ♖e1+ ♔f5 87 ♖a1 ♘c6 88 ♖a6 ♗e5 89 ♖xc6 ♗xb2 90 ♖c5+ ♔g6 91 ♔f4 ♗g7 **Black resigned.**

A titanic battle!

Akopian - Magomedov
Minsk 1990

15...♘d5

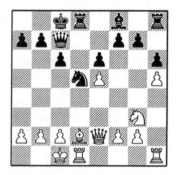

16 f4 ♗e7

In the game Spassky-Botvinnik, Moscow 1966, was played 16...c5 17 c4 ♘b4 18 ♗xb4 ♖xd1+ 19 ♖xd1 cxb4 20 ♘e4 ♗e7 21 ♘d6+ ♔b8, when, instead of the impulsive 22 ♘xf7?! ♖f8 23 ♘d6 ♖xf4, White could have held on to his advantage in two ways: 22 g3 ♖f8 23 ♔b1 a6 24 ♕g4 or 22 ♕e4 ♕c6 23 ♕xc6 bxc6 24 c5.

17 ♘e4 ♕b6 18 ♖h3 c5 19 ♖f1 ♖he8 20 ♖hf3 ♕c7 21 g4

While Black is forced to adopt waiting tactics, White methodically prepares the break f4-f5.

21...♖h8

Possibly stronger is 21...♘b4, followed by 22...♘c6.

22 ♗e1! ♖d7 23 ♗g3 ♘b4 24 f5 ♕c6 25 a3 ♘d5 26 fxe6 fxe6 27 ♖f7 ♖hd8 28 c4 ♘b6 29 ♘d6+

♔b8 30 ♖xe7 ♖xe7 31 ♗h4 ♖ed7 32 ♗xd8 ♖xd8 33 ♖f7 ♘c8 34 ♖xb7+ ♔a8 35 ♖xg7 ♘xd6 36 exd6 ♖xd6 37 ♕f1 ♖d8 38 ♔b1 ♕e4+ 39 ♔a1 e5 40 ♔a2 ♕c6 41 ♕f7 ♕b6 42 g5 a5 43 ♖g8 ♖xg8 44 ♕xg8+ ♔a7 45 ♕g7+ ♔a8 46 ♕xh6 ♕c7 47 ♕f8+ ♔b7 48 g6 **Black resigned.**

In the Panov Attack against the Caro-Kann Defence 1 e4 c6 2 d4 d5 3 exd5 cxd5 4 c4 ♘f6 5 ♘c3 after 5...♘c6 6 ♘f3 we frequently meet the following practically forced variation: 6...♗g4 7 cxd5 ♘xd5 8 ♕b3 ♗xf3 9 gxf3 e6 10 ♕xb7 ♘xd4 11 ♗b5+ ♘xb5 12 ♕c6+ ♔e7 13 ♕xb5 ♕d7 14 ♘xd5+ ♕xd5 15 ♕xd5 exd5

In the arising endgame White's doubled f-pawns are compensated by the possibility of an attack on the weak black pawns on d5 and a7. The question is whether White is able to exploit the time required by Black to develop his bishop, though the overall structure of the position is such that it is more difficult for Black to defend his weaknesses than for White to attack them.

Beliavsky - Wells
London 1985

16 0-0

The main plan is considered to be queenside castling after 16 ♗e3, though the open position of the white king allows Black to create counterplay.

A.Beliavsky endeavours to deprive Black of these possibilities and prove the worth of his plan.

16...♔e6 17 ♖e1+ ♔f5 18 ♖d1!

A fine prophylactic manoeuvre. White gains time for an attack on the isolated d5 pawn and at the same time prevents it from advancing. In the event of the routine 18 ♗e3 ♗e7 19 ♖ac1 Black has time to support the d-pawn: 19...♗f6! 20 ♖c5 ♖hd8 21 b4 ♔g6 22 b5 d4.

18...♖d8

If he attempts to support the d5 pawn with the other rook, 18...♔e6 19 ♖d3 ♗c5 20 ♗f4 ♖hd8, White advantageously exploits the c-file: 21 ♖c1 ♗b6 22 ♖c6+ ♔f5 23 ♗c7.

19 ♗e3 ♖d7 20 ♖ac1 ♗e7

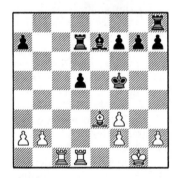

21 ♖d4!

A deep penetration into the position. It is obvious that Black plans to place his bishop on f6 and advance the d-pawn. With a fine rook manoeuvre White intends not only to attack the a7 pawn but also to check on f4, since the open position of the king allows maximum exploitation of the activity of the rooks.

21...♗f6

Black does not sense the danger. It was necessary to prevent the threat of check by 21...g5!, while on 22 ♖c6 possible is 22...♖hd8 23 ♔f1 ♗f6 22 ♖b4 ♗e5, preparing the advance of the d-pawn.

22 ♖f4+ ♔e5

Upsetting the harmony of the king and bishop. But on the natural 22...♔e6 follows 23 b3 ♖hd8 (not possible is 23...d4 because of 24 ♖e4+ ♔d5 25 ♗xd4 ♗xd4 26 ♖xd4+ ♔xd4 27 ♖d1+ winning a pawn) 24 ♖e1 ♔d6 25 ♖a4 ♖a8 26 ♗f4+ and the king is in danger.

23 ♖a4 d4

Also here this move is premature. More stubborn was 22...♖b8 24 b3 ♖bb7.

24 ♖a5+! ♔e6

Not possible was 24...♖d5 because of 25 ♗xd4+.

25 ♗f4 ♖b7

After 25...♗d8? winning is 26 ♖e5+ ♔f6 27 ♖c6+.

26 b3 ♖d8 27 ♔f1 d3

It is a natural reaction to prevent the transfer of the king to d3, but nevertheless worth considering was 27...h6 followed by ...g7-g5. Now White gets the chance to carry out a roundabout manoeuvre along the open fourth rank.

28 ♖e1+ ♔d7 29 ♖e4! ♗e7

Watching out for his opponent's rook threats he reconciles himself to exchanging a pair of rooks which reduces the potential of the d3 pawn. It was necessary to hold on by 29...♔c6.

30 ♖d5+ ♔e8

Also here, more active was 30...♔c6, intending, on 31 ♖xd8

罩xd8 32 罩d4, the possibility
32...罩d7.

31 罩xd8+ ♔xd8 32 ♔e1 ♗b4+
33 ♗d2 ♗c5 34 ♗e3 ♗b4+ 35 ♔d1
♗c3 36 罩c4 ♗e5 37 f4 ♗f6 38 罩a4
♗c3 39 ♗xa7 罩b4?

The bishop ending is won without
difficulty and so better was
39...罩b5, aiming at the kingside
pawns.

40 罩xb4 ♗xb4 41 ♗d4 g6 42 h3
♔d7 43 ♗b2 ♔c6 44 a3 ♗c5 45 f3
♗d6 46 f5 ♗f4 47 a4 gxf5 48 ♗d4
♔d5 49 ♗f2 ♔c6 50 b4 ♔d5 51 a5
Black resigned.

In modern practice a small advantage is not infrequently a consequence of tournament strategy,
when the choice of opening
variation is made according to the
principle: play for a win with White,
for a draw with Black. Upon this,
the defending side strives for an
early exchange of queens,
reconciling himself to definite
concessions, considering these insufficient for the opponent to play
for a win. Most frequently these
concessions reveal themselves in the
form of a significant lag in development or disruption of the pawn
structure with the formation of an
isolated pawn, and also to separate
pawn islands.

For the first type—an advantage
in development—it is possible, by
way of an example, to cite the so-
called "English endgame" obtained
after **1 c4 c5 2 ♘c3 ♘c6 3 ♘f3 ♘f6
4 g3 d5 5 d4 e6 6 cxd5 ♘xd5 7
♗g2 cxd4 8 ♘xd4 ♘xc3 9 bxc3
♘xd4 10 ♕xd4 ♕xd4 11 cxd4**,
which Vladimir Kramnik handles in
virtuoso style.

Kramnik - Lautier
Horgen 1995

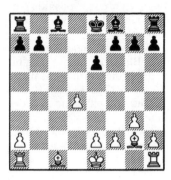

11...♗d6

11...♗b4+ 12 ♗d2 ♗xd2+ 13
♔xd2 ♔e7 14 罩hc1 罩d8 15 罩c7+
罩d7 16 罩ac1 ♔d8 17 罩xd7+ ♔xd7
is frequently played, although even
here the endgame is not quite so
simple for Black. For example,
Kramnik-Lautier, Belgrade 1995,
continued 18 g4 h6 19 f4 罩b8 20 g5
b6 21 gxh6 gxh6 22 罩c3 ♗b7 23
♗xb7 罩xb7 24 罩h3 罩c7 25 罩xh6
罩c4 26 罩h3 when after 26...罩xd4+?
27 罩d3 White won the pawn ending, exploiting the distant passed
h-pawn. Necessary was 26...罩a4!,
provoking 27 a3, which allows him,
after 27...罩xd4+ 28 罩d3 罩xd3+ 29
♔xd3 ♔e7, to create a rival passed
pawn more quickly.

12 0-0 罩b8

"It is impossible to understand..."
said V.Kramnik, in evaluating the
present situation, "...at what point
Black made a mistake. It is quite
possible that there wasn't one and
J.Lautier's defeat was simply the
consequence of an unpleasant position, which is very difficult to defend". He considered 12...0-0 more
flexible, after which 13 e4 can be
met by 13...e5 14 d5 f5 or 13...罩d8.

13 e4 0-0

After 13...b6 14 ♗b2 ♗b7 15 ♖ac1, in connection with the threat of e4-e5 he will not manage to avert the invasion of the rooks, since, on 15...♔d7, unpleasant is 16 d5! exd5 17 exd5 f6 18 ♗h3+ ♔d8 19 ♗e6.

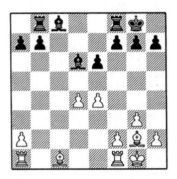

14 e5!

With this move White not only guarantees himself control over the the c-file but also prepares the breakthrough with a pawn to d6.

14...♗e7

Weaker is 14...♗c7?!, after which 15 ♗a3 ♖d8 16 ♖ac1 ♗b6 17 ♗d6 leads to a difficult position.

15 ♗e3 ♗d7 16 ♖fc1 ♖fc8 17 ♖xc8+ ♗xc8 18 ♖c1 ♔f8 19 ♗h3 ♔e8 20 d5 ♗d7 21 d6 ♗d8 22 ♗g2 b6 23 f4 ♖c8 24 ♔f2 ♖xc1 25 ♗xc1

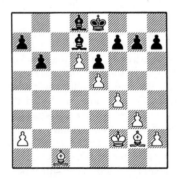

The result of the virtually forced ten-move operation is a four-bishop endgame where White retains a slight but firm advantage. This is how V.Kramnik himself evaluated the position: "At first sight Black seems to have great chances of a draw but upon closer examination it does not appear quite so simple: the picture is spoiled by the very bad bishop on d8; another trump for White is the strong pawn on d6. The only problem is to formulate and carry out a break on the king's or queen's flank. For this reason Black, as far as possible, should not touch his pawns. Over the next moves White's plan is quite clear: he must transfer his king to the region of the b4 square, possibly try to advance a4-a5 or undertake other active operations. In reply to this Black has no real argument: he simply has to wait".

25...♗b5 26 ♗e4 h6

After 26...g6?! Black would have to reckon on the weakness of the f7 pawn.

27 ♗e3 ♔d7 28 ♔e1 ♗c6 29 ♗d3 ♗d5 30 a3 f6

The alternatives: should he continue to hold on passively or, as it were, rid himself of the weak f7 pawn? Black decides on the second.

31 ♔d2 fxe5 32 fxe5 ♔c6

32...♗g5 is a loss of time after 33 ♗f4, followed by h2-h4, since it is unfavourable for Black to exchange on f4.

33 ♔c3 ♗f3 34 ♗c4 ♗d5 35 ♗a6 ♗f3 36 ♔d4 ♗d5 37 a4 ♗b3

Possibly it is worth voluntarily abandoning the c6 square: 37...♔d7 38 ♗b5+ ♔c8, though even here White has an obvious advantage.

38 ♗b5+ ♔b7 39 ♗d7!

The first part of the operation has been completed: the black king is cut off from the kingside to which White now directs his attention.

39...♗d5 40 ♔c3 ♗a2 41 ♔b4

Bearing in mind the intended plan, more accurate was an immediate blockade of the king's flank with the move 41 h4!, since now Black could prevent this by 41...g5!.

41...♗d5 42 h4!

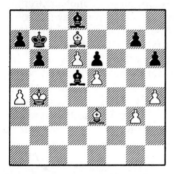

Beginning the second phase of the operation. Now, with the g7 and h6 pawns fixed, White can prepare the transfer of the dark-squared bishop along the route ♗c1-a3-f8 and, though he has to sacrifice the d6 pawn for this, the prospects of creating an outside passed pawn on the kingside clearly increase White's chances.

42...♗a2 43 ♗d2

A struggle for tempo, the point of which is revealed three moves later. As pointed out by V.Kramnik, after the direct 43 ♗c1 ♗d5 44 ♔c3 ♗a2 45 ♗a3 ♗d5 46 ♗e8?!, Black has 47...♗c6 and White loses a tempo compared to what happens in the game. However, even here, he could lose a move by 46 ♗b4.

43...♗d5 44 ♗c1 ♗a2 45 ♔c3 ♗d5 46 ♗a3 ♗a2

After 46...a6 White continues the struggle for tempo by 47 ♗b4, since after 47...a5 48 ♗a3 ♗a2 appears the possibility of the manoeuvre 49 ♗b5 ♗d5 50 ♗c4 ♔c6 51 ♔d4.

47 ♗e8 ♗d5 48 d7 ♗c6 49 ♗f8 ♗xa4 50 ♗xg7 ♔c7 51 ♗xh6 ♗xd7 52 ♗f7 ♔c6 53 h5

Now the h-pawn will cost a piece, but all the same an even quicker way to victory was 53 ♗g5 ♗c7 54 ♔d4, when the king is denied any activity.

53...♔d5 54 ♗g7 ♗g5 55 g4 ♔e4 56 h6 ♗xh6 57 ♗xh6 ♔xe5 58 g5 ♔f5 59 g6 ♔f6 60 ♗g5+ ♔g7 61 ♔d4 ♗a4 62 ♔e5 ♗c2 63 ♗f6+ ♔f8 64 ♔f4 Black resigned.

Many treatises have been written on the theme of the isolated pawn. The overall verdict is that this pawn needs to be blockaded and steps taken to show its defects in the endgame.

We come across this again when examining the game Ivanchuk-Korchnoi, Lvov 2000 (chapter 8). Here we restrict ourselves to an example of another approach to this problem. In one of the variations of the Tarrasch French: **1 e4 e6 2 d4 d5 3 ♘d2 c5 4 exd5 exd5 5 ♗b5+** a passive but quite reliable way of achieving a draw is reckoned to be the continuation **5...♗d7 6 ♕e2+ ♕e7 7 ♗xd7+ ♘xd7 8 dxc5 ♕xe2+ 9 ♘xe2 ♗xc5 10 ♘b3 ♗b6 11 ♗f4 ♘gf6 12 f3 0-0 13 0-0-0 ♖ac8**

A classical way of playing the position with the isolated pawn on d5 is considered to be the blockading 14 ♘bd4 followed by a siege. Thus say the majority. But the possibilities of chess are far broader and bring out those players who go beyond traditional thought. Like Bent Larsen who, having failed to win a series of games after blockading the "isolani", noted: "You don't need to blockade the isolated pawn—you need to win it".

Beliavsky - Bareev
Munich 1994

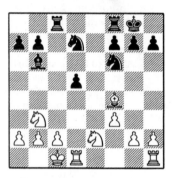

14 ♘c3!

Larsen's thoughts in action. As Beliavsky revealed, this move occurred to him only during the game. White attacks the pawn and after it advances to the d4 square it becomes clear that Black still does not free himself of his problems. Things are not so simple but of course such a move is linked to concrete calculation.

14...♖c4 15 ♗g3 ♖fc8 16 ♔b1!

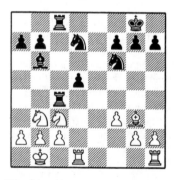

16...d4

Black compensates for the threat to his d5 pawn with an attack on the c2 pawn. With his king move, White provokes the advance of the d-pawn, since upon the passive 16...♘f8 17 ♖he1 ♘e6 18 ♗e5 still

the move has to be made: 18...d4 19 ♘b5! ♖xc2 20 ♘d6 and White begins to hunt it with his rooks: 20...♖8c6 21 ♘f5!. The mobility and energy of this knight is quite a good illustration of the theme "perpetual motion": Black is forced to part with the exchange— 21...♖6c4 22 ♘d2 ♖c5 23 ♗d6 ♖xb2+ (23...♖xd2 24 ♘e7+) 24 ♔xb2 ♖xf5 25 ♖e5 with an obvious advantage in the endgame (A.Beliavsky).

17 ♘b5 ♖xc2 18 ♘d6 ♖8c6 19 ♘f5!

And again White is "on horseback"! Black is in no position to defend himself against the forks on e7 and d4.

19...♘d5

On 19...♖6c4 would have followed 20 ♘d2 ♖c5 21 ♘xd4.

20 ♘bxd4 ♖xg2 21 ♘xc6 bxc6 22 ♖he1 ♘7f6 23 ♘h4 Black resigned.

He can only avoid the loss of a second exchange by 23...♖f2 24 ♗xf2 ♗xf2, but after 25 ♘f5 ♗xe1 26 ♖xe1 ♔f8 27 ♖c1 he loses the c6 pawn.

In the Introduction we have already touched upon the theme of small advantages in respect of the number of the opponent's pawn islands, on the basis of the illustrative game, Petrosian-Botvinnik (Moscow 1963). Let's also look at some examples from contemporary practice.

In one of the variations of the Slav Defence **1 d4 d5 2 c4 c6 3 ♘f3 ♘f6 4 ♘c3 dxc4 5 a4 ♗f5 6 ♘e5 e6 7 f3**, upon the attempt to create counterplay in the centre by **7...c5** (the main continuation is reckoned to be 7...♗b4) White can forcibly transpose to a favourable endgame, **8 e4 cxd4 9 exf5 ♘c6 10 ♘xc6 bxc6 11 fxe6 fxe6 12 ♕e2** (after the natural 12 ♗xc4 dxc3 13 ♕xd8+ ♔xd8 or 13...♖xd8 are more comfortable for Black) **12...dxc3 13 ♕xe6+ ♕e7 14 ♗xc4 ♕xe6+ 15 ♗xe6 cxb2 16 ♗xb2 ♗b4+ 17 ♔e2** and White, besides the better pawn structure (two pawn islands against three for Black), also has the advantage of the two bishops, controlling important diagonals. Not even the most stoic "defenders" will always succeed in holding a position with such enduring negative statics.

Topalov - Gelfand
Dos Hermanas 1996

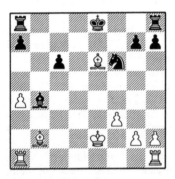

17...♔e7 18 ♗c4 ♖hd8
Black can block the a2-g8 diagonal by 18...♘d5, but after 19 ♖ac1! White's pressure is quite unpleasant.
19 ♖hd1 ♖ab8 20 g3 h5 21 ♖d4!
Fighting for the d-file.
21...♗a5
He should not give up the important diagonal, although 21...♗c5 22 ♖xd8 ♖xd8 23 ♖c1 is likewise in White's favour.
22 ♗a3+ ♔e8?!
It was necessary to go back, 22...♗b4, though after 23 ♖xd8

♔xd8 24 ♗b2 (24 ♖b1 a5) 24...♗d6 25 ♗c3 White undoubtedly has the preferable position. Now, however, he takes the d-file free of charge and his king becomes hostage to the white pieces.
23 ♖ad1 ♖xd4 24 ♖xd4 ♖b1
This pseudo-activity leads to the loss of the a7 pawn. But also an exchange of rooks is contra-indicated for Black. After 24...♖d8 25 ♖xd8+ ♗xd8 26 ♔e3 ♗c7 27 ♗b4 White advances his a-pawn with decisive effect in a situation where the exchange of either of his bishops leads to a winning endgame.
25 ♗d3! ♖e1+ 26 ♔f2 ♔f7 27 ♗c5 ♖a1 28 ♗c4+ ♔e8 29 ♗d3
Repeating the position, since after 29 ♗xa7? ♗c3 30 ♖d3 ♖xa4 Black wins back the pawn.
29...♔f7 30 ♗xa7 ♖a2+ 31 ♔g1 ♖a1+ 32 ♔g2 ♖a2+ 33 ♔h3 ♖a3 34 f4 ♗e1 35 ♗c5 ♖c3 36 ♗c4+ ♔e8 37 ♗b4 ♖c1 38 ♗xe1 ♖xe1 39 a5 ♖a1 40 a6 ♔e7 41 ♖d2 Black resigned.

Similar positions with a weak c-pawn also frequently arise in other openings after the pawn tension has been liquidated. For example, quite topical is the theme of the English Opening **1 c4 c5 2 ♘c3 ♘c6 3 ♘f3 ♘f6 4 g3 d5 5 d4** Here 5...e6 is usually played, but also met is the liquidation of the centre **5...cxd4 6 ♘xd4 dxc4 7 ♘xc6 ♕xd1+ 8 ♘xd1 bxc6 9 ♗g2 ♘d5 10 ♘e3 e6 11 ♘xc4 ♗a6 12 b3 ♗b4+ 13 ♗d2 ♔e7**
White's small advantage lies in his better pawn structure: he has two pawn "islands" compared to three for Black, where the c-pawn can become a quite real object of attack. This is how V.Kramnik exploited it.

Kramnik - Hjartarson
Clichy 1995

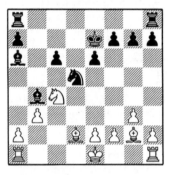

14 ⬜c1 ⬜ac8

Also possible is 14...⬜hc8 and if he follows the path in the game, 15 ♗xb4+ ♘xb4 16 a3 ♘d5, then White, just the same, retains a small advantage. For example, the game, Gelfand-Kramnik, Belgrade 1995, continued 17 e4 ♗xc4 (also after 17...♘b6 18 ♘a5 c5 19 e5 White has the initiative) 18 ⬜xc4 ♘b6 19 ⬜c5 ♘d7 20 ⬜c3 and, as before, White's chances are superior.

15 ♗xb4+ ♘xb4 16 a3 ♘d5 17 ♘a5 c5 18 0-0 ⬜hd8 19 ⬜c2

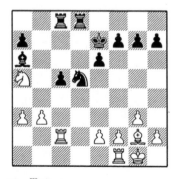

19...⬜c7

Despite White's unpleasant pressure, Black has sufficient defensive resources. As pointed out by V.Kramnik, he feared the pawn sacrifice 19...c4! 20 ♘xc4 (20 bxc4 ⬜c5 21 ⬜fc1 ⬜dc8) 20...♘b6 21 ⬜fc1 ♘xc4 22 bxc4 ⬜c5.

20 ⬜fc1 ⬜dc8 21 e4 ♘f6

It is more logical to look towards 21...♘b6, so as after 22 f4 to have the possibility of 22...c4. It seems that better for White here is 22 ♗f1 ♗xf1 23 ♔xf1, after which the knight is riveted to the b6 square (the threat is b3-b4). Nevertheless this is the lesser evil, since now Black lands in a cramped position.

22 f4! ♗d3

Black endeavours to rid himself of the c-pawn through the advance ...c5-c4.

23 e5 ♘d5

The advance 23...♘e4, after 24 ⬜b2 f5 25 exf6+ ♘xf6, only widens the archipelago of pawn 'islands'.

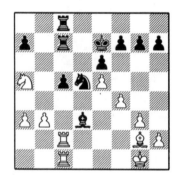

24 ⬜b2!

White prepares to open the b-file and prevents 24...c4. As pointed out by V.Kramnik, after 24 ⬜d2 c4 25 bxc4 (on the obvious 25 ♔f2 Black has a tactical reply: 25...cxb3! 26 ⬜xc7+ ⬜xc7 27 ♗xd5 b2! 28 ⬜xb2 exd5 with a probable draw) 25...♗xc4, White retains the advantage both in the minor piece endgame: 26 ⬜dc2 ♗b5 27 ⬜xc7+ ⬜xc7 28 ⬜xc7+ ♘xc7 29 ♔f2, and in the rook ending: 26 ⬜xc4 ⬜xc4 27 ♘xc4 ⬜xc4 28 ♗xd5 exd5 29

♖xd5 ♖a4 30 ♖d3 f6 31 exf6+ ♔xf6 32 ♔f2, though its drawing tendencies are quite great.

24...c4?

Persistence worthy of a better application; the text can only be explained by time-trouble since the following series of moves is easy to miscalculate. White forcibly transposes to a rook ending with an extra pawn. He should restrict himself to 24...♗b5, though after 25 ♔f2 and the doubling of rooks by ♖b2-c2, White retains the advantage.

25 bxc4 ♗xc4 26 ♖xc4 ♖xc4 27 ♘xc4 ♖xc4 28 ♖b7+ ♔e8 29 ♗xd5!

Retaining the bishop by 29 ♖xa7 ♖c1+ 30 ♔f2 ♖c2+ 31 ♔f3 after 31...♘e3 32 ♗h3 ♘c4 leaves Black possibilities of counterplay.

29...exd5 30 ♖xa7 d4 31 ♔f1 d3

Black endeavours to prevent the king coming out since on 31...♖c1+ 32 ♔e2 ♖c2+ 33 ♔d3 ♖xh2 34 ♔xd4 ♖g2 decides 35 e6! fxe6 36 ♖xg7.

32 ♔e1 ♖c2 33 a4 ♖xh2 34 a5 h5

After 34...g6 35 a6 the a-pawn moves on with support from the e6 pawn: 35...♔f8 36 ♖b7 ♖a2 37 a7 ♔g7 38 e6 or 35...♖a2 36 ♖a8+ ♔e7 37 a7 h5 38 e6. This same idea is also realised in the game.

35 a6 ♖a2 36 f5 ♔f8

Also losing is 36...♖e2+ 37 ♔d1 ♖xe5 38 ♖b7, followed by 39 a7.

37 ♔d1 g5 38 f6 ♔g8 39 ♖a8+ ♔h7 40 e6 Black resigned.

2 Crucial Decisions

In this chapter we look at examples showing crucial individual moves, which at first sight look insignificant, but which represent positional concessions and, as a consequence, hand over a small advantage to the opponent.

Exchange of Queens

In Chapter 1 we looked at examples of an early exchange of queens, which led to definite concessions even in the opening stages. But the cost of an inopportune exchange of queens can be high also in the middlegame.

Kasparov - Topalov
Amsterdam 1995

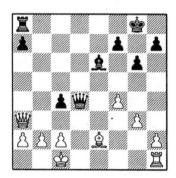

White's extra pawn results from a sacrifice in one of the topical sprawling variations of the Dragon Sicilian. As compensation Black has possibilities of attack on the queen's

flank. He might display activity by 22...♗d5 23 ♖d1 ♕f2 24 ♗g4 (after 24 ♖xd5 ♕xe2 the white king cannot relax) 24...♗e4 25 ♕c3 h5 26 ♗h3 ♕xh2 27 ♕xc4 ♗xc2 etc.

However, Black prefers a transfer to the endgame, since he exchanges queens from a position of strength.

22...c3?! 23 ♕xc3 ♕xc3 24 bxc3 ♗xa2 25 ♔b2 ♗e6 26 c4!

White's doubled pawns show their teeth: they are not only a bonus, they also cut off the black bishop from its support of the passed a-pawn. It becomes clear that Black overestimated his chances in the ending.

26...♔f8 27 ♖a1 a5 28 c5 ♔e7 29 c4 ♗d7

Or 29...♔d7 30 ♗f3 ♖a6 31 ♔c3 with advantage.

30 ♗f3 ♖b8+

On 30...♖a6 could follow 31 ♔c3 f6 32 ♗b7 ♖a7 33 ♖e1+ ♔f8 34 c6.

31 ♔c3 a4 32 ♖a3

White does not hurry with 32 c6, though after 32...♖b3+ 33 ♔d4 his advantage is obvious.

32...♖c8 33 ♔d4 h5 34 ♗b7 ♖d8 35 ♔c3 h4 36 gxh4 ♖h8 37 ♗d5 ♖xh4 38 ♔b4 ♖xh2 39 c6 ♗e6 40 ♗xe6 fxe6

Also losing is 40...♔xe6 41 ♔c5 ♖h8 42 ♖xa4.

41 ♔c5 ♔d8 42 ♖xa4 Black resigned.

How difficult it is to evaluate the consequences of an exchange of queens is demonstrated by a game of another world champion.

Gelfand - Karpov
Vienna 1996

White has only a symbolic advantage, characteristic of positions with an isolated d5 pawn. In order to reveal its weakness B.Gelfand offers an exchange of queens on which the natural reply would seem the retreat 18...♕e7. However A.Karpov reckons White's threats are immaterial and exchanges queens with the idea of worsening White's pawn structure.

18...♕xf4 19 gxf4

Now White's position deserves the preference. The doubled f4 pawn controls the centre, while the rest of his pieces are ready to attack in the centre and on the queen's flank.

19...♔f8 20 e3 ♖d6

More natural is 20...♘fe4.

21 b4

White prepares the advance of the a-pawn, in accordance with Nimzowitsch's dictum: to realise an advantage it is necessary to create a second weakness. Now already 21...♘ce4 is not good because of 22 ♘a4.

21...♘e6 22 ♘ce2 ♖e7 23 a4 ♘d8 24 a5 ♗c6 25 ♘c3 ♗e8 26 ♗f1 bxa5 27 bxa5 ♖b7

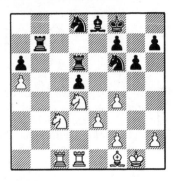

28 ♖a1!!

A move in the style of T.Petrosian. Removing any worries about the a5 pawn, White "unties the hands" of his other pieces for an attack on the weak a6 and d5 pawns.

28...♖c7?!

A colourless move, only urging on the knight to b4, where it wants to go anyway. It was necessary to move his forces to the centre by 28...♔e7 or 28...♘e6, whereas the obvious 28...♘e4 stumbles to the reply 29 ♘db5!!.

29 ♘a2 ♖b7 30 f3 ♘e6 31 ♖db1

Now, after the capture of the b-file, the game is decided and the struggle is only prolonged because of Karpov's high-level defensive technique.

31...♖e7 32 ♘b4 ♘c5 33 ♖c1 ♖b7 34 ♖ab1 ♘fd7 35 ♘bc6 ♖c7 36 ♘e5 ♔e7 37 ♖c3 f6 38 ♘xd7 ♔xd7 39 ♖b8 ♘e6 40 ♖xc7+ ♘xc7 41 ♔f2 ♔e7 42 f5 g5 43 ♔e1 ♗b5

Placing his last hopes on a rook ending. But in vain!

44 ♗xb5 ♘xb5 45 ♘xb5 axb5 46 ♖xb5 ♖c6 47 ♖xd5 ♖c3 48 ♔d2 ♖a3 49 ♔c2 ♖xe3 50 ♔b2 ♖e2+ 51 ♔b3 ♖xh2 52 a6 ♖h1 53 ♔b4 ♖a1

54 Ia5 Ib1+ 55 ♔c5 Ib8 56 a7 Ia8 57 ♔c6 and soon White won.

Kramnik - Ivanchuk
Las Palmas 1996

White has the somewhat preferable position due to the fact that he exerts a certain amount of pressure in the centre. Nevertheless, after an exchange of queens, 17...♕xg3, White's position would prove to be difficult. However V.Ivanchuk does not like the open f-file—18 fxg3!. Nevertheless it is worth going for this, with the idea 18...♗e6 19 If6 ♗xd5 20 exd5 e4!.

But V.Ivanchuk wants more and decides, before exchanging queens, to provoke the move f2-f3. But here he underestimates the fact that White obtains extra time to double rooks on the d-file, which foreshadows his advantage.

17...♗g4?! 18 Id2 Ied7 19 f3 ♕xg3 20 hxg3 ♗e6 21 Ifd1

Now it becomes clear that temporary factors are at work—an important constituent in the struggle for the advantage. Black cannot prevent the threat to double the e- or c-pawns.

21...h5
Preventing 22 g4.

22 a3 ♔b8

Black anticipates the possibility of a check on b7, together with an exchange on c6. He cannot arrange 22...♗xd5 23 exd5 ♘e7 24 ♘xe5 Ixd5 25 Ixd5 Ixd5 26 Ixd5 ♘xd5 27 ♔f2, since then he has to part with one of the pawns on the king's flank.

23 ♔f2 a6 24 ♗xc6!
This is stronger than 24 ♗xe6 Ixd2+ 25 Ixd2 Ixd2+ 26 ♘xd2 fxe6, when the knight on c6 maintains its influence on the centre.

24...Ixd2+ 25 Ixd2 Ixd2+ 26 ♘xd2 bxc6 27 f4!
An important exchange of the centre pawn, broadening the radius of action of the white pieces.

27...exf4 28 gxf4 ♔c8 29 ♔g3 ♔d7 30 ♔h4 f6 31 e5!
White removes his opponent's control of the g5 square.

31...fxe5
No help is 31...♔e7, in view of 32 ♘e4. V.Kramnik showed the possible development of events: 32...fxe5 33 fxe5 ♗d5 34 ♘c5 ♗xg2 35 ♔g5 ♗f1 36 a4! ♗e2 37 a5 ♗f1 38 b3 ♗e2 39 c4 ♗d1 40 b4 ♗e2 41 ♘xa6 ♗xc4 42 ♘c5 and White wins.

32 fxe5 ♗d5 33 g3 ♔e6 34 ♔g5 ♔xe5
More stubborn was 34...♔f7.

35 ♔xg6 h4 36 gxh4 ♔f4 37 h5 ♔e3 38 c4 ♗g2 39 ♘b3 ♗f1 40 h6 ♗xc4 41 ♘c5 ♗a2 42 ♔g7 ♗b1 43 ♘xa6 ♔d4 44 ♘xc7 ♔c4 45 ♘e6 ♔b3 46 ♘d4+ ♔xb2 47 ♘xc6 ♔xa3 48 ♘e5 ♔b4 49 ♘g6 ♗xg6 50 ♔xg6 Black resigned.

In the following examples we look at methods of exchanging queens, from a position of strength, to gain a definite positional advantage.

Atalik - Gufeld
Beijing 1996

In this double-edged position, with his last move **15...c4!** Black sacrifices a pawn, upon the acceptance of which—16 bxc4 b4 17 ♘b1 ♘c5—the blockaded white pawns and the activity of the black pieces offers sufficient compensation. S.Atalik prefers to exchange queens, which allows Black to gain a slight advantage by force in a complicated ending.

16 ♘b1 ♕xd2 17 ♘xd2 c3!

With a temporary pawn sacrifice Black forces a transfer to an ending where the dark-squared bishop cooperates excellently with the rooks. Of course White cannot allow the clamp 18 ♘b1? b4.

18 ♖xc3 ♘xd5 19 ♖xc8 ♖bxc8 20 exd5 ♖c2 21 ♘de4 ♖xa2 22 ♘xd6 ♖exe2 23 ♘xe2 ♖xe2 24 ♖d1

Weaker is 24 ♖c1 ♗d4+ 25 ♔f1 ♖f2+ 26 ♔e1 ♘c5 27 ♖d1 ♖xg2.

24...f5

It is possible to sum up the results of the "skirmish": the white knight is restricted in its manoeuvres, the d5 pawn is firmly blockaded, whereas Black has the potential possibility of creating a passed a-pawn, supported by the bishop on

g7. This allows us to assess Black's chances as preferable.

25 ♔f1 ♖a2

Black forcibly transfers to a favourable minor piece ending. On 25...♖b2 possible is 26 ♖c1.

26 ♖c1 ♖a1 27 ♖xa1 ♗xa1 28 ♘b7 ♗d4 29 ♔e2 ♘c5 30 ♘xc5?

After this exchange White gets a lost endgame. As pointed out by S.Atalik, the only way to save the game was by sacrificing the b3 pawn for real activation of his passed pawn: 30 ♘a5! ♗c3 31 ♘c6! and now after 31...♘xb3 32 d6 ♘c5 33 ♘b8 ♘e6 34 d7 ♗a5 35 ♘c6 ♘xg5 36 ♘xa5 ♘e6 37 ♘c6 ♔f7 38 ♔d2 White wins the knight.

30...♗xc5 31 ♗d2 ♔f7 32 b4 ♗d6 33 g3?

After 33 h3 ♔e7 34 g4 ♗g3 the bishop attacks from the rear and Black wins the d5 pawn: 35 ♔d3 ♔d6 36 gxf5 gxf5 37 ♗c3 ♔xd5.

33...♔e7 34 ♔d3 ♔d7 35 ♔d4 h5! 36 ♗e1 h4 37 ♔e3

Zugzwang.

37...h3

After 37 gxh4 ♗xh2 38 ♔c5 ♗g1+ also wins.

38 f4 ♗f8 39 ♔f3

The pawn cannot be held: 39 ♔d4 ♔d6 and 40...♗g7+.

39...♔d6 40 g4 ♔xd5 41 gxf5 gxf5 42 ♔g3 ♔c4 White resigned.

And here is another example on the theme of offering a queen exchange, in fact even with a pawn less.

Gufeld - de Guzman
Cordoza 1998

Here, White has some space advantage and chances of an attack on the king's flank but Black's position has no weaknesses.

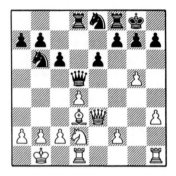

17 ♘e4!

As proclaimed by the great Lasker, the side having the initiative must attack.

17...♛xd4?!

It is difficult to blame the opponent for this move. The subsequent events were far from obvious and moreover, on general considerations, to exchange a flank pawn for a centre one is not at all bad.

But to be fair we should mention that more circumspect would have been the counterthrust 17... ♘c4!? 18 ♕e2 ♘cd6, although even here White is left with the preferable chances.

18 ♘f6+ ♚h8 19 ♘xh7 ♛xe3 20 fxe3 ♖g8

With the threat of 21...♖xd3, which cannot be played at once because of 22 ♘xf8.

21 g6 f6

Black goes over to a god-forsaken defence since there are problems for him also after 21...fxg6 22 ♘g5.

22 h4!

Not only to defend the g6 pawn, but to prepare the return of the knight, which is helped by the rook on h1—without leaving its place.

22...♘d6 23 ♘g5 ♖ge8 24 ♘f7+!
♘xf7 25 gxf7 ♖f8 26 ♗g6 ♘d7

26...♘c4 27 ♖xd8 ♖xd8 28 ♚c1 ♖f8 29 ♖d1 ♘e5 30 h5 leads practically to a transposition of moves.

27 h5 ♘e5 28 ♖xd8 ♖xd8 29 ♚c1

This is a slight error. More accurate is 29 b4, since now Black could hold up White's advance by 29...a5.

29...♖f8 30 ♖d1 ♘xf7 31 ♖d7

Absolute control of the seventh rank. Black is a pawn ahead, but his king is paralysed. On the other hand, White has a rook on the seventh rank and one king more!!

31...♘d8 32 b4 f5 33 ♚d2 e5 34 ♖e7 e4

More active, but just as hopeless is 34...f4 35 ♚e2 f3+ 36 ♚f2.

35 ♚e2 ♚g8 36 a4 a6 37 a5 ♖f6 38 ♖e8+ ♖f8 39 ♖e5

The clearest, though also possible was 39 ♖xf8+ ♚xf8 40 ♗xf5 c5 41 c3 cxb4 42 cxb4 ♘c6 43 ♗xe4.

39...♘f7

Nor is there any salvation in 39...f4 40 exf4 ♖xf4 41 ♖e8+ ♖f8 42 ♖e7.

40 ♖xf5 ♘d6 41 ♗h7+ Black resigned.

And here is an example of a poor deployment of forces.

Tegshsuren - Gufeld
Los Angeles 1998

Despite his backward pawn on d6, Black's position is quite solid. In order to get at this pawn

E.Tegshsuren makes a firm decision and offers an exchange of queens, reconciling himself to the doubling of his g-pawns. But precisely from such "trifles" are also created small advantages.

35 ♕g3 ♕xg3 36 hxg3 ♖ad7 37 a4?!

With the exchange of queens White has achieved nothing, since, instead of a queen, in its place will soon arrive the king. But why then did he create the weakness on b3? Now the assessment of the position is about to turn in Black's favour.

The obvious move is 37 g4, fixing the f6 pawn (in the future Black can prevent this by ...h7-h5), though after 37...♔f7 38 ♖f1 ♔e6 39 ♘d5 ♖f7 equality is maintained.

37...♔f7 38 ♔f2 ♔e6 39 ♔e3 ♔e5 40 ♖d3 ♖b8 41 ♘b5

While here also we see the consequences of the careless 37 a4?!. He has to give up a pawn, since after 41 ♘d5 ♖db7 (after 41...f5? 42 exf5 gxf5 43 ♔f3 threatens mate by 44 ♖e1) 42 ♘xf6 ♖xb3 43 ♘xh7 ♗xe4 cannot be considered.

By "punching a hole" through d6, White counts on the activity of his rooks.

41...♗xe4 42 ♖xd6 ♖xd6 43 ♖xd6 ♗xg2 44 ♖d7 ♖b7 45 ♖d8 ♗c6 46 ♖c8 ♖b6 47 ♖c7 h5 48 ♖a7 g5 49 ♖xa5 f5!

On 49...h4 50 gxh4 gxh4 comes 51 ♘d4! ♔d6 52 ♘f5+ ♔d7 53 ♘xh4 and White saves himself. Now on 50 ♘d4 Black has 50...f4+ 51 gxf4+ gxf4+ 52 ♔d3 ♗e4+ 53 ♔c3 ♔d6 with a clear advantage.

50 ♖a7 ♖b7 51 ♖a6

The minor piece endgame after 51 ♖xb7 ♗xb7 52 a5 h4 53 gxh4 gxh4 54 ♔f2 f4 55 ♘c7 h3 56 a6 ♗c6 is lost for White.

51...♗e4 52 ♖h6 ♖d7! 53 ♖xh5 ♖d3+ 54 ♔f2 ♖f3+ 55 ♔g2

Also losing is 55 ♔e2 ♖xg3.

55...♖xb3+ 56 ♔f2 g4 57 ♖h8 ♖f3+ 58 ♔g2 ♖a3+ 59 ♔f2 ♖xa4 60 ♖e8+ ♔f6 61 ♘d6 ♖a2+ 62 ♔e1 ♗f3 63 ♖c8 f4 White resigned.

In conclusion of the theme it remains to add that it is not always painless to refuse an exchange of queens.

Anand - Karpov
FIDE World Championship,
Lausanne 1998

Is it not right that the familiar pawn structure outflanks the kingside? However, in fact, the chances of the two sides are roughly level. And this is not only due to the fact that White has weaknesses of his own, but above all due to the fact that he has insufficient resources for a piece attack on the king.

18...f5!

A.Karpov immediately cuts White's "Gordian knot", showing the futility of his hopes.

19 ♕e2?!

V.Anand, apparently still under the impression of his past initiative, turns down the exchange of queens. After the natural 19 exf6 ♕xf6 20 ♕d4 the position is simplified and a drawn outcome is highly likely. Now, however, the cramping h5 pawn becomes weak and the initiative passes firmly to Black.

19...♗d7 20 ♖d1 ♗b5!

The 12th world champion starts to build up the pluses of his position.

21 ♕f3 ♕e8! 22 ♗f4

Too risky is 22 ♕xb7 ♗c6. Now the retreat 23 ♕a6 ♕xh5 24 ♗xh6 ♖ac8 25 ♗e3 ♕g6 26 ♕f1 f4! leads to a dangerous initiative for Black, while on 23 ♕c7 follows 23...♖c8 24 ♕xa7 ♕xh5 and now 25 f3?! is not good because of 25...♗xf3! with a very strong attack for Black.

22...♖c8 23 ♖d4 ♖c4

More accurate is 23...♕f7 24 ♖ad1 ♖c4, since now White could take the pawn, 24 ♕xb7, intending after 24...♖xc3 25 a4 ♗c6 26 ♕b4 ♖c2 27 ♕b3 ♖e2 28 ♕c4 ♖b2 29 ♕c3 to pursue the black rook. Missing this chance, it remains for White only to await the development of events.

24 ♖ad1 ♕f7! 25 ♖xc4 ♗xc4 26 a3 ♖c8 27 ♖d4

After 27 ♖d6 ♗d5 28 ♕h3 ♖c4, Black supercharges the situation by cutting off the white rook.

27...♔h7 28 ♗d2 ♗d5 29 ♕h3 b5 30 a4 bxa4 31 ♖xa4 ♖c4! 32 ♖xc4 ♗xc4 33 ♕h4 ♗b5 34 c4 ♗e8

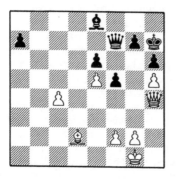

A.Karpov demonstrates the advantage of a more active opposite-coloured bishop over its "opposite number". We go into this theme in more detail in a separate chapter of this book.

35 c5

More active is 35 ♕d8!? ♕xh5 36 ♗e3, but, as pointed out by the well-known analyst I.Zaitsev, after 36...g6! (there is nothing in 36...♗c6 37 ♕d6 ♗a8 38 ♕d8, 36...a6 37 ♕b6 or 36...♕f7 37 ♕a8) 37 ♕d6 f4! 38 ♗xf4 (38 ♗xa7? f3) 38...♕b1+! (an important finesse; after an immediate 38...♕e4 39 ♕xe6 ♗c6 40 f3 White saves himself) 39 ♔h2 ♕e4 40 ♕d2 (or 40 ♗e3 ♗c6) 40...♕xc4, Black's practical chances of victory are no less than White's of a draw.

35...♕d7!

Not tempted by the pawn: 35...♕xh5 36 ♕xh5 ♗xh5 37 c6 ♗e8 37 c7 leads to a draw.

36 ♗c3 ♕d3

More resolute is 36...♕d1+ 37 ♔h2 ♕c1! 38 ♗b4 ♕b2 39 ♕f4 ♗xh5 40 c6 ♕c2, holding on to the pawn.

37 ♕d4?

White offers an exchange of queens, being unable to resist the lure of an endgame with opposite-coloured bishops, which turns out to be lost. It is worth confusing the issue with 37 ♗a5!.

37...♕xd4 38 ♗xd4 a5 39 c6?!

More stubborn was 39 f3 a4 40 ♗b2 ♗xh5 41 c6 ♗e8 42 c7 or 39 ♗e3 a4 40 ♗c1 ♗xh5 41 c6 ♗e2! 42 c7.

39...♗xc6 40 f3 f4!

The key move, after which White cannot prevent the creation of two distant passed pawns on opposite flanks.

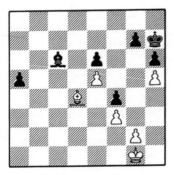

41 &b2 &e8 42 &c1 a4 43 &xf4 a3 44 &e3 &xh5 45 &f2 &e8 46 &d4 &c6 47 &c3 a2 48 g3 h5 49 g4 h4 White resigned.

Strategical Concessions

And now a few examples on the theme of poor moves, creating strategical minuses in the position, which lead to an upsetting of the balance.

Lasker - Eliskases
Moscow 1936

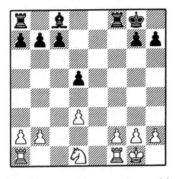

In this roughly equal position Black made an at first sight imperceptible strategical mistake.

17...d4?!

In an attempt to restrict the knight, Black creates a weak pawn on d4, which is finely exploited by

the 2nd world champion. After the natural 17...&f5 18 d4 &ae8 19 &e3 c6, White would already be pre-occupied with the weak pawn on d4.

18 f3 &e8 19 &f2 &e3

Of course it is tempting to rivet the knight to the pawn, but more active is 19...&e2, not fearing the counterattack 20 &fe1 &xb2 21 &e8+ &f7 22 &ae1 in view of the resource 22...&b1! 23 &8e7+ &f6.

20 &ac1 c6 21 &c4 &e6 22 &xd4 &xa2 23 &d7

Chasing the rook by 23 &e4 &e2 24 &b4 b5 25 &c3 a5 26 &xb5 cxb5 27 &xe2 b4 would give Black chances of creating a distant passed pawn.

23...b5 24 &e4 &d5 25 &d1 &e2

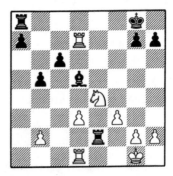

26 &c3!

A move in the style of the classical school. In the four-rook ending, absolute control of the seventh rank compensates for material loss.

26...&xb2 27 &xd5 cxd5 28 &c1!

Yet another finesse, the point of which becomes clear two moves later.

28...&h8?

This and the last move shows how much lower defensive technique was half a century ago. Black loses time, while the modern master, not worrying about material loss, would have advanced the distant passed pawn: 28...a5! 29 ♖cc7 a4 30 ♖xg7+ ♔f8 31 ♖xh7 ♔g8.

29 ♖cc7 ♖g8?

Even here it was still not too late for 29...a5, not fearing 30 ♖a7 because of 30...♖c8 31 ♖dc7 ♖e8 32 h4 a4.

30 ♖xa7 h6

If White transfers the rook via the e-file (28 ♖e1), then the d5 pawn would not be attacked and Black could have played here 30...♖d2.

31 h4 b4 32 ♖ab7 b3 33 ♔h2 ♖d2

An irreparable situation. It has become clear that the b-pawn is not so mobile as it is lost just like its predecessor, the a-pawn.

34 ♖xb3 ♖e8 35 ♖bb7 ♖xd3 36 ♖xg7 ♖d8 37 ♖h7+ ♔g8 38 ♖xh6 ♖e3 39 ♖hh7 d4 40 ♖hd7 ♖ee8 41 h5 d3 42 h6 ♖xd7 43 ♖xd7 ♖e6 44 ♖xd3 ♖xh6+ 45 ♔g3 Black resigned.

Beliavsky - Romanishin
USSR Championship 1978

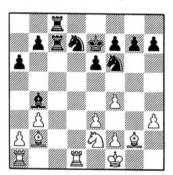

White's small advantage lies in his advantage of the two bishops, controlling both long diagonals. As compensation Black controls the c-file. For a rook invasion on c2 he needs to take care of the b7 pawn which he can do by the move

18...b6. However, Black plays more energetically, thereby making a strategical mistake.

18...b5?

This pseudo-activity allows White to open the a-file and create new objects of attack.

19 a4 bxa4 20 ♖xa4 a5 21 ♗a3 ♗xa3 22 ♖xa3 ♘c5 23 ♘d4

It is well known that one of the constituent advantages of the two bishops is the possibility of a timely exchange of one of them. Now White wins a pawn. The threat is 24 ♖a5, while the a5 pawn cannot be defended with the rook from a7 in view of the fork on c6.

23...♘ce4 24 ♖xa5 g6 25 b4 ♖c4 26 b5 ♔f8 27 ♗xe4!

With this exchange White brings his king into the game.

27...♘xe4 28 ♔g2 ♘c3 29 ♖c1 ♘d5 30 ♖xc4 ♖xc4 31 ♔f3 ♖b4 32 ♖a7

The continuation 32 ♖a8+! ♔g7 33 ♖c8 might save White extra time.

32...♖b2 33 ♖a8+ ♔g7 34 ♖c8

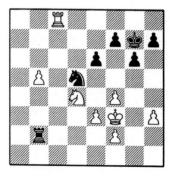

34...♘e7?!

With this move White allows the knight to be cut off from participation in the game. More tenacious was 34...♖b1.

35 ♖c2 ♖b1 36 e4 g5 37 ♖c7 ♔f8 38 fxg5 e5 39 ♘f5 ♘xf5

On 39...♘g6 would have followed 40 ♘d6 with the transfer to a winning rook ending.

40 exf5 ♖xb5 41 f6 ♔e8 42 ♖e7+ ♔f8 43 ♖a7 ♖b8 44 ♔g4 h6 45 h4 ♔g8 46 ♔h5 hxg5 47 hxg5 e4 48 g6 Black resigned.

Gulko - Kramnik
Novgorod 1995

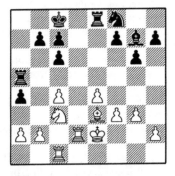

White has a small advantage. He has a superiority in the centre and the better pawn structure. However, the activity of the black pieces after ...♘f8-e6, allows him to reckon on obtaining counterplay. For example on 18 ♗d4 possible is 18...♗h6 19 f4 g5. Worth considering is 18 ♔f2, intending to place the rooks on c2 and d1.

However, White plays on general considerations—blockading the a-pawn by **18 a3?!**, which is a serious positional mistake. The assessment of the position is thus reversed—the small advantage passes to Black. For the weakness of the a4 pawn, White has two: the weakness of the b2 pawn and the b3 square. Apart from this, Black has clear play associated with ...f7-f5, whereas it is not clear what White can extract from the d-file.

18...♘e6 19 ♔f2

Premature is 19 f4 because of 19...♘c5, while on 19 h4 Black undermines the centre by 19...f5!.

19...g5 20 ♖cd1?

Again a move made on general considerations. But White is already experiencing difficulties in his choice of moves. For example, on 20 ♘e2 he has to reckon on both 20...f5 and 20...g4. But nevertheless he should not allow doubled pawns.

V.Kramnik recommends the prophylactic 20 ♔g2!, moving the king off the f-file.

20...f5 21 exf5 ♗xc3 22 bxc3 ♖xf5

Black has an obvious advantage, he threatens not only ...g5-g4, but also ...♖e8-f8. 23 g4 ♖f7 24 ♔g3 ♖ef8 leads to new weaknesses.

23 ♖d7 h5 24 ♖h7 g4 25 f4 ♘g5 26 ♖g7 ♘e4+ 27 ♔f1

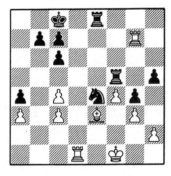

27...♘d6!

White can only dream about such redemption as 27...♘xc3 28 ♖dd7. Now, however, Black manages to neutralise the active rook on g7, whereas it is not clear how to defend the ruined pawns on the queen's flank. He does not succeed in ridding himself of the doubled pawns by 28 c5?, since in the four-rook ending, 28...♖xe3 29 cxd6 cxd6 30 ♖xd6 ♖xc3 31 ♖dd7 ♖b5, the white rooks are on a dry run, whereas Black threatens mate after 32...♖c2.

28 ♗b6?!

This unnecessary activity makes possible an exchange of rooks. It is worth limiting himself to 28 ♗f2.

28...♖f7! 29 ♖xf7 ♘xf7 30 ♗d4?!

Playing on general considerations quickly ends the game. More stubborn was 30 ♗f2, retaining after 30...♘d6 the possibility of 31 ♖d4.

30...♘d6 31 c5 ♘c4! 32 ♔f2

The rook ending after 32 f5 ♘e3+ 33 ♗xe3 ♖xe3 34 ♔g2 ♖xc3 is hopeless.

32...b5!

Black closes in on the a3 pawn.

33 cxb6

On passive defence of the a3 pawn by 33 ♖a1 V.Kramnik had prepared the encirclement of the c5 pawn: 33...♖f8 34 ♔e2 ♔d7 35 ♔d3 ♖f5 36 ♔e4 ♔e6 37 ♖a2 ♖d5 followed by ...♘c4-a5-b3.

33...cxb6 34 ♗f6 b5 35 ♖d4 ♘xa3 36 ♖d6 ♔c7 37 ♗e5 ♘c4 38 ♖e6+ ♔d7 White resigned.

3 Exploiting a Small Positional Advantage

How frequently we come across situations where one of the sides has a slight positional advantage! In comments to games the reader is told: "...an insignificant advantage (most often positional) that is hardly enough for victory" or "with energetic moves, Black neutralises White's small positional advantage". There is also another: "with a series of energetic moves an insignificant advantage leads to victory, but upon this the side conducting the defence does not make full use of his defensive resources". In short, very capacious is this concept of positional advantage.

Usually the whole exploitation of a positional advantage is the achievement of a material one. And, in fact, the theme of realisation of a small advantage in any of its forms leads to the playing of positions having a technical character. We can convince ourselves of this from the examples in the first chapters where we looked at the prerequisites for obtaining a small advantage. In the following chapters we look at other examples of this realisation. The majority of these assume a character which is found in complicated endgames.

Our study does not include an elucidation of all aspects of problems touching on the subject. We would rather interest ourselves not in rules, but exceptions: games on the edge of a draw with positions where everything sometimes depends on a single move. We do not stress the final result of the game, ending in a win for one of the sides. The question is not only that but also the duel, replete with a full-blooded struggle, where the side possessing a positional advantage does not always manage to gain victory.

A large number of the illustrative examples are arranged according to increasing complexity but also according to the principle of corresponding material, which can have definite methodological value. We suggest it is appropriate to take poetic licence and also arrange them under transfer to more simple endgames. From the point of view of the reliability of the realisation of the advantage "according to Gufeld" it is possible to arrange them in the following order: pawns, queens, knights (many would contemplate placing this in the second place), same-coloured bishops, rooks, and opposite-coloured bishops.

Struggle with Queens

The presence of queens usually brings to the struggle elements of the middlegame since, in individual cases, arise opportunities of organising an attack on the king. Usually the side with the initiative has the possibility of choosing between an attack and a transfer to a favourable endgame.

Timman - Larsen
Montreal 1979

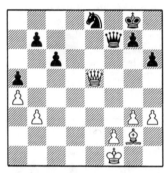

White's positional advantage is conditioned by the more active placement of his pieces and the unreliable sanctuary of the black king. The b7 and c6 pawns are in the sights of the bishop and are qualitatively devalued. Black has in prospect a difficult defence.

33 ♗e4 ♔f8 34 ♕xa5 ♕xb3 35 ♕c5+ ♔f7 36 ♗c2 ♕d5 37 ♕b4!

Upon the exchange of queens, 37 ♕xd5+ cxd5 38 ♔e2 ♘d6 39 ♔e3 ♔e6 40 ♔d4 b6 41 f4 ♘c8 42 g4 ♘e7, despite his space advantage, White will hardly manage to realise it. Therefore J.Timman gropes for new weaknesses in the opponent's position, while retaining prospects of attack on the black king.

37...♕d7 38 ♗b3+ ♔g6

After 38...♔f6?? 39 ♕f8+ White forces mate.

39 ♕e4+ ♔f6 40 ♕h4+ ♔g6 41 ♕e4+ ♔f6 42 ♔g2 ♘c7?!

He should decide on 42...g5! and after 43 f4 gxf4 44 ♕xf4+ ♔g7! Black constructs a defence on new lines.

43 ♕f4+ ♔e7 44 ♕b4+ ♔d8 45 ♕xb7

How often it happens that a positional advantage is transformed into a material one.

45...♕d3 46 ♕b4 c5

47 ♕c4!

Transposing to a minor piece ending is the quickest way to victory.

47...♕xc4 48 ♗xc4 ♘e8 49 ♔f3 ♔c7 50 a5 ♘d6 51 ♗d5 ♔b8 52 ♔f4 ♔a7 53 ♔e5 ♘b5 54 ♗c4

Also leading to victory is 54 ♔f5 ♘c3 55 ♗c4 ♘d1 56 ♔g6.

54...♔a6 55 ♔d5!

Winning as well is 55 ♗xb5+ ♔xb5 56 ♔d5 with the "production" of queens: 56...c4 57 a6 c3 58 a7 c2 59 a8=♕ c1=♕ 60 ♕b7+, but the plan chosen by White leaves Black no chances.

55...♔xa5 56 ♔xc5 ♘c3 57 ♗d5 ♘d1 58 f4 ♘f2 59 ♔d4!

The *leitmotiv* of White's attack is the active king!

59...♔b4 60 ♗f3 ♘xh3 61 ♔e3 g5 62 f5 g4

There is also no salvation in 62...♔c5 in view of 63 ♗g4 ♘g1 64 ♔f2 h5 65 ♗xh5 ♘h3+ 66 ♔f3!.

63 ♗xg4 ♘g5 64 ♔d4 ♔b3 65 ♗h5 ♔c2 66 f6 ♔d2 67 f7 ♘e6+ 68 ♔e5 ♘f8 69 ♔d6 Black resigned.

We present our first summing up. This is how schematic J.Timman's victory looks:

1 Creation of new weaknesses in the opponent's position in conjunction with threats to the king.

2 Transformation of a positional advantage into a material one.

3 Transfer to a winning minor piece ending.

Very simple. Isn't that right?

Ljubojević - Karpov
Linares 1981

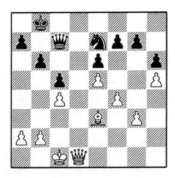

In the diagram position is the already familiar to us pawn structure from the Caro-Kann Defence. As we know from Chapter 1, the advance 28 g4, completing the encirclement of Black's kingside pawn chain, can consolidate White's advantage. The dangers in store for Black might be demonstrated by the example of the natural move 28...♕c6?. In this case White can transpose to a favourable minor piece endgame: 29 ♕d6+! ♕xd6 30 exd6 ♘g8 31 g5 ♔b7 32 b4! ♔c6

(32...cxb4 broadens the sphere of activity of the bishop: 33 ♗d4 f6 34 g6 ♔c6 35 c5 bxc5 36 ♗xc5! and the bishop gets to the g7 pawn) 33 bxc5 bxc5 34 ♗xc5 g6 35 hxg6 fxg6 36 ♔d2 h5 37 ♔e3 a6 38 ♔e4 ♔d7 39 ♔e5 and White should win. Of course Black could avoid the exchange of queens by 28...♕b7, but he still has in prospect a difficult defence.

However White delays, which allows A.Karpov immediately to undermine one of the cramping pawns.

28 ♕d3?! g6! 29 hxg6

Here already 29 g4? gxh5 30 gxh5 ♘f5 is a blank shot.

29...fxg6 30 a3

"Harder" is 30 ♕e4 ♘f5 31 ♗f2 h5 32 ♔c2.

30...a5!

The picture has changed. After the exchange of the cramping h5 pawn Black's chances are already preferable and he has a "better" knight in comparison with the bishop, restricted by its own pawns.

Additional factors are also the circumstance that at the end of the game the queen and knight cooperate more harmoniously than queen and bishop: this circumstance "covers" the squares of the opposite colour.

For a start it is important to lay down a clear strategical line leading to an endgame and depriving the opponent of possible counterplay. A.Karpov carries out this complicated task in virtuoso style.

31 b3

Also here White should play more actively by 31 g4, since now Black restricts him on the kingside as well.

31...h5! 32 ♕e4 ♘f5 33 ♗f2 ♕d7

Now Black has control over the d-file, though, for the present, the squares of invasion are not apparent.

34 a4?!

He should not needlessly create new weaknesses. More accurate is an immediate 34 ♔c2.

34...♔c7! 35 ♔c2

The pseudo-active 35 ♕a8? allows Black to increase his advantage still further: 35...♕d3! 36 ♕a7+ ♔c8 37 ♕a8+ ♔d7 38 ♕b7+ ♔e8 39 ♕b8+ ♔f7 40 ♕b7+ ♘e7.

35...♕d8!

It is necessary to activate the queen and to this end the break ...g6-g5 is highly appropriate.

36 ♔c1

It's also not easy after 36 ♕d3 ♕a8! or 36 ♕f3 ♕d4!.

36...g5!

Broadening the sphere of activity of the queen, since on 37 ♔c2 it is necessary to reckon on 37...g4.

37 fxg5 ♕xg5+ 38 ♔c2 ♘e7!

White can only dream about 38...♘xg3? 39 ♗xg3 ♕xg3 40 ♕h7+ .

39 ♕h7 ♔d7

Also worth considering is an immediate exchange of queens: 39...♕g6+ 40 ♕xg6 ♘xg6 41 ♗e3 ♔d7 42 ♗g5 ♘xe5 etc., but Black goes for an even more favourable solution.

40 ♕e4 ♕f5 41 ♕d3+ ♔c6 42 ♕xf5 exf5 43 ♗e3 ♘g6 44 e6

This pawn is doomed. White's last chance is a breakthrough with the bishop to the opponent's queen's flank.

44...♔d6 45 ♗g5 ♔xe6 46 ♔d2 f4! 47 gxf4 h4

Simpler is 47...♔f5.

48 ♔e3 h3 49 ♔f3 ♔f5 50 ♔g3

On 50 ♗h6 decides 50...h2 51 ♔g2 ♘xf4+ 52 ♔xh2 ♔e4.

50...♘xf4! 51 ♗d8 ♘e2+ 52 ♔xh3 ♘d4 53 ♗xb6

No better is 53 ♔g2 ♔e4 54 ♔f1 ♔d3 55 ♔e1 ♘xb3 56 ♔d1 ♔xc4.

53...♘xb3 54 ♗d8 ♔e4 55 ♔g4 ♔d3 56 ♔f4 ♔xc4 57 ♔e4 ♔c3 58 ♗f6+ ♔c2 59 ♗e5 c4 60 ♔e3 c3 61 ♗f6

The alternative, 61 ♔e4 ♘c5+ 62 ♔d5 ♘xa4 63 ♔c4 ♘b2+ 64 ♔b5 a4, hardly solves White's problems.

61...♘c5 62 ♔e2

After 62 ♔d4 ♘xa4 63 ♔c4 Black has to find the straightforward 63...♘b6+ 64 ♔b5 a4, since on the mistaken 63...♘b2+? 64 ♔b5 a4 65 ♔b4 White surprisingly saves himself.

62...♔b3 White resigned.

And now an example on the theme of the "better" bishop in the performance of the "late" A.Karpov.

Karpov - Cu.Hansen
Groningen 1995

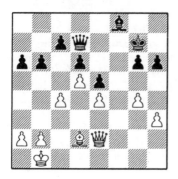

The endgame looks quite harmless for Black but already with his next move A.Karpov demonstrates that White has the advantage. It lies in the presence of the "better" bishop.

30 c5! dxc5

From such little things comes forth an advantage: Black is forced to reconcile himself to a deterioriation of his pawn structure. It is clear that not good is either 30...bxc5 31 ♕xa6, which presents White with an outside passed a-pawn, or 30...b5 because of 31 c6!. And on 30...♕a4 A.Karpov immediately pointed out two favourable continuations:

a) 31 c6!? ♗e7 32 ♗c3 ♗g5 33 a3! with the threats of ♔b1-a2 and b2-b3.

b) 31 cxb6 cxb6 32 b3 ♕d4 33 ♕e3 ♕xe3 34 ♗xe3 b5 35 ♔c2 ♗e7 36 ♔c3 with the threat of a breakthrough on the queen's flank.

31 ♕xa6 h5

Suicidal is 31...c6? 32 ♗c3 cxd5 33 ♗xe5+ and 34 ♕xb6.

32 ♕e2 hxg4 33 ♕xg4

It might be worth retaining queens by 33 hxg4, since now Black easily holds his passive position.

33...♕xg4 34 hxg4 ♔f7 35 a4 ♔e8 36 a5 ♔d7 37 axb6 cxb6 38 ♗c3

After 38 b4 c4 39 b5 ♗c5 Black "plugs" all the holes.

38...♗d6

On 38...♔d6 White breaks through with 39 b4 c4 40 b5 ♔c5 41 ♗xe5, creating two connected passed pawns.

39 b4!

The pawn sacrifice is the only way to victory. Since Black is prohibited from transferring to a pawn ending (White has a passed d5 pawn), he is forced to play a bishop ending with separate pawn islands.

39...cxb4

Not possible is 39...c4 40 b5! ♔e7 41 ♔c2 ♔f6 42 ♗d2 ♗c5 43 ♔c3 and Black loses a pawn. After 39...♔c7 40 ♔c2 ♔b7 41 ♔b3 ♔a6 42 bxc5 bxc5 43 ♔c4 ♔b6 44 ♗d2! ♗e7 45 ♗e3 ♗d6 46 ♗g5 ♔a6 47 ♗d8 Black falls into zugzwang.

40 ♗d2 ♔c7 41 ♔c2 b5 42 ♔b3 ♔d7 43 ♗xb4 ♗c7 44 ♗c3 ♗d6 45 ♗b2! b4

Zugzwang. Black is forced to repulse the threat of ♗b2-a3. In the event of 45...♔c8 46 ♗a3 ♗c7 47 ♗f8 ♔b7 (47...♗a5 48 ♗d6) 48 ♔b4 ♔b6 49 d6 ♗b8 50 d7 ♔c7 51 51 ♗d6+ White wins.

46 ♗c1 ♗c5 47 ♗d2 ♗g1 48 ♔xb4

White wins a pawn, but it is not so simple to realise it.

48...♗f2 49 ♔c4 ♗g1 50 ♔d3 ♗c5 51 ♗e3 ♗e7 52 ♔c4

52...♗a3?

This move allows the bishop to be cut off to a passive position. According to an analysis by A.Karpov, after 52...♗h4 53 ♗c5 ♗g5 54 d6 ♔c6 55 d7 ♗d8 56 ♗b4 ♔d7 57 ♔d5 ♗f6 58 ♗c3 ♗g7 59 ♗xe5 ♗h6, White improves the position of his king but at the cost of reducing the pawn material, which leaves Black definite hopes of saving himself.

53 ♗d2!

Cutting off the way of the enemy bishop to White's rear.

53...♗e7 54 ♗c3 ♗d6

In the event of 54...♗f6 55 g5! ♗g7 56 ♗b4 the bishop lands in a cage and the roundabout journey of the king decides.

55 ♗b4 ♗b8 56 ♔b5 ♗a7

After 56...♗c7 57 d6 ♗xd6 58 ♗xd6 ♔xd6 59 g5, White wins the pawn ending.

57 ♗c5 ♗b8 58 d6! Black resigned.

With rooks on the board, as well as queens, we have elements of the middlegame, since it is possible to create threats against the enemy king.

Gheorghiu - Larsen
London 1980

White's chances are linked to the outside passed b-pawn, but his king is not secure which gives Black the possibility of attacking it.

46...♖h5 47 ♔c3!

Quickly under cover! Getting the king out of danger is the first priority. F.Gheorghiu solves this problem very elegantly.

47...♖h3 48 ♔b4 ♕f2

It is clear that the rook ending after 48...♕xe3 49 ♕xe3 ♖xe3 50 b6 is hopeless for Black.

49 ♖a3!

The rook provides excellent defence for his king from the rear.

49...♕b2+ 50 ♔a4 ♕c2+ 51 ♔a5 ♕d2+ 52 ♔a6 ♕b4

Now Black tries to get close to the opponent's king from the other side, but so unsuccessfully. The rook is on its guard!

53 ♖a5! ♔g5 54 c5!

A decisive break! White creates a second passed d-pawn—after 54...dxc5 it is irrepressible, while after 54...♕xc5 55 ♕xc5 dxc5 the advance of the b-pawn decides.

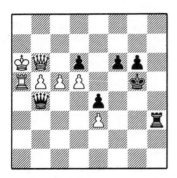

54...♖h8 55 ♕c6! ♖d8 56 b6 dxc5 57 b7 c4 58 ♖b5 ♕a3+

In case of 58...♕f8, winning is 59 d6+ f5 60 ♔a7.

59 ♔b6! f5

On 59...♕xe3+ follows 60 ♔c7.

60 ♕c5 Black resigned.

Of course we did not discover America, when we say that the king is the most active piece in the endgame. In the following example it proves exceptionally mobile even in the queen ending, where it wages an offensive action against the very ... king. It is necessary to assume that the chess king is still not familiar with the conclusions of a number of sociologists, asserting that the world is going matriarchal.

Gufeld - Spiridonov
Tbilisi 1970

White has a small positional advantage in view of his fewer pawn islands and the possibility of forming another one for his opponent.

34 f4! ♘e6 35 fxe5 ♘d4 36 ♕e4

Even stronger was 36 b4! fxe5 37 b5 ♕e6 38 a4, preparing the creation of an outside passed pawn. But insufficient was the obvious 36 ♘f3 fxe5, since no good is 37 ♘xe5?? ♕xe5!, while on 37 ♔g2 possible is 37...♕b7 38 ♔g3 ♘xf3 39 ♕xf3 e4 with equal chances.

36...fxe5 37 ♔g2 h5 38 ♘f3 ♘xf3 39 ♔xf3 ♕f6+ 40 ♔e2 hxg4 41 ♕xg4

The game passes to a queen ending, where White's small advantage manifests itself in the form of the greater activity of his queen and the centralised king. The alternative ending after 41 hxg4 ♕e7 42 ♕e3 ♔g7 43 g5 is also pleasant for White, but requires separate analysis.

41...e4?!

Black strives to activate his queen, counting on checking the white king which has no cover. But, as becomes clear, it does not need cover, preferring to play an active role. Therefore more circumspect would be "to stay put" by 41...♕d6 (it is also possible to provoke the weakening a2-a4: 41...♕a6 42 a4

♕d6) 42 ♕e4 ♔h6 43 ♕d5 and, although his queen is more actively placed, it is not easy to increase his advantage.

42 ♕xe4 ♕b2+ 43 ♔f3 ♕xa2 44 ♕e7+ ♔h6 45 ♕e3+ ♔h7 46 ♔e4!

46...♕c2+

Now the king is included in the attack on the queenside pawn islands. But also after 46...♕g2+ 47 ♔e5! ♕c6 48 ♕g5, Black's defence is very difficult. No use either is 46...♕a5 47 ♕g5. In all these varieties of endgame White's advantage will be manifested above all in the fact that, after the exchange of the c5 pawn for the b3 pawn, the passed pawn on c4 can get to the queening square significantly quicker than the a-pawn. To the point, this is a striking example which confirms the view, expressed above, that queen endings are very similar to pawn endings, except that they take considerably longer to realise.

47 ♔d5 ♕f5+ 48 ♔d6 ♕f6+ 49 ♕e6 ♕d4+

The pawn ending after 49...♕xe6+ 50 ♔xe6 ♔h6 51 ♔d5 ♔h5 52 ♔xc5 ♔h4 53 ♔d6 is hopeless for Black.

50 ♔c6 ♕c3 51 ♕e7+ ♔h6 52 ♕f8+ ♔h7 53 ♕xc5 ♕f3+ 54 ♕d5! ♕xb3 55 c5

Black's position is lost. The h3 pawn is immune from capture (55...♕xh3? 56 ♕d7+). On 55...♕a4+ follows 56 ♔c7 and the c5 pawn gets the green light. Relatively stronger is 55...♕e3 56 h4 ♕f4 57 ♔d7 ♕g4+ 58 ♔d6 ♕g3+ 59 ♕e5 ♕d3+ 60 ♔e7, but even this doesn't save him.

But here occurred a paradoxical situation, with its source probably going back to the distant chess past, when upon a threat to the king "check" was announced, and upon a threat to the queen—"garde". My rival got "mixed up" as to which of his principal pieces White was attacking...

55...♔h6?? 56 ♕xb3 Black resigned.

Krasenkov - Beliavsky
Lvov 2000

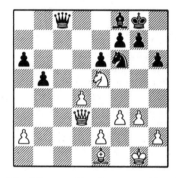

Black's small advantage lies in the more active position of his queen, controlling the only open line, and the potential possibility of creating an outside passed pawn on the queen's flank. White can do away with the first problem by offering an exchange of queens with 30 ♕c3, but it seemed to him that this did not solve the second.

M.Krasenkov preferred to continue the game with queens and...fell under attack.

30 ♕b3 ♕c1 31 ♔f2

Even here it is not too late for 31 ♕c3, but Black did not sense the danger.

31...♘d5 32 e4 ♕a1!

A surprising manoeuvre. By attacking the d4 pawn, A.Beliavsky seizes the initiative.

33 ♘c6

33 exd5? leads to a loss of time: 33...♕xd4+ 34 ♕e3 ♗c5 35 ♕xd4 ♗xd4+ 36 ♔e2 ♗xe5.

33...♘b6 34 ♔e2 h5!

This not only hands over the move to White, for whom it is not easy to decide whether to make a rearguard raid with the knight, but also threatens to attack the opponent's weakened king's flank.

35 ♘b8 ♕xd4 36 ♘xa6

On 36 ♗f2 decides 36...♕d6 37 ♘xa6 ♘a4 with irresistible threats.

36...♘c4 37 ♘c7 ♕g1 38 ♗f2 ♕g2

"Taking" the pawn, 38...♕xh2!?, is worth considering, since after the move in the game White can apparently defend himself. Here, however, after 39 ♕xb5 ♗d6 40 ♘xe6 (also in Black's favour is 40 ♕xc4 ♗xg3 41 ♕c5 ♗xf2 42 ♕xf2 ♕xc7) 40...♗xg3 41 ♕e8+ ♔h7 42 ♘f8+ ♔h6, Black retains the advantage.

39 ♕xb5 ♘d2 40 ♕xh5?

Confusion. After this the game is quickly over. It was necessary to decide on 40 ♔xd2 ♕xf2+ 41 ♕e2 ♗b4+ (if he wants, there is a perpetual check by 41...♕d4+ 42 ♕d3 ♕f2+ 43 ♕e2) 42 ♔d3 ♕b6 43 ♕b2 ♕a5 44 ♕b3 ♗c5 45 ♘b5 ♗g1 and, though Black, as before, has the initiative, White's main difficulties are behind him.

40...♗b4! 41 ♘xe6

On 41 ♔e3 possible is the simple 41...g6.

41...♕f1+ 42 ♔e3 ♘c4+ 43 ♔f4

More tenacious is 43 ♔d4, but even this does not save him after 43...♘b2.

43...♕xf2 44 ♕b5 ♗d6+ 45 ♔g5 ♕xf3 White resigned.

The struggle with rooks

In the absence of queens there is a reduced danger of an attack on the king, which therefore has the opportunity of taking an active part in the game. First let us look at an example of a classic complicated endgame played in the early 20th century.

Réti - Rubinstein
Göteborg 1920

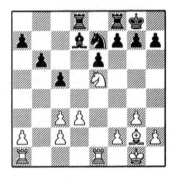

The knight on e5 looks very imposing but in the present position far more significant is the weakness of White's pawns on the queen's flank. With the following fine manoeuvre A.Rubinstein underlines this.

20...♗a4! 21 ♖e2 ♘d5 22 ♗xd5

This exchange makes White's defence difficult. He should decide on 22 c4!?, after which possible is 22...♘b4 23 ♖c1 f6 (23...♘xa2 24 ♖a1 ♘c3 25 ♖ee1) 24 ♘f3 ♔f7 25

♘e1 ♘xa2 26 ♖a1 ♘c3 27 ♖e3 b5 28 cxb5 ♖d4 with a passive, but sufficiently solid position for White. Now the superiority of the black bishop over the white knight will be noticeable.

22...exd5 23 ♖ae1 ♖fe8 24 f4 f6

The exchange of rooks is to Black's advantage.

25 ♘f3 ♔f7 26 ♔f2 ♖xe2+ 27 ♖xe2 ♖e8 28 ♖xe8 ♔xe8 29 ♘e1

A.Rubinstein has assessed deeply the arising minor piece ending. The knight is forced to a passive position, and now for the black king arises the possibility of invading the opponent's camp along the weakened white squares.

29...♔e7 30 ♔e3 ♔e6 31 g4

Otherwise Black plays 31...♔f5 and then the march of the h-pawn will weaken White's position on the king's flank.

31...♔d6 32 h3 g6 33 ♔d2

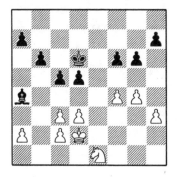

33...♗d7!

The bishop handles its mission excellently. The threat to the c2 pawn is no longer very effective; now the pawns of the opposite flank are in the bishop's sights.

34 ♘f3 ♔e7!!

Excellently played. With such moves you feel the hand of a true master! The hurried 34...h5 would allow White an easier defence—35

g5 fxg5 36 ♘xg5. For example: 36...♔e7 37 h4 ♔f6 38 ♔e3 ♔f5 39 ♘f7 ♗a4 40 ♘d6+ ♔e6 41 ♘c8 ♔d7 42 ♘xa7 ♔c7 43 c4 and White gains equal chances.

35 ♔e3 h5! 36 ♘h2

A forced decision. After 36 gxh5 gxh5 37 h4 ♔e6 the black king breaks through to the white pawns.

36...♔d6 37 ♔e2 d4!

Cutting off the white king from the important e3 square and fixing the white pawns on the same coloured squares as his bishop. Black has in prospect the possibility of ...g6-g5 and an invasion of the king via the e5 square.

38 cxd4

After 38 c4 it is necessary to reckon on 38...hxg4 39 hxg4 g5!.

38...cxd4 39 ♔d2 hxg4 40 hxg4

The pawn ending is hopeless for White: 40 ♘xg4 ♗xg4 41 hxg4 g5!.

40...♗c6! 41 ♔e2

The attempt to free himself by 41 c3? would lead White to a sad and highly instructive end: 41...dxc3+ 42 ♔xc3 ♗g2! 43 ♔d4 b5 44 ♔e3 a5 45 a3 ♔d5—zugzwang!

41...♗d5! 42 a3 b5 43 ♘f1 a5

By forcing White to play a2-a3, A.Rubinstein obtains the possibility of creating a passed pawn on the a-file.

44 ♘d2 a4 45 ♘e4+

White unsuccessfully tries to save himself in the pawn ending, though even after 45 ♔d1 g5! he is not left with any chances of salvation.

45...♗xe4 46 dxe4 b4 47 ♔d2 bxa3 48 ♔c1 g5 White resigned.

A.Rubinstein's play in this ending is a really aesthetic delight. An analogous feeling is aroused in the technique of the great J.R.Capablanca, who, in the following game, demonstrates an excellent text book example on the theme of positional pressure.

Capablanca - Yates
New York 1924

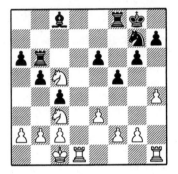

White's position is better—he controls the d-file; the black pieces are passive but the presence of a great number of pawns makes the position "viscous", settled for Black. However, Capablanca finds a way to break up the pawn chain on the queenside, after which his knight gains space for operations.

25 a4! ♘h5 26 b3! cxb3 27 cxb3 bxa4 28 ♘3xa4 ♖c6 29 ♔b2 ♘f6

Black attempts to anticipate White's activity after the possible doubling of his rooks on the central file.

30 ♖d2 a5

Clearly Black wants to move the pawns away to an invulnerable position, but even on a5 it will not be easy to defend it. Let us recall one of the basic chess laws: do not move pawns on that flank where the opponent is stronger. More accurate was an immediate 30...♘d5!? or 30...♔f7!?, endeavouring to give the position more solidity and improve the coordination of his pieces.

The whole of Capablanca's following play is a brilliant example of

methodical   and   purposeful positional pressure.

31 ♖hd1 ♘d5 32 g3 ♖f7 33 ♘d3!

White strives to exchange rooks in order to transfer the knight to c4 to attack the a5 pawn.

33...♖b7 34 ♘e5 ♖cc7 35 ♖d4

Now, after the inevitable e3-e4, the backward e6 pawn becomes yet another tangible weakness.

35...♔g7 36 e4 fxe4 37 ♖xe4! ♖b5 38 ♖c4!

The logical continuation of the plan begun with the move 33 ♘d3!—Capablanca endeavours to exchange rooks, rightly assuming that his positional advantage is stable.

38...♖xc4 39 ♘xc4 ♗d7

On 39...♔f6 likewise follows 40 ♘c3 and if 40...♘xc3 41 ♔xc3 g5 42 hxg5+ ♔xg5 43 ♖a1 White consolidates his advantage.

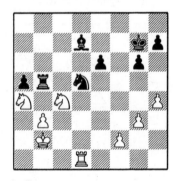

40 ♘c3!

The start of a five-move raid on the a5 pawn.

40...♖c5 41 ♘e4 ♖b5 42 ♘ed6 ♖c5 43 ♘b7 ♖c7 44 ♘bxa5 ♗b5

Black's pieces have come to life a little, but this is only temporary.

45 ♘d6 ♗d7 46 ♘ac4 ♖a7 47 ♘e4

In the hands of the world champion, the finish is superb.

47...h6 48 f4 ♗e8 49 ♘e5 ♖a8 50 ♖c1 ♗f7 51 ♖c6 ♗g8 52 ♘c5 ♖e8 53 ♖a6 ♖e7 54 ♔a3 ♗f7 55 b4

Capablanca strengthens his position to the utmost.

55...♘c7 56 ♖c6 ♘b5+ 57 ♔b2 ♘d4 58 ♖a6 ♗e8 59 g4 ♔f6 60 ♘e4+ ♔g7 61 ♘d6 ♗b5 62 ♖a5 ♗f1 63 ♖a8!

With the idea of weaving a mating net—64 ♘e8+ ♔h7 65 ♘f6+ ♔g7 66 g5.

63...g5 64 fxg5 hxg5 65 hxg5 ♗g2 66 ♖e8! ♖c7

Also losing is 66...♖xe8 67 ♘xe8+ ♔f8 68 g6 ♔xe8 69 g7.

67 ♖d8 ♘c6 68 ♘e8+ ♔f8 69 ♘xc7+ ♘xd8 70 ♔c3 ♗b7 71 ♔d4 ♗c8

Black prepares to give up his minor pieces for the white pawns to obtain a theoretically drawn ending, but Capablanca is inexorable.

72 g6 ♘b7 73 ♘e8! ♘d8 74 b5 ♔g8 75 g5 ♔f8 76 g7+ ♔g8 77 g6 **Black resigned.**

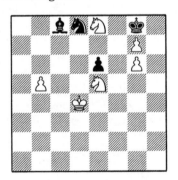

The final position undoubtedly deserves a diagram. Black is in total zugzwang: neither his knight nor his bishop can move because of inevitable mate. It only remains for us to applaud White's splendid knight duet and keep in the heart the indelible talent of one of the greatest masters of the ending.

The following game between outstanding endgame study composer Genrikh Kasparyan and the brilliant attacking romantic Vladimir Simagin is reflective of the fighting tradition of the Soviet chess school which excused any refusal to struggle only by the exhaustion of a player's resources.

Kasparian - Simagin
Sochi 1952

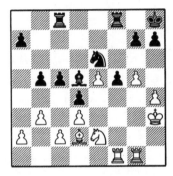

Black has not so much a small advantage as a moral one—he has the more active bishop and the possibility of advancing on the queenside. White is also in a belligerent mood —in fact it is difficult to imagine what can shake the momentum of his resolve.

30...a5! 31 g6 h6 32 ♘f4 ♘xf4+ 33 ♗xf4 ♖fe8 34 ♖f2 a4 35 ♖c1 b4 36 ♖e1 ♗e6 37 h5 ♖a8 38 ♖ee2!

White prophylactically over-protects his only real weakness, the c2 pawn.

38...♔g8!

Black shows that there is no need to hurry and sets about improving the position of his king. Such outwardly unremarkable moves not infrequently have a strange effect on an opponent, inducing him into active operations without particular reason.

39 ♔g3 ♔f8 40 ♗c1 ♖a6 41 a3?

With the enemy king approaching the centre, G.Kasparian makes the decision to complicate the struggle. Otherwise he would have to stick to waiting tactics: 41 ♔f4 ♔e7 42 ♖e1 ♗d5 43 ♖ee2 ♔e6 44 ♖e1 and though Black, as before, has the preferable game, there is nothing really concrete.

41...axb3 42 axb4 ♖a1

The rook aims at the d3 pawn from the rear. However stronger was 42...♖b8! 43 cxb3 ♖xb4 after which White might be sorry for opening lines.

43 ♗b2 ♖g1+ 44 ♔g2 ♖h1 45 ♖h2

Also possible was 45 bxc5 ♖xh5 (weaker is 45...♔e7?! 46 ♖h2 ♖d1 47 ♔f4 with advantage to White) 46 cxb3 ♗xb3 47 ♗xd4 ♖d8 with equal chances.

45...♖d1 46 bxc5 bxc2 47 ♖xc2 ♖xd3+ 48 ♔f4

White is just as actively placed as Black. And, although the active position of the king entails some risk, upon the retreat 48 ♔f2 Black's attack might develop more dangerously: 48...♗b3! 49 ♖e2 ♗d1 50 ♖e1 ♖c8.

48...♖b8 49 ♖cd2

Upon the impulsive 49 c6? White loses—49...♖bb3 50 ♖hf2 ♖h3.

49...♖e3!

The culminating moment of the struggle. In a situation where the fate of the position swings to and fro, V.Simagin sets the opponent a complicated problem and he is not up to the task.

50 ♖de2?

It was not easy to decide on 50 ♗xd4 ♖e4+ 51 ♔f3 ♖b4, after which he has to go over to godforsaken defence: 52 ♗e3 ♖b3 53 ♖he2 ♖xe5 54 ♔f2 etc. And so, as decisions are often made, he then switched to another move.

Further events show, that stronger was 50 ♖he2!, but then after 50...♖bb3 51 ♖xe3 dxe3 he has to decide the fate of the "hanging" rook. Where can it go? No good is 52 ♖e2? ♗c4!. There remains 52 ♖c2 ♖d3 53 ♗c1 ♗b3 when he is faced with finding the only move 54 ♖b2! (losing is 54 ♖e2? ♗d1! 55 ♖e1 e2!) and after 54...e2 55 ♖xe2 ♗d1 56 ♖f2 ♗xh5 57 ♔xf5 White has an active king, but the position comes down to 59...♖g3 58 ♔e6+ ♔e8 59 ♖a2 ♖xg6+ 60 ♔f5 ♖g1, when objectively the result is a draw.

Now however an unpleasant surprise awaits White.

50...♖b4! 51 ♖xe3 d3+!!

Black sacrifices a rook, but this is a "Greek" gift: 52 ♔f3? ♗d5+ 53 ♔f2 ♖xb2+ 54 ♔g3 f4+ and White is left a piece down.

52 ♖e4 ♖xe4+ 53 ♔g3 f4+ 54 ♔f3 ♗d5!

The position assumes a technical character. With rooks on the board the "opposite-coloured" bishops are clearly in Black's favour. We will return to this theme in an appropriate place in chapter 5.

55 ♔g4 f3+ 56 ♔g3 ♖c4 57 c6

57 ♗a3 ♖c2 58 ♖xc2 dxc2 does not create any illusions of a pleasant outcome.

57...♔e7 58 ♖d2 ♗xc6 59 ♖xd3 ♖c2 60 ♗a3+ ♔e6

Clearer is 60...♔e8!.

61 ♖d1

Also losing is 61 ♖d6+ ♔f5 62 ♖xc6 ♖xc6 63 ♗f8 ♔g5 64 ♗xg7 ♔xh5 65 ♔xf3 ♔xg6.

61...f2 62 ♗f8 ♗b5 63 ♗xg7 f1=♕ 64 ♖xf1 ♗xf1 65 ♗xh6 ♗e2 66 g7 ♔f7 67 ♔h4 ♖c6!

The shortest way to victory, since now, after the natural 68 ♔g5, even 68...♔g8 wins as he has to part with the bishop.

68 ♗f4 ♔xg7 69 ♔g5 ♗d3 70 ♗e3 ♔f7 71 h6 ♔e6 72 ♗f4 ♗h7 White resigned.

Kasparov - Kramnik
Linares 1998

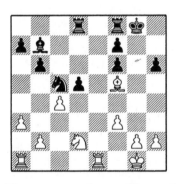

If we assess the position only from the point of view of Black's damaged kingside pawn formation then White appears to have a very tangible advantage. Undoubtedly, on passive play, Black could well lose. However White's pieces are for the present insufficiently well coordinated. V.Kramnik exploits this fact energetically. Then his opponent's advantage is only small.

20...♗a6!

Black attacks the c4 pawn, not giving White time to put right the coordination of his pieces.

21 ♖ac1

After 21 ♖e7 dxc4 22 ♘e4 ♘xe4 23 ♗xe4 ♖fe8 24 ♖xa7 ♗c8 25 ♖c7 f5 26 ♗c2 b5, Black's rooks control the central file.

21...dxc4 22 ♘xc4 ♘b3 23 ♖c3 ♘d4

Not a second's peace!

24 ♗h3

Hardly better is the retreat along the b1-h7 diagonal. On 24 ♗d3 Black can repeat the position by 24...♘b5 25 ♖b3 ♘d4 26 ♖c3 ♘b5, while after 24 ♗b1 he can offer an exchange of rooks by 24...♖fe8 25 ♔f2 ♖xe1 26 ♔xe1 ♖e8+.

24...♖fe8 25 ♔f2 ♖xe1 26 ♔xe1 ♖e8+ 27 ♔d2

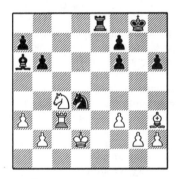

27...♘e2

All in the same style—Black's pieces continually hound White's. And yet, as shown by V.Kramnik, even stronger was 27...f5! (cutting off the h3-bishop) 28 ♘e3 ♖d8 (impetuous is 28...f4?! 29 ♘c2 with simplification, since 29...♖e2+?! 30 ♔d1 ♘e6? is not possible because of 31 ♘b4) 29 ♔e1 ♖e8, giving the king no rest.

28 ♖e3

On 28 ♖c2 would have followed 28...♘f4!.

28...♖d8+ 29 ♔xe2 ♗xc4+ 30 ♔e1 ♔f8 31 ♗f5

A true sign of poor form, Black would still have to labour for the half point after the more exact 31 ♖c3. Black would have to move away the bishop by 31...♗b5, since if 31...b5 32 b3! ♖d3 33 ♖xd3 ♗xd3 34 ♔d2, awaiting him is a far inferior ending than that in the game. Now, however, Black hurries not only to exchange rooks, but also to move up his king to the centre, which makes his position practically unassailable.

31...♖e8 32 ♖xe8+ ♔xe8 33 ♔d2 ♔e7 34 ♔e3 ♗d5 35 ♔d4 ♔d6 36 ♗e4 ♗e6

Of course not the pawn ending after 36...♗xe4 37 ♔xe4 ♔e6 38 g4!.

37 ♗d3 ♗c8 38 ♗c4 ♔e7

Also here, no good is 38...♗e6 39 ♗xe6 fxe6 40 g4!. It should be mentioned that, upon accurate defence, Black will hardly succeed in breaching his position. The fact of the matter is that White will not manage to create a second weakness, while the one, the f7 pawn, is not enough to realise his small advantage.

39 ♔e4 ♗b7+ 40 ♗d5 ♗c8 41 ♔d4 ♗d7 42 ♔c4

Or 42 ♗b7 ♔d6.

42...♗e8 43 b4

The attempt to break through with the king on the queenside by 43 ♔b4 ♗d7 44 ♗c4 ♗c6 45 ♗b5 is refuted by 45...♗d5 46 ♗a4 ♔d6.

43...♗d7

Also good is 43...♔d6 44 ♔d4 f5!.

44 f4 f5!

White will not be able to penetrate any further with his king.

45 ♗f3 ♔d6 46 ♗h5 f6 47 ♗d1 ♗c6 48 g3 ♗d7 49 ♗c2 ♔e6 50 a4 ♔d6 51 a5 ♔e6 52 ♔d4 Draw.

Spassky - Ljubojević
Montreal 1979

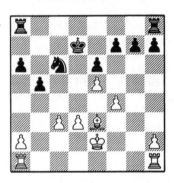

Black's position looks quite pleasant—he has no pawn weaknesses while the half-open d- and c-files promise quite good prospects. Apparently L.Ljubojević also assessed the arising endgame quite optimistically and at first he makes no attempt to create counterplay. But meanwhile White has a significant positional plus: a compact and potentially mobile pawn mass in the centre.

The first part of White's plan consists of the demolition of the distinctive barrier—the black b5 pawn. It must become a weakness.

21 ♖hb1!

With the idea of a2-a4.

21...♖ab8 22 ♗c5 ♖hc8 23 ♗d6

This bishop has no apparent objects of attack, but its unpleasant "X-Ray" is already felt—the black pieces are limited in mobility.

23...♖b7 24 a4 ♘d8 25 axb5 axb5 26 ♔d2 f6

Rather belated activity. White is already hurrying to create a weakness for his opponent on b5 and to control the important strategical principal a-file.

27 d4

On 27 ♗f8, simplest is 27...♔e8 (weaker is 27...fxe5 28 fxe5 ♔e8 29

♗d6) 28 ♗b4 ♘c6 29 ♗d6 and we are back to where we started.

27...♘f7 28 ♗b4 fxe5

He should bide his time with this exchange—28...♘h6!?.

29 fxe5 ♘h6 30 ♖a5 ♘f5 31 ♔d3 g6

Black counts on defence, with an original fortress, but also worth considering is 31...♖cb8!?.

32 ♗c5 ♖cb8 33 ♖a6 ♖c8 34 ♔e4 ♖cc7 35 ♔f4!

Threatening to invade with the king by ♔f4-g5. White needs to weaken the kingside pawns.

35...h6 36 ♔e4 g5

More stubborn was 36...♖c8. Now, if 37 d5 exd5+ 38 ♔xd5 ♘e7+ 39 ♗xe7 ♔xe7, Black has chances of defending himself, both after 40 ♖e6+ ♔f7 41 ♖f1+ ♔g7 42 ♖ff6 ♖d7+, and also upon 40 ♖xg6 ♖d7+ 41 ♖d6 ♖xc3 42 ♖xd7+ ♔xd7 43 ♖xb5 ♖d3+ 44 ♔e4 ♖h3, when he has sufficient counterplay.

Nevertheless, by playing 37 c4 ♖cb8 38 d5 bxc4 39 ♖xb7+ ♖xb7 40 dxe6+ ♔d8 41 ♗d6, White should win.

37 ♖ba1 ♖c8 38 ♖xe6! ♖xc5

Of course, also hopeless was 38...♔xe6 39 ♖a6+ ♔d7 40 ♔xf5.

39 ♔xf5 ♖xc3 40 ♖xh6

The game is decided, White's connected passed pawns in the centre are irresistible.

40...♔c7 41 ♖h7+ ♔b6 42 ♖xb7+ ♔xb7 43 e6 ♔c7 44 ♖a7+ ♔b6 45 ♖a8 Black resigned.

Z.Almasi - Zuger
Horgen 1995

Here, White's slight positional advantage lies, first and foremost, in the superiority of his knight, occupying the "eternal" d4 square, over the bishop. This situation is characteristic of the French Defence, since from the very beginning the pawn structure is determined.

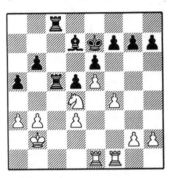

25 ♖e3!

A fine rook manoeuvre, forcing Black to worsen his kingside pawn structure.

25...h5 26 ♖h3 g6 27 ♖e3

By forcing the kingside pawns to move to squares of the colour of his own bishop, White obtains a slight but enduring advantage, though it is not easy to breach Black's position.

27...♖5c7 28 ♖e2 ♖c3 29 ♖d1 ♖3c7 30 g3 ♖g8 31 ♖f1 ♖gc8

Convincing himself that the break 31...g5 32 f5! exf5 33 ♘xf5+ ♗xf5 34 ♖xf5 boomerangs, Black continues with waiting tactics. You see, White has no other alternative but to exchange rooks.

32 ♖d2 ♗e8 33 ♖c2 ♖c5

After 33...♖xc2+ 34 ♘xc2 ♗b5 35 ♖f3 f6 36 ♘d4 ♗d7 37 exf6+ ♔xf6 38 ♖e3 appears the traditional "French" pawn-pair brake, d5-e6.

34 ♖fc1 ♗d7 35 ♖f1 ♗e8 36 ♖ff2! ♗d7 37 ♔c1!

While Black marks time the white king transfers to the centre.

37...♖8c7 38 ♔d2 ♖c8 39 ♖f1 ♖a8 40 ♖fc1 ♖ac8 41 ♘f3!

Freeing the d4 square for the pawn.

41...♔d8 42 ♘g5!

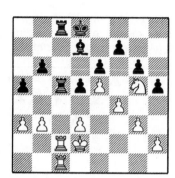

42...罝xc2+

Black is forced to exchange rooks, since after 42...當e7 43 罝xc5! bxc5 44 d4! 罝b8 (it's no easier after 44...c4 45 bxc4 dxc4 46 ②e4 or 44...a4 45 罝xc5!) 45 罝xc5 罝xb3 46 罝xa5 罝b2+ 47 當e3 罝xh2 48 罝a7! and Black lands in an unpleasant pin (Z.Almasi).

43 罝xc2 罝xc2+ 44 當xc2

The game goes into an ending where the knight is clearly stronger than the bishop.

44...當e7 45 當c3 皋b5 46 ②f3 當d7 47 ②e1 當c6 48 ②c2 當c7 49 b4 皋a4 50 ②d4 當d7 51 ②f3

Stronger is 51 bxa5! bxa5 52 ②f3, threatening to penetrate with the king via c5.

51...當c7

Stronger is 51...axb4+.

52 ②g5 皋e8 53 ②h7 皋a4 54 ②f6 皋b5 55 bxa5 bxa5 56 f5!

A decisive break. Black cannot entertain either 56...exf5 57 ②xd5+ 當d7 58 h4, or 56...gxf5 57 ②xh5.

56...當b6 57 fxg6 fxg6 58 ②h7! 皋e8 59 ②f8 皋f7 60 h4! 當b5 61 d4!

In "crippling" the bishop, White fixes the black pawns. Black is in zugzwang.

61...當a4 62 當b2 當b5 63 當b3 當b6 64 ②d7+ 當b5 65 ②c5 當b6

On 65...皋g8 follows 66 ②b7 and 67 ②d6.

66 當c3 當c6 67 ②d3!

White conducts the ending very accurately. While sealing off the way to a4, he transfers the knight to the kingside.

67...當b5 68 ②b2 當c6 69 當d2 當d7 70 當e3 當e7 71 當f4 皋e8 72 當g5 當f7 73 ②d3 皋a4 74 ②c5 皋c2 75 ②b7 a4 76 當h6 當f8 77 ②c5 當f7 78 當g5 皋b3 79 當f4 皋d1 80 當e3 Black resigned.

Korchnoi - Kasparov
Wijk aan Zee 2000

Black's small advantage lies in his undivided control of the d-file. However White has sufficient defensive resources.

23...罝cd4! 24 b3!

Restricting the knight on b6.

24...罝d3 25 當e2

Here the king also finds no peace. Worth considering is 25 罝g1, with the idea of exchanging rooks after 26 罝g3, on which Black might reply 25...罝h3 26 罝g2 e5!, maintaining the initiative.

25...罝d2+ 26 當f3 罝7d3+ 27 當g2 e6

Also possible was 27...e5 28 fxe5+ 當xe5, but the world champion does not hurry to force the game, reckoning on more weighty dividends.

28 罝he1 當e7

This allows White to demonstrate activity. Worth considering is 28...h6!? and, after 29 ♖cd1 ♖xd1 30 ♘xd1 g5 31 fxg5 hxg5, his control over the f4 square guarantees Black the advantage. 29 h4 does not stop this in view of 29...e5!.

29 f5! ♘d7 30 fxe6 fxe6 31 ♔f1 ♘e5 32 ♖e2 g5

Black can win a pawn by 32...♘g4!? 33 h3 ♖xh3 34 ♖xd2 ♖h1+ 35 ♔e2 ♖xc1, but he prefers to increase the pressure.

33 ♘a4 ♖d1+ 34 ♖e1 ♖xe1+ 35 ♔xe1 ♖d7

Black does not like 35...b6 because of the possible exchange of rooks, 36 ♖c7+ ♖d7 37 ♖xd7+ ♘xd7, with real chances of a draw. But, as G.Kasparov pointed out, better is 35...♔d6! and on 36 ♘c5 there is 36...b6!, forcing a transfer to a clearly better pawn endgame. White would have to limit himself to 35 ♔e2.

36 ♔e2 ♘d3

The knight on e5 is too well placed to be removed. More logical is 36...b6!? or 36...g4.

37 ♖c3 ♘f4+ 38 ♔f3

38 ♔e3 ♔f6 39 ♘b2 h5 40 f3 looks more solid.

38...♔f6 39 ♘c5 ♖c7

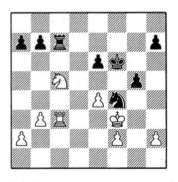

40 h4?

At the time control V.Korchnoi makes a serious strategical mistake, leading to the creation of an outside passed h-pawn for his opponent. It was necessary to return with the knight, 40 ♘a4, and after 40...♖xc3+ 41 ♘xc3 ♔e5 42 ♔e3 h5 43 f3, although Black's chances, as before, are preferable, it is easier for White to fight for the draw.

40...e5 41 hxg5+ ♔xg5 42 ♖c4

On 42 ♘a4 could follow 42...♖f7, followed by the advance of the h-pawn.

42...b5

Why not 42...b6 43 ♘a4 ♖xc4 44 bxc4 h5 ? You see, it is well known that knight endings are close to pawn endings in content—and the outside passed pawn plays a great role in them. But at the present moment an exchange of rooks is premature, since, after 45 c5 bxc5 46 ♘xc5, the number of pawns is reduced and, besides, there is the threat of ♘c5-d7, hunting the a-pawn. Therefore Black prefers to devalue White's queen's flank.

43 ♖c1 b4! 44 ♖c4

After 44 ♖g1+ ♔f6 45 ♘a4 ♖c2 (also good is 45...♖c8) 46 ♖g8 and the black rook, working from the rear, is more effective than White's. For example, 46...♘e6 47 ♖b8 ♘d4+ 48 ♔g3 a5 49 ♖f8+ ♔g7 50 ♖a8 ♖xa2 or even 46...♖xa2 47 ♖f8+ ♔g5.

44...a5 45 ♘a4 ♖f7!

Also here 45...♖xc4 46 bxc4 h5 47 c5 might prove insufficient to realise the advantage.

46 ♔e3

On 46 ♔g3 would have followed 46...♘d3 47 ♖c2 h5 48 ♖d2 ♘e1.

46...♘g2+ 47 ♔e2 ♘f4+ 48 ♔e3 h5 49 ♖c5 ♘g2+

After 49...♘g6 50 ♘b2 h4 51 ♘d3 White manages to put right the coordination of his pieces.

50 ♔e2 h4!

One of the methods of realising a material advantage—is not to cling on to it at the expense of new positional achievements.

51 ♖xe5+ ♔g4 52 ♖e8

White misses the chance to exchange rooks—52 f3+ ♖xf3 53 ♖g5+ ♔xg5 54 ♔xf3 ♘e1+ 55 ♔f2 ♘d3+ 56 ♔f3, which would allow prolonged resistance. For example, there is nothing to gained by 56...♘c1? 57 ♘b6 ♘xa2 58 ♘c4. And yet, as pointed out by G.Kasparov, after 56...♘e5+ 57 ♔g2 ♔g4 58 ♘c5 h3+ 59 ♔f2 (59 ♔h2 ♔h4 loses more quickly) 59...♔h4 60 ♘e6 ♘d3 61 ♔f3 ♘e1+ 62 ♔f2 h2, Black must win.

Now, however, the game is quickly over.

52...♘f4+ 53 ♔e3 h3 54 f3+ ♔h4 White resigned.

On 55 ♖h8+ follows the simple 55...♘h5 56 ♔f2 ♖g7 and the pawn promotes to a queen.

That it is not easy to defend against an opponent with a spatial advantage is well known by everyone. However, nowadays, when defensive technique is high, this is often the lot of the Black player. Such champions as Lasker, Petrosian and Karpov, quite often demonstrated their cold-bloodedness in protracted defence. However, for players of an aggressive style, a passive stand proved more agonising. Here is an example of single combat involving present day leaders.

Kramnik - Kasparov
BrainGames World Championship,
London 2000

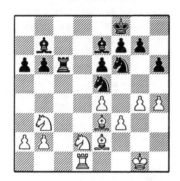

White has a space advantage and, with an advance of the h- and g-pawns, plans to increase this. However, the absence of real pawn weaknesses in Black's position makes it sufficiently fire-proof.

With the prophylactic retreat, 21...♘e8!? 22 f4 ♘d7 23 ♘d4 ♖c7, Black's forces are like a spring ready to uncoil at an appropriate moment (for example on 24 h5 possible is 24...e5). However, this was not the best of days for the world champion.

21...♗c8?! 22 g5 hxg5 23 hxg5 ♘fd7

Also here not bad is 23...♘e8!?.

24 f4 ♘g6 25 ♘f3!

On the routine 25 ♘d4 ♖c7, Black is ready for counterplay by ...e6-e5. Taking into account the overloaded bishop on c8, defending the knight and a6 pawn, White "invites" the rook as a guest. Kasparov accepts the invitation and wrongly, it seems. By continuing to stick to passive tactics of the type 25...♘e8!? 26 ♘fd4 ♖c7 27 ♗h5 ♘gf8 28 ♘e4 ♗b7, Black can count on a successful defence.

25...♖c2 26 ♗xa6 ♗xa6 27 ♖xd7 ♖xb2 28 ♖a7 ♗b5

Sobering—a single active rook can hardly compensate for the weakness of the b6 pawn and the periphery (the back rank!).

29 f5 exf5 30 exf5 ♖e2

Starting to play move by move— 30...♘h8? 31 ♗xb6 ♗c6 32 ♗d4 clearly does not sort out Black.

31 ♘fd4

Also possible is the prosaic 31 ♗xb6 ♘e5 (bad is 31...♘f4? 32 ♘bd4) 32 ♘fd4 ♖e1+ 33 ♘h2 ♗e8 34 ♗c5 ♗xc5 35 ♘xc5, but Kramnik draws his opponent into a forcing game, counting on exploiting his hanging pieces.

31...♖e1+

31...♖xe3?? 32 ♘xb5 loses a piece.

32 ♔f2 ♖f1+ 33 ♔g2 ♘h4+ 34 ♔h3 ♖h1+ 35 ♔g4 ♗e8

Again the only move, since losing is 35...♘g2 36 ♘xb5 ♘xe3+ 37 ♔f4.

36 ♗f2 ♘g2 37 ♖a8!

This pin is a psychological attack in a time-trouble situation, although it is not easy for Black even after 37 ♘f3, with an attack on the b6 pawn.

37...♖f1 38 ♔f3 ♘h4+?

Tarrasch's dictum that the edge of the board is a relatively poor position for a knight, applies also to champions! After 38...♘f4 39 ♘d2 ♖d1 40 ♘c4 ♘d5, or 40 ♘e4 ♘d5, the knight is a little more active. Now White succeeds in deriving real benefit from the pin of the rook on a8.

39 ♔e2 ♖h1 40 ♘b5 ♗xg5 41 ♘c7 ♔e7 42 ♘xe8 ♘xf5 43 ♗xb6

As a result of the activity Black has ended up losing a piece. Is this the end? No. It is never too late to resign, particularly in conditions of limited material where White has

still to overcome certain technical difficulties. And, as it turns out, the miracle is still ahead.

The ending of the game might also fully serve the theme of the final chapter of this book.

43...♔d7 44 a4

Kramnik censured this move, reckoning that 44 ♘c5+! ♔c6 45 ♖a6, with the threat of various discovered checks, would lead more quickly to victory.

44...♖h3!

Kasparov does not miss such opportunities—the rook is most active on the 3rd rank.

45 ♘c5+ ♔c6 46 a5

46...♖e3+?!

Kramnik considered this move a mistake, pointing out as strongest 46...♗e3!. Putting right the coordination of this bishop and rook will make the white king rather nervous, since it is not easy to assess consequences of the type, 47 ♖c8+ ♔d5! 48 ♘d3 (on 48 ♘c7+ there is 48...♔c6! 49 ♘e8+ ♔d5) 48...♖h2+ 49 ♔f3 ♖h3+ 50 ♔g2 (not 50 ♔g4?? ♖g3+ 51 ♔xf5 ♖g5 mate) 50...♖g3+ 51 ♔h2 ♘e4 52 ♘e5 (Kramnik).

47 ♔d1 ♖e7?

He should not take the rook away from its active position. It is worth trying 47...♔b5!?, attempting a break with the king—Kramnik.

48 ♖c8+ ♔b5 49 ♘e4 ♖xe4 50 ♖c5+ ♔a6 51 ♘c7+ ♔b7 52 ♖xf5 ♗e3 53 ♗xe3 ♖xe3

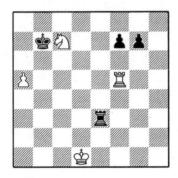

54 ♖xf7?

The start of a series of mutual errors, showing that even the greats make their own mistakes. Winning is 54 ♘d5! ♖a3 55 ♘b4 f6 56 ♖b5+ ♔c7 57 a6.

54...♖e5?

After 54...♔c6! Black would already be close to a draw. For example: 55 a6 ♖a3 or 55 ♔d2 ♖e5!.

55 a6+?

White again misses an easy win: 55 ♘d5+! ♔a6 56 ♘b4+ ♔b5 57 ♖f4 g5 58 ♖d4 ♖f5 59 a6. An inopportune advance of the pawn, with the knight attached to it, leads to a theoretically drawn position. But, as becomes clear, it's not over yet!

55...♔b6 56 ♖xg7 ♖a5! 57 ♔d2 ♖a1 58 ♔c2 ♖h1?

No way was it possible to take the rook off the a-file. After this gift the pretender, already at the start of the match, was able to make the score 2-0 in his favour: 59 ♖g8! ♖a1 (on 59...♖h7 follows mate—60 ♖b8+ ♔a7 61 ♖b7 mate) 60 ♘d5+! ♔c5 61 ♖g5! ♔c4 62 ♘c7 and the rook

is forced from the a-file—62...♖a2 63 ♔b1 ♖a3 64 ♔b2 (Zaitsev). But in turn White makes a mistake.

59 ♔b2? ♖h8!

The "limit" of the mistakes has been exhausted—this time a draw is inevitable.

60 ♔b3 ♖c8 61 a7 ♔xa7 62 ♔b4 ♔b6 63 ♘d5+ ♔a6 64 ♖g6+ ♔b7 65 ♔b5 ♖c1 66 ♖g2 ♔c8 67 ♖g7 ♔d8 68 ♘f6 ♖c7 69 ♖g5 ♖f7 70 ♘d5 ♔d7 71 ♖g6 ♖f1 72 ♔c5 ♖c1+ 73 ♔d4 ♖d1+ 74 ♔e5 Draw.

One of the co-authors of the following game, L.Kavalek, said that "...playing over this game is more thrilling than reading a detective story".

Larsen - Kavalek
Montreal 1979

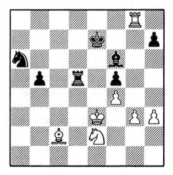

A prosaic and quite boring endgame position, isn't that true?

Black's chances are in no way worse—he has a passed pawn, opposite-coloured bishop and in general there is not quite enough material on the board. But, together with this, is also included the skill of the master, who can "breathe life" even into these kind of positions, if he discovers the slightest tactical nuance to continue the struggle. Those pessimists who maintain that endings are quite boring, we advise to play through, time and time again, this ending in which a fascinating and uncompromising struggle fluctuates to and fro.

34 g4! fxg4 35 hxg4 h6 36 ♖g6 ♘c5

Only three moves have been made and the not obvious start has made things obvious—White has a quite tangible positional advantage.

37 ♘g3!

With few forces B.Larsen manages to create dangerous threats against the enemy king.

37...♗d4+ 38 ♔f3 b4 39 ♘f5+ ♔f8 40 ♖b6!

Accuracy is essential. The h6 pawn is doomed and it is necessary to control the b-pawn.

40...♗c3 41 ♖b8+ ♔f7 42 ♘xh6+ ♔e7 43 ♘f5+ ♔d7

The position is defined. White's chances are linked to the exploitation of the unstable position of the black knight and the advance of the connected passed pawns (Particularly dangerous is the g-pawn). Black's only, but sufficient, counterchance is the passed b-pawn, supported by the active pieces.

44 ♘e3

Also good is 44 ♖b5 ♔c6 (or 44...♖d2 45 ♖xc5 ♖xc2 46 ♖b5 etc) 45 ♘e7+ ♔xb5 46 ♘xd5 ♔c4 47 ♘xc3 ♔xc3 48 ♗f5 b3 49 g5 ♘d3 50 ♔e3 ♘b4 51 g6 ♘c2+ 52 ♔f2 b2 53 ♗xc2 ♔xc2 54 g7 b1=♕ 55 g8=♕ with advantage to White.

44...♖d4 45 ♗f5+ ♔c6 46 g5 ♘d3 47 ♘g2 ♖d5! 48 ♗e4 ♔c7!

Black defends himself very resourcefully.

49 ♖g8 ♖d4 50 ♖g6

A further advance of the g-pawn suggests itself, but in this case the defence is facilitated: 50 g6 ♘c5 51 g7 ♖xe4 52 ♖c8+ ♔xc8 53 g8=♕+ ♔c7.

50...♔d7 51 ♖b6 ♘c5 52 ♗f5+ ♔c7 53 ♖b5 ♔c6 54 ♖b8 ♘d7

Also in White's favour is 54...b3 55 g6 ♖a4 56 ♘e3 ♗g7?! (56...b2 57 ♘d1) 57 ♖g8 ♖a7 58 ♗b1.

55 ♖e8 ♘c5 56 g6 ♖d2

Playing such endings is in no way less complicated than calculating forcing combinations. The cost of a single mistake is too high.

57 ♘e3 ♘d3 58 ♘g4

Even stronger was 58 ♘c4!.

58...♖d1 59 ♖c8+ ♔b7 60 ♔e2 ♖d2+ 61 ♔e3 ♘e1!

The black pieces are activated to the maximum and the f4-pawn is now in need of defence.

62 ♖c4 ♘g2+ 63 ♔e4 ♘h4 64 ♗c8+ ♔b8 65 f5 ♖e2+ 66 ♔d5!

The only move to retain the advantage. On 66 ♔d3 good is 66...♖e8! 67 ♗a6 (67 ♗e6 ♘xg6!) 67...♘xf5, while on 66 ♔f4 follows 66...♗d2+ 67 ♔g3 ♗e1+ and 68 ♔h3?? is not possible because of 68...♘f3.

66...♖d2+ 67 ♔e6 ♖d4

Let us turn our attention to the arrangement of the pieces. All White's are on white squares, while all Black's are on black.

Now White should break up his light-squared formation and play 68 ♖xd4 ♗xd4 69 ♘f6 when 69...b3 loses after 70 ♗a6 b2 71 ♗d3. However he misses this possibility and Black obtains excellent chances of a draw.

68 ♗a6? ♘xf5!! 69 ♔xf5 ♖d5+ 70 ♔e4

There is nothing in 70 ♔e6 ♖g5 71 ♔f7 ♖f5+ 72 ♔g8 ♖g5 73 ♔h7 ♖h5+ when, on 74 ♘h6, follows 74...♗d2.

70...♖g5 71 ♗c8 ♖xg6 72 ♘e3 ♖h6 73 ♔d5 ♗d2 74 ♘f5 ♖b6

The draw becomes quite real; it merely requires accuracy from Black.

75 ♘d6 b3 76 ♗f5

The game approaches the final phase. White has still not exhausted his attacking resources on the enemy king and the opposite-coloured bishops make possible White's plan.

76...♗b4 77 ♘f7 b2 78 ♗b1 ♗a3 79 ♖c3 ♖b7 80 ♘e5 ♖b5+ 81 ♔e6 ♗b4 82 ♖b3 ♔c7??

Here is a fatal mistake, Black still "holds" the draw by 82...♖b6+.

83 ♘d7! ♔d8

There is no saving himself by 83...♔c6 84 ♗e4+ ♔c7 85 ♗f3.

84 ♗e4 ♖a5 85 ♘e5

Far simpler was 85 ♖xb4 ♖a6+ 86 ♖b6.

85...♖a6+ 86 ♘c6+ ♔c7 87 ♖xb4 ♖b6 88 ♖xb6 ♔xb6 89 ♔d5 ♔b5 90 ♗c2 Black resigned.

A dramatic and far from faultless struggle. This ending once again graphically confirms that there are no boring positions, it is only routine play that makes it possible to castrate any position.

The cost of being influenced, in making a decision for the evaluation of a position, we have already come across in chapter 2. In the following example White retains his advantage after inaccuracies by both sides..

Gufeld - Sokolin
New York 1996

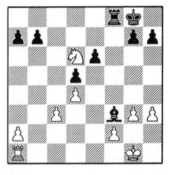

How strange it is that this position, with its "French" weakness, the e6-pawn, was reached from the Petroff Defence. In this sort of position the manoeuvrability of the knight usually makes it stronger than the bishop.

By way of compensation the bishop keeps the king "tense" but this is only temporary whereas the weaknesses are lasting.

Here, White is faced with several alternatives: both 25 ♘xb7 and 25 ♖e1 look equally attractive. But precisely his choice defines his assessment of the position. I decided to take the pawn immediately and not guess the cost of my preferance. I should have preferred 25 ♖e1!, acting according to the proverb: "a bird in the hand is worth two in the bush" (two pawns are under attack at the same time).

25 ♘xb7

Now White's advantage has been reduced to a minimum. The opening of the b-file allows Black to activate his rook: 25...♖b8!. If White does not want voluntarily to enter a pin by 26 ♖b1?! (after which Black frees himself by 26...a5! 27 ♔f1 e5!), then he has to allow the rook behind his lines: 26 ♘c5 ♖b2, which gives Black good counterplay. For example: 27 ♘d3 ♖c2 28 ♖b1 h5 (for the time being, 28...♖xc3? is not possible because of 29 ♖b8+ ♔f7 30 ♘e5+) 29 ♘e5 ♖xc3 and Black maintains equality both after 30 a4 ♗e4!, and in the rook ending after 30 ♘xf3 ♖xf3.

Fortunately, my opponent was preoccupied with the idea of ridding himself of the backward e6 pawn and...the assessment of the position was reestablished in White's favour.

25...e5?! 26 dxe5 d4

Forced moves follow. All this is good, but...for White, who obtains a mobile passed e-pawn.

27 ♘d6 dxc3

If 27...d3 28 e6 d2 29 e7 and White is winning.

28 e6 ♖b8 29 e7 ♗c6 30 ♖c1 c2

Black had great hopes for this move.

31 ♔h2! ♖b1 32 e8=♕+ ♗xe8 33 ♖xc2 ♖b8

33...♗d7 loses the bishop after 34 ♖c7 ♗e6 35 ♖e7.

34 ♖c7 a6 35 g4!

35 ♘xe8 ♖xe8 with chances to draw the rook and pawn ending.

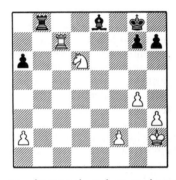

35...♗b5 36 ♔g3 ♗d3 37 ♔f4 h6 38 h4

38 ♖c8+ ♖xc8 39 ♘xc8 g5+! and Black has good chances to draw.

38...♗b1 39 a3 ♖b6 40 ♘e8 ♖b3 41 ♘xg7 ♖xa3 42 ♘f5! ♖a4+ 43 ♔e5 h5 44 f3 hxg4 45 fxg4 ♔h8 46 ♘h6! a5 47 h5 ♖b4 48 ♖a7 a4 49 ♔f6 ♗d3? 50 ♘f7+ ♔h7 51 ♘g5+ ♔h6 52 ♖h7+! Black resigned.

In this game the knight, in cooperation with the rooks, confidently outplayed the bishop. In general in my practice such an alignment often occurs for Black, and not infrequently I have had to prove the value of the knight.

Atalik - Gufeld
Los Angeles 1999

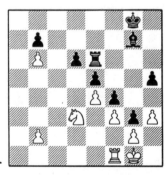

How to assess this position? The first impression is that it is in favour of White, who can quickly organise a rook invasion along the c-file. But all is not so simple. The feature of the position—the presence of the g3 pawn, pushed far up the board—nevertheless gives a basis for an optimistic assessment and chances for Black: the white king is in some danger and in any ending the g2 pawn will be an object of attack. Therefore White's advantage can be rated as small.

31 ♘b4

The knight is aimed at d5, reckoning on "filling" the position, after which it is possible to set about realising White's positional advantage.

31...♖e8 32 ♖c1

White had a choice between taking the a- or c-file and he went for the more important one: after 32 ♖a1 ♖c8 Black's position is apparently preferable.

There is no need for White to keep the rook on f1, as it is doing nothing there. It is necessary to free the king from the danger zone, while the rook drifts towards a possible invasion into Black's camp.

32...♖a8 33 ♔f1 ♗f6!

Precisely this! If 33...♔f7, then after 34 ♘d5 the black bishop prepares for a difficult life.

34 ♘d5 ♗d8

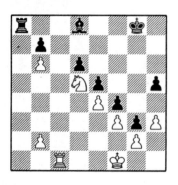

35 ♔e2

The attempt to decide the outcome of the game with "strong measures" by 35 ♖c7 does not change the assessment of the position. Of course, 35...♗xc7? 36 bxc7 would lead to victory for White, however after 35...♖a1+! 36 ♔e2 ♖g1 37 ♖xb7! (on 37 ♖c8?! ♖xg2+ 38 ♔d3 ♖f2 39 ♖xd8+ ♔g7 40 ♖d7+ ♔h6 41 ♖d8 ♔g5 Black already has chances of victory) 37...♗xb6! 38 ♖xb6 ♖xg2+ 39 ♔d3 ♖f2 40 ♖b7 g2 41 ♖d7 g1=♕ 42 ♘f6+ ♔f8 43 ♘h7+ ♔e8 44 ♘f6+ achieves a draw.

35...♔f7 36 ♔d3 ♖a6

After the automatic 36...♔e6? 37 ♘c7+ ♗xc7 38 ♖xc7, despite the equal material, the endgame is in White's favour. Therefore the attack on the b6 pawn is the only means of holding the position, otherwise White improves it with the transfer of the knight to the queenside.

37 ♖c8 ♗xb6 38 ♖b8 ♗g1 39 ♖xb7+ ♔g6 40 ♖d7 ♔g5 41 h4+ ♔g6 42 ♔c2 ♗d4 43 ♔b1 ♗c5 44 ♖b7

Clearly unfavourable for White is 44 b4? ♗xb4 45 ♘xb4 ♖b6.

44...♖a4 45 ♖b3 ♔f7 46 ♖c3 ♔e8 47 ♖d3 ♖a7 48 ♔c2 ♔d7 49 b4 ♖a2+!

The most resolute, but also possible is 49...♗d4.

50 ♔b3 ♖xg2 51 bxc5 ♖f2 52 ♘c3

He has to reckon with the passed g-pawn, since after 52 cxd6? g2 it cannot be stopped. Now, however, on 52...g2 appears 53 ♖xd6+ and 54 ♖g6.

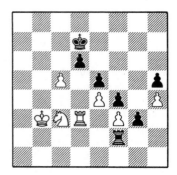

52...♔c6!!

What is the idea of this king move, which makes way, as it were, after 53 cxd6, for the passed pawn? The piquant point lies in the fact that the king goes back—53...♔d7!!, and the g3 pawn reaches the queening square quicker than its antagonist on d6, after which White seems to be losing: 54 ♘a4 g2 55 ♘c5+ ♔c6 56 d7 g1=♕ 57 d8=♕ ♕b1+ with two echo-mates 58 ♔c4 ♖c2+ 59 ♔c3 ♕b5 mate or 58 ♔a4 ♖a2+ 59 ♔a3 ♕b5 mate.

53 ♖xd6+ ♔xc5 54 ♖d5+

Otherwise the black pawn cannot be stopped.

54...♔c6 55 ♖xe5 ♖xf3 56 ♖g5

If 56 ♖xh5?, then 56...♖xc3+! 57 ♔xc3 g2 58 ♖g5 f3 and Black wins.

56...♖f2

57 ♘d5

57 e5!? looks more active. If Black does not take serious measures against the e-pawn, then he risks losing:

a) 57...♖h2 58 e6 ♔d6 59 ♖e5 with a win;

b) 57...♔d7 58 ♔c4! ♖d2 (losing quickly is 58...♖c2 59 ♔d3 ♖c1 60 ♘e2 or 58...♔e6 59 ♘e4 ♖h2 60 ♘c5+ ♔e7 61 ♖g7+) 59 ♘e4! ♖d1 60 ♘f6+ ♔e6 61 ♘xh5 with a great advantage for White;

c) 57...g2 58 ♖g6+ ♔d7 (58...♔c7 59 e6 f3 60 ♖g7+) 59 e6+ ♔e8 60 ♘e4! ♖e2 (60...♖f3+ 61 ♔c4 ♖g3 62 ♘xg3 g1=♕ 63 ♖g8+ ♔e7 64 ♔f5 winning) 61 ♘f6+ ♔f8 (61...♔d8 62 ♖g8+; 61...♔e7 62 ♘d5+) 62 ♖g8+ ♔e7 63 ♘d5+ ♔d6 (63...♔xe6 64 ♘d4+) 64 ♘xf4 ♖e3+ 65 ♔c2 ♖e4 66 ♘xg2 ♔xe6 67 ♔d3 and White wins.

And yet Black saves himself by countering the e-pawn with the rook: 57...♖f1! 58 ♔c4 ♖e1 59 ♖g6+ ♔d7 60 ♔d5 f3 61 ♖g7+ ♔e8 62 ♔e6 ♔d8 63 ♘b5 ♔c8 64 ♘a7+ ♔b8 65 ♘c6+ ♔c8 66 ♘e7+ ♔b8 Draw.

57...g2 58 ♘b4+ ♔d6 59 e5+

Or 59 ♖g6+ ♔e7 60 ♘c6+ ♔f8 61 ♘d4 f3 Draw.

59...♔d7 60 ♖g7+ ♔e8 61 ♘d3 ♖f3 62 ♖xg2 ♖xd3+ 63 ♔c4 ♖g3 64 ♖a2 f3 65 ♔d5 ♖g2 66 ♖a3 f2 67 ♖f3 ♔e7 68 ♖f4 ♖g4 69 ♖xf2 ♖xh4 70 ♖a2 ♖b4 71 ♖a7+ ♔e8 72 ♔c6 h4 73 ♖h7 ♖d4 74 ♔c5 ♖d1

Black transposes to a theoretically drawn position. Of course also 74...♖a4 is sufficient for a draw.

75 ♖xh4 ♔e7 and **Drawn** on the 89th move.

Rohrbaugh - Gufeld
Oklahoma 2000

In this position Black has a classic small advantage: all his pieces, and also the pawn structure, are qualitatively superior to White's. But a particularly important point is the possibility of attacking the weak h-pawn, which, in the event of an exchange of rooks, is practically doomed. And yet White has sufficient defensive resources.

31...♖e4 32 b3

This move is by no means forced, it was possible to organise an "outpost": 32 ♗e2 ♔f6 33 ♔d2 ♔e5 34 b4 ♔d4 35 ♖g3.

32...♔f6 33 ♔d2

Also here it is more accurate to look at (in comparison with the game) the transfer of the bishop to the b1-h7 diagonal: 33 ♗e2 ♔e5 34 ♗d3 ♖f4 35 ♗g6 ♔d4 36 ♖e2 and White, if the opportunity arises, will penetrate with his rook to the seventh rank.

Apparently, also possible was 33 ♗c8 b6 34 ♔c2 ♔e5 35 ♔d3, not fearing 35...♖d4+ 36 ♔e3 ♖h4 37 ♖f2 and again the rook is ready to invade.

33...♔e5 34 ♗d1?!

Even here it is still not too late for 34 ♗c8, and if 34...b6, then White acts according to the above-

mentioned scheme: 35 ♔d3 ♖d4+ 36 ♔e3 ♖h4 37 ♖f2. And if 34...♘f3+ 35 ♔c3 ♖e3+ 36 ♔b4 or 35...♖h4 36 ♖g7 the advantage passes to White. But now the black king becomes dangerous.

34...♔d4 35 ♔c2 ♖f4 36 ♖d2+ ♔e5 37 ♖e2+ ♘e4 38 ♖g2 ♔d4

Strangely enough, a loss of time: 38...♖f2+! 39 ♖xf2 ♘xf2 40 ♗e2 ♔f5 41 b4 ♔g5 and, with his active king in the endgame, Black has achieved his goal.

39 ♔b2 ♖f2+ 40 ♖xf2 ♘xf2 41 ♗c2 ♘d3+ 42 ♔a3 ♘f4 43 ♗d1

Weaker is 43 ♗g6 ♔e5 44 ♗e8 ♔f6 and, due to the threat of ♔f6-e7, the h5 pawn is lost.

43...♔e5 44 ♗g4 ♔f6 45 ♔b4 ♔g5 46 ♗c8

46...♘xh5

After 46...b6 47 ♔b5 ♘xh5 48 ♔c6, with the fall of the c-pawn he has to reckon on the possibility of the break b3-b4 and c4-c5.

47 ♗xb7 ♘g3 48 ♗c8 ♘f5 49 c5!

Only by activity can he retain hopes of saving himself. Upon the passive 49 ♔c3 h5 50 ♔d3 h4 51 ♔e4 h3 52 ♔f3, Black switches over to the queenside pawns: 52...♘d4+ 53 ♔g3 ♘e2+ 54 ♔xh3 ♘c1 55 b4 ♘xa2 56 b5 ♔f4, retaining winning chances.

49...h5

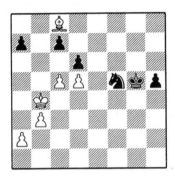

50 cxd6?

White's salvation, though not obvious, lies in the approach of his king to the c7 pawn: 50 ♔b5! h4 51 ♗xf5 ♔xf5 52 ♔c6 h3 53 ♔xc7 h2 54 cxd6 h1=♕ 55 d7 and Black is in no position to prevent the appearance of a new queen: 55...♕c1+ 56 ♔b7 ♕g5 57 ♔c8.

50...cxd6

Only this, after 50...♘xd6? 51 ♗h3 he can hold on.

51 ♗a6 h4 52 ♗f1 ♘e3 53 ♗h3 ♔f4 54 ♔b5 ♔g3!

The final blow.

55 ♗e6

Also losing is 55 ♗c8 ♘g4 56 ♔c6 h3 57 ♗f5 h2 58 ♗e4 ♘f2.

55...♘g4 56 ♔c6 h3 57 ♔xd6 h2 58 ♗xg4 ♔xg4 59 ♔c7 h1=♕ 60 d6 ♕h2 White resigned.

Nevertheless, on a general plane, in an endgame with no queens on the board, and particularly in positions bearing an open character, it is reckoned that rook and bishop cooperate more harmoniously than rook and knight: this is explained not only by the long-range bishop, but also the influence of the geometrical factors of "straight-line" pieces.

Here is a classic example on this theme from the work of the genius Robert Fischer.

Fischer - Taimanov
Candidates match, Vancouver 1971

White has a small but enduring positional advantage. His pieces are operating on important arteries of the board, whereas Black cannot display activity. R.Fischer demonstrates a clear plan to realise his advantage: first he fixes the queenside pawns, securing a passage for his king, and then, by advancing the pawns on the opposite flank, strives to create new weaknesses there.

32 ♖e3 ♔d6

Black sticks to waiting tactics but possibly he should free his rook from its defence of the f7 pawn, even at the cost of weakening the light squares: 32...f6!? 33 ♖e6 ♖d8 34 ♗b5 ♖d6 and it is not easy for White to exploit the weaknesses.

33 a4! ♘e7 34 h3 ♘c6 35 h4

Black cannot allow the further advance of the pawns, h4-h5, g3-g4, and after the transfer of the king to g3, g4-g5. But, together with this, he has to place his pawns on squares of the colour of his bishop.

35...h5 36 ♖d3+ ♔c7 37 ♖d5 f5

On 37...g6 might follow 38 ♗b5 ♖e8 39 f5. But now the weakness of the e6 square is felt.

38 ♖d2 ♖f6 39 ♖e2 ♔d7 40 ♖e3 g6 41 ♗b5 ♖d6 42 ♔e2

In order to get close to the pawns White needs to exchange rooks, but an immediate 42 ♖d3 ♖xd3+ 43 ♗xd3 ♘d8! 44 ♗c4 ♔e7 45 ♔e3 (45 ♗d5 ♘f7) 45...♘b7 46 ♔d3 ♘d6 47 ♗d5 ♔f6 allows Black to close the way to his rear.

42...♔d8

He must wait with the exchange, since after 42...♖f6 43 ♔d3 ♖d6+ 44 ♔c4, the king breaks through, while on 42...♔c7 43 ♖e8, the rook...

43 ♖d3 ♔c7 44 ♖xd6 ♔xd6 45 ♔d3

Already a transfer to a winning pawn endgame is threatened: 46 ♗xc6 ♔xc6 47 ♔c4 ♔c7 48 ♔b5 ♔b7 49 c4.

45...♘e7 46 ♗e8 ♔d5 47 ♗f7+ ♔d6 48 ♔c4 ♔c6 49 ♗e8+ ♔b7 50 ♔b5 ♘c8 51 ♗c6+ ♔c7 52 ♗d5 ♘e7

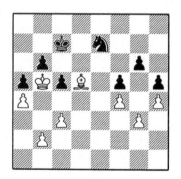

The first stage of the winning plan is linked to the penetration of the king to the a6 square, but he does not manage to maintain the bishop on the long diagonal since on 53 ♗f3 follows 53...♘g8 with the idea

of transferring the knight to e4. After 53 ♗b3 follows 53...♔b7 54 ♗f7 ♔a7! and, as shown by Y.Balashov, insufficient for victory is 55 ♗xg6 ♘xg6 56 ♔c6 c4 57 ♔d5 b5! 58 ♔e6 ♗xa4 59 ♔f7! (59 ♔xf5? ♘f8) 59...♘h8+ 60 ♔g7 ♔b6 61 ♔xh8 ♔b5 62 ♔g7 a3 63 ♗xa3 ♔a4 64 ♔f6 ♔xa3 65 ♔xf5 ♔b3 66 ♔g6 a4 67 f5. Therefore the only way is linked to the gain of a tempo. This is achieved by the "star" method with the tieing of the knight to the e7 square.

53 ♗f7! ♔b7 54 ♗b3 ♔a7 55 ♗d1 ♔b7 56 ♗f3+ ♔c7

Now the king penetrates to a6, since bad is 56...♔a7? 57 ♗g2 ♘g8 58 ♔c6.

57 ♔a6 ♘g8 58 ♗d5 ♘e7

The second stage of the plan lies in the construction of zugzwang, with the bishop on e8. Then, on ♔c7-d8, follows the sacrifice of the bishop on g6 and capture of the b6 and a5 pawns.

59 ♗c4

Beginning a new struggle for tempi. Insufficient is 59 ♗f7 ♔c6 60 ♗e8+ ♔c7 61 c4 ♔d8 62 ♗xg6 ♘xg6 63 ♔xb6 ♔d7 64 ♔xc5 ♘e7 65 ♔b6 ♘c6 66 c5 ♘b8! 67 ♔xa5 ♔c6 68 b4 ♘d7 69 ♔a6 ♘b8+ 70 ♔a7 ♘d7 71 a5 ♔c7 72 a6 ♔c6 (Y.Balashov).

59...♘c6 60 ♗f7 ♘e7 61 ♗e8!

The crowning of the manoeuvre begun on the 53rd move. The rest requires no commentary.

61...♔d8 62 ♗xg6 ♘xg6 63 ♔xb6 ♔d7 64 ♔xc5 ♘e7 65 b4 axb4 66 cxb4 ♘c8 67 a5 ♘d6 68 b5 ♘e4+ 69 ♔b6 ♔c8 70 ♔c6 ♔b8 71 b6 Black resigned.

To conclude the "rook" theme let us look at examples of play with minor pieces of the "same name".

Suetin - Gufeld
Tbilisi 1969

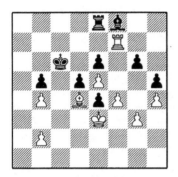

In this position, the game was adjourned. Analysis showed that Black should maintain equality, though there are definite difficulties in achieving a draw.

41...♗xb4 42 ♖f6 ♔d7 43 ♖xg6 ♖c8 44 ♖g7+

Not dangerous for Black is 44 f5 exf5 45 ♔f4 ♗c5!.

44...♔e8

Only not 44...♗e7 45 h4! and White has an enormous advantage.

45 ♖g8+

On 45 f5 follows 45...♖c2.

45...♔d7 46 ♖g7+ ♔e8 47 ♖g8+ ♔d7 48 ♖xc8 ♔xc8 49 g4!

This exclamation mark does not relate to the move itself, which should not lead to any upsetting of the balance on the board. This evaluation is for the excellent fighting qualities of A.Suetin, who even in a drawn position searches for concealed paths to continue the struggle.

49...hxg4 50 ♔f2!

If 50 h5 ♗f8 51 ♔f2 ♗h6 52 ♔g3 ♔d7 53 ♔xg4 ♔e7 the draw is obvious.

50...♗d2

Simpler was 51...♔d7.

51 ♔g3 e3

Black achieves an easy draw after 51...♔d7 52 h5 ♔e7 53 ♔xg4 (after 53 h6? ♔f7 54 h7 ♔g7 55 f5 e3 56 fxe6 e2 57 ♗f2 e1=♕ 58 ♗xe1 ♗xe1+ 59 ♔xg4 ♗b4 60 ♔f5 ♔xh7 might even lose) 53...♔f7 54 f5 ♗c1 and White cannot strengthen his position.

52 h5 e2 53 ♗f2 e1=♕ 54 ♗xe1 ♗xe1+ 55 ♔xg4 ♗b4 56 h6 ♗f8 57 h7 ♗g7

The last moves bear a forcing character. Here the game was again adjourned. A number of study-like situations now arise.

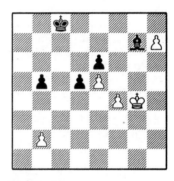

58 ♔g5 d4

58...♗h8 59 ♔g6 d4 leads only to a transposition of moves. Considerably worse is 58...♔d7? 59 ♔g6 ♗h8 60 ♔f7 d4 61 f5 d3 62 fxe6+ ♔c7 63 e7 d2 64 e8=♕ d1=♕ 65 ♕xh8 and Black does not have perpetual check.

59 ♔g6! ♗h8 60 f5 d3 61 fxe6 d2 62 e7 d1=♕

This is already the third black queen in a single game!

63 e8=♕+ ♕d8

After 63...♔c7 64 ♕xh8, Black again does not have perpetual check: 64...♕g4+ 65 ♔f7 ♕h5+ 66 ♔e7 ♕h4+ 67 ♕f6 ♕xh7+ 68 ♔f8.

64 ♕c6+ ♔b8

Losing is 64...♕c7 65 ♕xc7+ ♔xc7 66 e6.

65 ♔f7!!
A brilliant move!

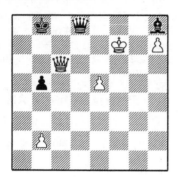

65...♔a7
The only move, since 66 ♕d6+ was threatened, while, on 65...♗xe5, winning is 66 ♕xb5+.
66 ♕d6 ♕c8
66...♕g5? does not achieve its objective: 67...♕c7+ ♔a6 68 ♕c8+ ♔a5 69 ♕xh8.
67 e6 ♕c2 68 e7! ♕xh7+ 69 ♔e8 ♗xb2 70 ♔d8 ♕h4 71 ♔c8
Worth considering is 71 ♕d7+!?, after which definite accuracy is required of Black: 71...♔b6 72 ♕d6+ ♔a7 (after 72...♔a5?! 73 ♕d2+ b4 74 ♕xb2 ♕g5 75 ♕a2+ ♔b5 76 ♕e6 White gains the advantage) 73 ♕d7+ ♔a6 74 ♕e6+ ♔b7.
71...♕e4!
The Black queen also shows its "teeth". Not possible is 72 ♕d7+ ♔b6 73 e8=♕? ♕a8 mate.
72 ♕c5+ ♔a6 73 ♕d6+ ♔a7?!
After 73...♔a5! 74 ♕d8+ ♔a6, Black would probably have every chance to count on a draw.
74 ♔d8 ♕h4 75 ♕d7+ ♔b6 76 ♕e6+ ♔b7
Here, on 76...♔a5, winning is 77 ♔c8.
77 ♕d5+! ♔b6 78 ♔d7 ♕h7 79 ♕e6+ ♔a7?
After such an inaccuracy it is no wonder that he loses the thread of

the defence. It seems it was possible to hold the position by 79...♔b7 with the possible variations 80 ♕c6+ ♔a7 81 ♕c7+ ♔a6 or 80 ♕d5+ ♔b6 81 ♕e6+ ♔b7.
80 ♔c8!
If 80 ♕a2+, then 80...♔b6 81 ♕xb2 ♕f5+ 82 ♔d8 ♕d5+ with a draw.
80...♕c2+ 81 ♔d8 ♔b7 82 ♕d7+ ♔b6 83 ♕d6+ ♔b7 84 e8=♕ ♗f6+ 85 ♔d7 and after a few moves **Black resigned**.

Anand - Karpov
Brussels 1991

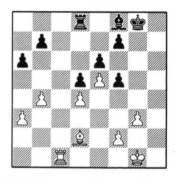

White's small advantage lies in his control of the c-file. However, it is not immediately apparent what he can extract from this: Black's queenside pawns are fully defended and moreover White has a "bad" bishop.
32...b5!
For active defence he needs space for the rook. After 32...♖d7 33 ♖c8 ♔g7 34 a4 ♗e7 35 b5, it would be much more difficult for Black to hold the position.
33 ♖c6
As is often the case, one object of attack is insufficient to achieve real gains: you see, it is not difficult to defend the a6 pawn. White's chances must be associated with

play on both flanks. Taking into account the passive role of the black knight, riveted to the f7 pawn, it is important to restrict the f8-bishop. This is achieved by the manoeuvre 33 ♖c7 ♖a8 34 ♖b7 ♖c8 35 ♖b6 ♖a8 (35...♖c2 36 ♗g5) 36 ♗g5, controlling the f6-square.

33...♖a8 34 ♖b6

Even here it was still not too late for 34 ♖c7!, with the same idea. After this lapse, Black includes his bishop in the defence and ridding himself of the backward f7 pawn becomes a real possibility.

34...♗e7 35 ♔f1 ♗d8 36 ♖b7 ♔g7

Upon the attempt to bring the king to the centre, 36...♔f8 37 ♔e2 ♔e8, he has to reckon on the possible manoeuvre, 38 ♗h6 followed by ♗h6-g7-f6.

37 ♔e2 ♖c8 38 ♔d3 ♖c6 39 ♖b8 ♗c7 40 ♖a8 ♔g6?

An automatic move, explained, apparently, only by having insufficient time before the control. Black misses the chance to solve all his problems with the move 40...f6!, but, to his good fortune, White did not find the winning manoeuvre.

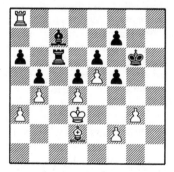

41 ♖c8?

Chances are retained only by 41 ♖g8+ ♔h7 42 ♖c8 ♔g6 (or 42...♖c4 43 ♖a8 ♖c6 44 ♗g5) 43

♗f4!, linked to the gain of an important tempo, preventing ...f7-f6. Now, after 43...♖c4 44 ♖g8+ ♔h7 45 ♖a8, Black is faced with the choice of the passive 45...♖c6 46 ♗g5 (with the threat to transfer the bishop via e7 to c5), and the active 45...♗b6 46 ♗e3 a5 47 bxa5 ♖a4 48 axb6 (or 48 ♖f8) 48...♖xa8 49 ♗d2 and the white king goes to the help of the b6 pawn. Matters are not changed by 45...a5, if only because of 46 ♗d2.

41...f6!

This time A.Karpov does not miss his chance. On 42 exf6 there is 42...♖c4 and 43 ♗g5 ♔xg5 44 f7 does not help because of 44...♗d6.

42 ♗c3 ♔f7 43 exf6 ♔xf6 44 ♗d2 ♖c4 45 ♖f8+ ♔g6 46 ♖a8 ♖c6 and after insipid play to the 63rd move a **draw** was agreed.

Minor Piece Endings

In endings of this type the decisive factor in the assessment of the position is the active positions of the pieces or pawns of one of the sides. It should be mentioned that there is also a sharp increase in the role of the king.

Rubinstein - Lasker
Moscow 1925

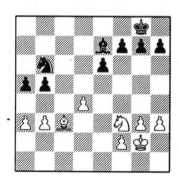

The positional advantage is on White's side—he has the more active pawn formation on the queen-side, whereas the white pawn on d4 is weak. Let us observe how the virtuoso E.Lasker exploits the pluses of his position.

33...a4! 34 bxa4

White has nothing else, on 34 b4 follows 34...♘c4, while, in reply to 34 ♗a5, E.Lasker had prepared the brilliant reply—34...axb3! 35 ♗xb6 ♗g5!!.

34...bxa4 35 ♔f1

Activating the king is White's only chance. The knight ending after 35 ♗b4 ♗xb4 36 axb4 a3 37 ♘d2 a2 38 ♘b3 ♔f8 is hopeless for him.

35...♗xa3 36 ♔e2 ♔f8 37 ♔d3 ♘d5 38 ♗e1 ♗d6 39 ♔c4 ♔e7 40 ♘e5 ♗xe5 41 dxe5 ♔d7 42 ♗d2 h5!

One feels the hand of a wise "die-hard" of the endgame. Black prudently reduces White's possibilities on the kingside.

43 ♗c1

After 43 ♔b5? a3 44 ♗c1 ♘c3+ 45 ♔c4 a2 46 ♗b2 ♘d1 the knight breaks through to the pawns on the kingside.

43...♔c6 44 ♗a3 ♘b6+ 45 ♔d4 ♔b5 46 ♗f8 ♘c4 47 ♔c3 g6 48 f4 ♘e3 49 ♔d3 ♘d5

Now the inevitable ...h5-h4 will break up White's pawn chain. He is not in a position to prevent this. If 50 h4 the black knight gets over to f5, and the pawns will be doomed.

50 ♗a3 h4 51 gxh4 ♘xf4+ 52 ♔e4 ♘h5

Of course, greed of the type 52...♘xh3 leads to no good—53 ♔f3 ♘g1+ 54 ♔f2 with a "perpetual" attack on the knight.

53 ♔f3

White's last hope is to break through with the king to the f7 pawn.

53...♔c4 54 ♗b2 ♔b3 55 ♗a1 a3 56 ♔g4 ♔c2 57 ♔g5 ♔d3! White resigned.

While the king is taking the f7 pawn, Black proceeds with his king to f5, and his knight gains unlimited freedom of action.

Vaganian - Rashkovsky
Moscow 1981

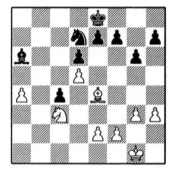

White's playing for a win in this ending can be shown to be unfounded. True, his passed pawn is more distant than his opponent's, but there are no other apparent real prerequisites. But there is a highly significant detail of which R.Vaganian has a fine appreciation. All of Black's pieces have abandoned the king's flank and, moreover, the pawns after the "fianchetto" are placed on white squares (don't forget there is a white-squared bishop!). All these little pluses R.Vaganian exploits to carry out an original plan of pawn pressure on Black's kingside.

31 f4! ♔d8 32 h4 ♔c7 33 a5!

Playing with pawns in such endings is exceptionally difficult and responsible. In order not to let out the king, White sacrifices his only passed pawn. But Black spends precious time on its capture which allows White to carry out his intended plan of a pawn blockade. After this, the role of a passive statistic is prepared for the enemy king—not an insignificant factor in an endgame.

33...♘c5 34 ♔f2 ♘b3 35 g4 ♔d8

White threatens to play h4-h5-h6 and after f4-f5 Black's h-pawn would become untenable. Therefore the black king is forced to return to the remaining unsupervised flank.

36 h5 ♔e8

N.Rashkovsky, under the spell of R.Vaganian's "psychic" attack, bows to the pressure, having doubts about the position after 36...gxh5 37 g5! (after 37 gxh5? h6 38 ♗c2 ♘xa5 there is no apparent compensation for the pawn). But he is wrong! After 37...♘xa5 38 ♗xh7 h4, the passed h-pawn becomes a distracting factor that allows Black to activate his king. Here, for example, is a possible, though also not forced variation: 39 f5 ♔e8 40 ♔f3 ♔f8 41 ♔g4 ♗c8 42 e4 ♔g7 43 g6 fxg6 44 ♗xg6 ♔f6 45 ♔xh4 ♔e5 46 ♔g3 ♔d4 47 ♘b5+ ♔e5 etc.

37 h6 ♘xa5 38 f5

White's threat is obvious—a double attack on g6 first with a pawn and then also with the bishop. The black king has to reconcile itself to the role of a statistic.

38...♔f8 39 g5 ♘b3 40 ♔e3 ♘c5 41 ♗c2 ♗c8

Black strives for a release of the pawn tension. We mention that he cannot prevent the move f5-f6, since on 41...♘d7 would have followed 42 ♔d4 followed by 43 ♗a4.

42 f6 ♗h3

N.Rashkovsky creates the threat 43...♘d7 44 ♘e4 ♗g2, not reckoning on the expediency of limiting

the bishop to the defence of the c4 pawn, though this was apparently possible: 42...♗a6 43 ♔d4 exf6 44 gxf6 ♔e8. For example: 45 ♗a4+ ♔d8 46 ♗c6 ♘b3+ 47 ♔e3 ♘c5 48 ♔d4 ♘b3+ and Black holds on.

43 ♗a4! exf6 44 gxf6 ♘xa4

He has to reckon on the threat of 45 ♗c6, after which the d6 pawn would be doomed.

45 ♘xa4 g5

A second passed pawn appears for Black and, though he is playing without a king, his defensive possibilities are still not exhausted.

46 ♘c3

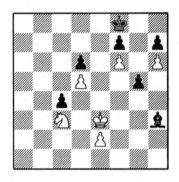

46...g4?

This advance, which N.Rashkovsky avoided on the 42nd move—so as not to limit the range of activity of the bishop—he makes on the 46th. After 46...♗d7! it is not easy for White to gain the advantage, since after 47 ♘e4 g4 the "support" from the c4 and g4 pawns would be more fire-proof. There is nothing in 48 ♘xd6 c3 49 ♘e4 c2 50 ♔d2 ♗a4 51 ♔c1 (in Black's favour is 51 d6?! ♔e8 52 e3 ♗c6 53 ♘g3 ♔d7) 51...♗b3 52 ♘g3 ♗xd5 53 ♔xc2 and the intrigue unfolds. On 48 ♔d4 (or 48 ♔f4) Black simply waits, 48...♗c8, since continuations of the type 49 e3?! ♗f5 50 ♘c3 ♗d3 or 49 ♔xc4?! ♗a6+ 50

♔d4 ♗xe2 51 ♘xd6 g3 are in Black's favour, while 49 ♘g3 ♗a6 50 ♘e4 ♗c8 leads to a repetition of position. And after 47 ♔d4 g4 48 e3 g3 49 ♘e2 g2 50 ♔xc4, White wins back the pawn, but Black hurries to latch on to the central pawns after 50...♗c8 51 ♔d4 ♗a6.

47 ♔f2!

Now the bishop, too, assumes the role of a statistic.

47...♔e8 48 ♘b5 ♔d7 49 e4 ♔d8

The alternative 49...g3+ 50 ♔xg3 ♗f1 51 ♔f2 ♗d3 52 ♔e3 is likewise to White's advantage.

50 ♘xd6 c3 51 ♘xf7+ ♔c7 52 ♘e5 g3+ 53 ♔xg3 c2 54 ♘d3 ♗f1 55 ♘c1 ♔d7 56 e5 ♗c4 57 d6 ♗e6 58 ♔f4 ♔c6 Black resigned.

Chess anthologies feature many cases showing both the advantage of two bishops over a pair of other minor pieces—and also the reverse.

From the aspect of our theme, frequently this same advantage is expressed in the fact that one of the bishops can be exchanged at an appropriate moment, with advantage.

Velimirović - Shipov
Belgrade 1998

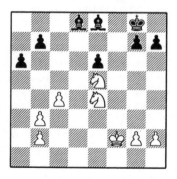

Black has the better position. Apart from the obvious advantage

of the two bishops over a pair of knights (by no means because of their numerical value!)—they have support points, Black also has the better pawn structure—on the queenside three white pawns are devalued by two white ones. Nonetheless the knights demonstrate fine resistance.

32...♗c7 33 ♘f3 h6

Prophylaxis against the advance of the knight to g5. On 33...♗f4 White harasses from the other side —34 ♘c5 ♗c6 35 g3 when 35...♗c1 is useless because of 36 ♘d3.

34 ♔e3 ♔f7

Worth considering is 33...a5.

35 ♔d4 ♔e7 36 b4 ♗f4 37 ♘c5

Also after 37 b3 ♗c6 White's defence is not easy.

37...♗c6 38 ♘e5!

White strives to exchange and thereby reduce the pressure of the bishops.

38...♗xg2

If 38...♗xh2 39 ♘xc6+ bxc6 40 ♘xa6, White quickly creates a distant passed pawn.

39 ♘g6+ ♔d6?!

The choice of move here seems to have no significance—the king still lands on f4—but in fact this is not so. More accurate would be 39...♔f6, since instead of the following "automatic" capture...

40 ♘xf4?!

...White could have played 40 ♘xb7+! ♗xb7 41 c5+ ♔d7 42 ♘xf4 g5 43 ♘g6 ♗d5 44 ♘e5 with approximately equal chances.

40...e5+ 41 ♔e3 exf4+ 42 ♔xf4 a5

Worth considering is 42...g5+, retaining some advantage, but also the move in the game looks highly ambitious.

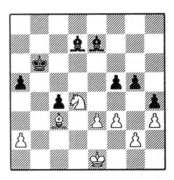

43 ♘xb7+!

Bravo, Velimirović! The knight sacrifice saves White.

43...♗xb7 44 bxa5 ♗c8

For the bishop White has only two pawns but it is not so easy for the black king to gobble up the white "trio". And after 44...♔c5 45 ♔f5 ♔xc4 46 ♔g6 ♔b5 47 ♔xg7 h5 48 ♔h6 ♗f3 49 b4 ♗e2 50 ♔g5 the bishop is in no position to capture the remaining surviving pawns.

Running ahead, we might mention that the tail-piece of this game can be broadened by a number of examples, looked at in chapter 7.

45 b4 g5+ 46 ♔e4 h5 47 b5! ♔c5 48 a6 ♔b6

Or 48...♔xc4 49 a7 ♗b7+ 50 ♔f5 g4 51 ♔g5 with a draw.

49 c5+! ♔a7 50 ♔e5! h4 51 ♔d6 g4 52 ♔c7 g3

He could even lose after 52...♗xa6? 53 b6+ ♔a8 54 c6.

53 hxg3 hxg3 Draw.

After 54 ♔xc8 g2 55 b6+ ♔xa6 56 b7 g1=♕ 57 b8=♕ ♕xc5+ 58 ♕c7 ♕xc7+ 59 ♔xc7 only the bare kings remain on the board.

V.Milov - Van Wely
Biel 2000

Despite Black's advantage of the two bishops, the following position at first sight seems drawish.

The attempt at pressure on the queenside by 47...♗b4 meets a firm refutation: 48 ♔d2 ♔c5 49 ♘c2. Nevertheless L. Van Wely finds a way to breathe life into this position.

47...g4!

With a pawn sacrifice Black exasperates White's redoubt on the kingside and the light-squared bishop gets the chance to draw close to the g2 pawn.

48 hxg4 fxg4 49 fxg4

Not good is 49 f4 h3 50 gxh3 gxh3 51 ♘f3 ♗b4 with advantage to Black.

49...♗xg4 50 ♗xa5+ ♔xa5 51 ♘c6+ ♔a4 52 ♘xe7 ♔a3 53 ♔d2 ♔b2

All this, of course, as also the following move, was foreseen by Black on the 47th move. His king shepherds the passed c-pawn and White's move is forced.

54 ♘d5

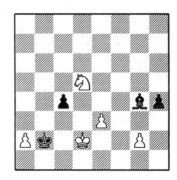

54...♗f3!!?

It is impossible to resist the temptation of such beauty! We give it two exclamation marks. White's reply, as also the following knight manoeuvre, is forced and constructs a very beautiful positional draw.

**55 gxf3 h3 56 ♘c3 h2 57 ♘d1+!
♚xa2 58 ♘f2 ♚b2 59 ♘d1+ ♚b3
60 ♘f2 ♚b2 Drawn.**

But returning to the position in the diagram. Why did we also add to the move 54...♗f3 a question mark? In the name of objectivity: you see, the sacrifice of the bishop turns out to be sufficient only for a draw, and not too complicated either, whereas there are still resources in the position for the bishop. Black could set his opponent far more difficult problems by the bishop manoeuvre **54...♗f5! 55 ♘c3 ♗d3!**, aiming to get the g2 pawn. In this case, in order to save the game, accurate defence is required of White—at every step he might break up on the reef (for example, there are no saving chances by 56 a4? ♗f1 57 a5 ♗xg2).

The main continuation is **56 e4 ♗f1**

57 ♘d1+!

It is important to encounter the h-pawn as soon as possible. Losing is 57 e5? ♗xg2 58 e6 h3 59 e7 ♗c6 60 ♘d1+ ♚xa2 61 ♚c3 h2 62 ♘f2 ♚b1 63 ♚xc4 ♗c2 and, thanks to the "lower" opposition, the king ousts the knight.

57...♚xa2 58 ♚c3! ♗xg2 59 ♘f2! ♚b1 60 ♚xc4 ♚c2 61 e5 ♚d2 62 ♚c5 ♗f3 63 e6 ♚e3 64 e7 ♗h5 65 ♘h3 (also possible is 65 ♘g4+ ♚f4 66 ♘h2 h3 67 ♚d6 ♚g3 68 ♘f1+ ♚g2 69 ♘e3+ ♚f2 70 ♘g4+ ♚g3 71 ♘e3 and the pawn remains on h3) **65...♚f3 66 ♚d6 ♚g3 67 ♘g1 ♚g2 68 ♘e2** and Black does not manage to advance the pawn to h3.

But he could be cunning: **57...♚b1!?**

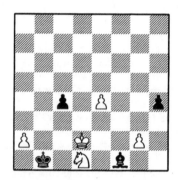

Now if 58 ♘e3?! ♗xg2 59 e5 h3 60 ♘g4 ♚b2 or 58 a4?! ♗xg2 59 ♘f2 ♚b2 60 ♘d1+ ♚b3, White loses. But also here there is still no saving himself—**58 ♚c3! ♗xg2 59 ♘f2 ♚xa2** (now the king does not succeed in getting the opposition) 60 ♚xc4 ♚b2 61 ♚d4 **Draw.**

This game and its analysis draws attention to the resources which are stored in what would seem a drawn position.

4 Exploiting a Small Material Advantage

What happens on the chessboard at that moment when, in an encounter between rated players, the game ends in victory for one of the sides? Generally, a positional advantage has assumed a decisive character. The most universal means of realising it is the achievement of a material advantage, sufficient for victory. But just as frequently met is the reverse, when the best way of realising a small material advantage is the transformation of it into a decisive positional one. This will be quite sufficient for victory.

We will look at examples from practical play in which a material advantage is so insignificant (for example when the activity of the enemy pieces virtually compensates for a pawn deficit), that many players reconcile themselves to a draw. Many, but not true masters! Usually they will not strive to hold on unfailingly to a material advantage. For them more important is activity, not only for the sake of material gain but more often for serious positional achievements. And quite often this thirst for battle will be rewarded.

In this chapter we look at examples with an extra pawn, against an attacking side, with material balance of other pieces. Other cases are looked at in the following chapters of the book.

1 Realisation of an extra pawn

Quite often a small material advantage will prove sufficient, if the opponent's counterplay can be neutralised. But this implies the possession of a high level of technique. The chess classics have amassed quite a lot of these examples. Let us look at a few fragments from the creative work of outstanding chessplayers of various times, who demonstrate to us various forms of filigree technique.

Capablanca - Alekhine
World Championship match,
Buenos Aires 1927

White's extra pawn and more active positions of his pieces are still insufficient to achieve victory. You see, the opponents' pawn chains are on one flank and, with each exchange, the chances of a win can be reduced.

J.R.Capablanca carries out the plan of creating a passed pawn, in conjunction with the threat to break up the opponent's king cover.

39 ♘e5!

White unequivocally threatens to sacrifice the knight on g6.

39...♗g7 40 ♕a8+ ♔h7 41 ♘f3 ♗f6

The white knight is limited in mobility, but, you know, there is also that extra pawn...

42 ♕a6!

With the threat of d4-d5.

42...♔g7 43 ♕d3 ♕b7 44 e4 ♕c6 45 h3!

Let us turn our attention to the characteristic details of the play of J.R.Capablanca in the ending—he does not hurry with active operations, but improves his position to the maximum and restricts his opponent's possible counterplay.

45...♕c7 46 d5! exd5 47 exd5

White realises his plan and creates a passed pawn. However A.Alekhine, understanding that the blockade of the passed pawn by 47...♕d6 48 ♕c4 ♕f8 49 ♘d4 is unpromising, prepares a remarkable defensive resource. He offers a queen exchange, counting on saving himself in the minor piece ending.

47...♕c3! 48 ♕xc3

On 48 ♕e4, A.Alekhine intended 48...♕c5!.

48...♗xc3 49 ♔f1 ♔f6 50 ♔e2 ♗b4!

Black intended to play 51...♗c5, in order not to allow the knight to c6.

51 ♘d4 ♗c5 52 ♘c6 ♔f5 53 ♔f3!

Upon the routine 53 f3, A.Alekhine would, of course, have played 53...h4!.

53...♔f6 54 g4 hxg4+ 55 hxg4

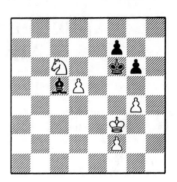

55...♔g5?

After an excellent defence, Black makes a mistake and in a trice leaves the f7 pawn undefended. This proves sufficient for realising the advantage. Defensive resources were retained by 55...♗d6! 56 ♘d8 (on 56 ♔e4, good is 56...♔g5!, with the idea ...f7-f5) 56...♗e7 or even 55...♗b6.

56 ♘e5! ♗d4?!

This simplifies White's task, but also the better 56...♗a3!? 57 d6 ♔f6 58 d7 would hardly have saved Black (58...♔e7 59 ♘xf7 ♔xd7 60 ♘e5+).

57 ♘xf7+ ♔f6 58 ♘d8 ♗b6

Not possible is 58...♔e5?, because of 59 ♘c6+.

59 ♘c6 ♗c5

And once again a familiar position arises, but this time without the f7 pawn—"a mysterious disappearance"...

60 ♔f4!

The king goes over to the attack, not worrying about the loss of the f2 pawn. If 60 ♔g3 ♗d6+ 61 f4, Black becomes active by 61...g5!.

60...♗xf2 61 g5+ ♔f7

On 61...♔g7 would have followed
62 d6.

**62 ♘e5+ ♔e7 63 ♘xg6+ ♔d6 64
♔e4 ♗g3 65 ♘f4 ♔e7 66 ♔e5 ♗e1
67 d6+ ♔d7 68 g6 ♗b4 69 ♔d5!**

But not 69 g7? ♗c3+!.

69...♔e8 70 d7+ Black resigned.

The triumph of centralisation!
—we frequently come across this
phenomenon when playing through
games of leading players of the past.

Rubinstein - Schlechter
Berlin 1918

White has an extra pawn, but one
of these is among the tripled(!) f-
pawns. However, upon a closer in-
spection of the position, we see that
White controls the d-file, and the f5
pawn, if the opportunity arises, can
become a battering ram; moreover
Black is, for the present, weak on
the back rank. Let us observe how
virtuoso A.Rubinstein exploits this
imperceptible temporary plus and
abruptly changes the picture of the
struggle by activating his pieces.

27 ♕d4!

Centralisation is more important
than a pawn, the more so a flank
one. Black, reckoning that his position is sufficiently solid, accepts the
sacrifice. However, as pointed out

by E.Lasker, more circumspect was
27...♘d7.

27...♘xa4 28 f6 ♘c5

The exchange of knights is the
only possibility of weakening the
onslaught of the white pieces.

**29 ♘xc5 bxc5 30 ♕g4 g6 31
♕g3!**

Finely assessing the arising pawn
ending, White offers an exchange of
queens. Black is forced to avoid the
exchange, but thereby lets go of the
important e5 square.

31...♕d8 32 ♕e5 a4 33 h4 h6

A painful necessity—Black is
obliged to take care of the safety of
his own king.

**34 ♔g2 ♕c8 35 ♔g3 ♕d8 36
♔g2 ♕c8**

A repetition of position—the
usual method of gaining time before
the control.

**37 ♕xc5 ♕e6 38 ♕e7! ♕c8 39 c5
g5**

Black actually finds himself in
zugzwang and makes a desperate
bid for freedom. But he does not
save himself. We mention that by
now even waiting makes no sense.
After 39...♕a8 40 ♕d7, White advances f3-f4-f5, breaking up the
cover of the enemy king.

Even tripled pawns can bring
great benefits!

**40 hxg5 hxg5 41 ♕e3 ♕e6 42
♕xg5+ ♔f8 43 ♕g7+ ♔e8 44
♕g8+ ♔d7 45 ♕g4! ♔e8 46
♕xe6+ fxe6 47 ♔g3 ♔f7 48 ♔f4
♔xf6 49 ♔e4 Black resigned.**

In the following chapters of the
book the reader can also see other
masterpieces of great masters of the
past. But here I return to the practice
of my colleagues. Here is an
example of fine manoeuvring and
brilliant defence.

Beliavsky - Polugaevsky
Moscow 1979

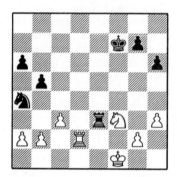

Black's pieces are so active that the extra pawn is hardly felt and it is by no means easy to find a way to realise it. A study of this ending is highly instructive.

39 ♘d4 ♖e4!

From here the rook controls both flanks.

40 ♘e2 ♔e7 41 ♔e1 h5!

One senses the hand of a great master. While observing the queenside, Black paralyses the kingside.

42 ♔d1 h4!

Having in view a possible knight ending and a march of the black king.

43 b3 ♘c5 44 ♖d4 ♔f6 45 ♖xe4 ♘xe4 46 ♔c2 ♔e5

The king has changed places with the rook on the observation point.

47 ♔d3 ♘f2+ 48 ♔e3 ♘d1+ 49 ♔d2 ♘f2 50 ♘d4 ♔f4

This is where the advance of the h-pawn comes in handy.

51 ♘e6+ ♔g3 52 ♔e3 ♘d1+ 53 ♔d4 ♔xg2 54 c4

It is clear that in the knight ending, as in the one with pawns, the principal energy is concealed in the passed pawns.

54...bxc4 55 bxc4 ♔xh3 56 c5 ♘b2!

The knight makes contact with the c-pawn, while the black h-pawn proves to be a quite worthy opponent for it.

57 c6 ♘a4 58 ♘f4+ ♔g3 59 ♘d5 h3 60 c7 h2 61 c8=♕ h1=♕ 62 ♕c7+

62...♔h4?

After conducting the defence excellently, Polugayevsky makes a mistake and "attaches" his king to the queen, which costs him his knight. After 62...♔f2! 63 ♕c2+ ♔g3 it is not apparent how White can strengthen his position.

63 ♕d8+ ♔g3

On 63...♔g4 or 63...♔h3 follows 64...♕d7+ and 65...♕xa4.

64 ♕g5+ ♔h2

After 64...♔f2 65 ♕e3+ ♔g2 66 ♘f4+ he could get mated.

65 ♕h5+ ♔g1 66 ♕d1+ ♔h2 67 ♕xa4 ♕a1+ 68 ♔c5 ♕c1+ 69 ♕c4 ♕a3+ 70 ♔d4 ♕b2+ 71 ♔e4 and after a few moves **Black resigned**.

On the theme of compensation for material deficit through active counterplay, we might also share with the reader some of our own experience.

Yurtaev - Gufeld
Helsinki 1992

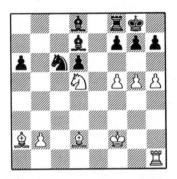

Black's extra pawn is offset by the more active deployment of the white pieces. Therefore, in order to realise his material advantage, the main task for Black is to parry White's initiative.

31 f6 ♗e6 32 ♔g3 ♖e8 33 fxg7 ♔xg7 34 ♖d1!

White "unravels" his forces in the direction of the centre and the weak d6 pawn.

34...♘e5 35 ♗f4 h6

Black must reckon with the threat of ♘d5-f6 and is ready to return the pawn in order to weaken this threat and achieve his objective. Though also not without help from the opponent...

36 gxh6+?!

L.Yurtaev overestimates his chances. After 36 ♘f6! ♗xf6 37 gxf6+ ♔xf6 38 ♖xd6 ♔f5 39 ♗xe5 ♔xe5 40 ♖xa6, the game is simplified with a probably drawn result.

36...♔h8 37 h7 ♔xh7 38 ♗b1+ ♔h8 39 ♘e3 ♖g8+ 40 ♔f2 ♗h4+ 41 ♔e2 ♗g3!

White missed this possibility in his calculations, when thinking over his 36th move. With the exchange of the dark-squared bishops, Black's advantage takes a real outline.

42 ♗xg3 ♖xg3 43 ♗e4

Capturing the d6 pawn leads to the loss of a piece: 43 ♖xd6?? ♖xe3+! 44 ♔xe3 ♘c4+.

43...♘g4! 44 ♖d3 ♘xe3 45 ♖xe3 ♖g5!

Upon the exchange of rooks, the draw becomes absolutely real: 45...♖xe3+ (or 45...♗g4+ 46 ♔d2 ♖xe3 47 ♔xe3 ♗xh5 48 b4! and White wins the b7 pawn) 46 ♔xe3 a5 47 h6 f5 48 ♗d3 ♔h7 49 ♔f4 ♔xh6 50 ♗xf5 Now, however, Black wins a second pawn.

46 h6 ♖b5 47 ♖a3 ♖xb2+

The rest is a matter of technique.

48 ♔d1 ♗c4 49 ♗c2 ♖b8 50 ♔d2 ♖g8 51 ♖e3 ♖g2+ 52 ♔c3 ♗e6 53 ♖e1 a5 54 ♖a1 ♖g5 55 ♗d3 ♖h5 56 h7 ♖c5+ 57 ♔b2 ♗f5 58 ♗xf5 ♖xf5 59 ♖h1 ♖f3 60 ♖h4 d5 61 ♔c2 d4 62 ♔d2 a4 63 ♖xd4 a3 64 ♖d7 a2 65 ♖a7 ♖h3 66 ♔c2 ♖h1 White resigned.

Gufeld - Fedorowicz
Reno 1999

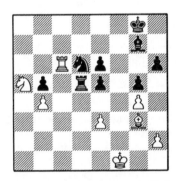

Notwithstanding the extra, if doubled, pawn, White has something of a symbolic advantage. Objectively speaking, the position has a double-edged character, though during the game I assessed my chances as rather higher. Nevertheless White's pieces are on the offensive, Black's confined to defence.

35 ♔e2 ♗f8 36 ♘b3 ♔f7 37 ♘c5

White logically improves the positions of his pieces, but also Black does not dawdle.

37...♘c4 38 ♗e1 ♗e7

Also worth considering is 38...♗xc5!? 39 bxc5 e4 40 ♖c7+ ♔f6! (not good is 40...♔e8? 41 c6 ♖d3 42 ♖c8+ ♔e7 43 ♗b4+ and White wins) 41 ♖h7 (in Black's favour is 41 ♗c3+ e5 or 41 c6 ♖d3) 41...♔g6 42 ♖e7 ♔f6 and everything is in order for Black. Now, however, White wins the b5 pawn.

39 ♖c7 ♖d8 40 ♖b7 ♖a8

Black rightly prefers activity to clinging on to the pawn. After 40...♘d6 41 ♖a7 White can return to a siege of the e5 pawn.

41 ♖xb5

41...♖a3

The plan to win the pawns on the kingside also looks tempting: 41...♖a2+ 42 ♔d3 ♘d6! (of course not 42...♘b2+? 43 ♔e4) 43 ♖a5 ♖xh2 and Black creates an alternative distant passed g-pawn. Let us look at the possible continuations:

a) 44 ♗c3?! ♖h4 45 ♘d7 (or 45 ♗xe5 ♖xg4 and the b4 pawn is under threat) 45...e4+ 46 ♔d4 h5 with the better chances for Black.

b) 44 ♘d7 e4+ 45 ♔d4 h5 46 ♘e5+ ♔f6 and there is apparently nothing real.

42 e4 ♖e3+

Black could win the e4 pawn—42...♗xc5 43 ♖xc5 (weaker is 43 bxc5?! ♖e3+ 44 ♔f2 ♖xe4) 43...♖e3+ 44 ♔f2 ♖xe4, but apparently the endgame did not suit him after 45 ♖c7+ ♔f6 46 h3 ♘b2 47 ♗d2. The position is simplified which plays into the hands of the distant passed pawn.

43 ♔f2 ♖h3 44 ♔g2 ♖a3

It is worth repeating the position by 44...♖e3, retaining, in addition, the possibility pointed out in the previous note. Now, however, White puts right the coordination of his pieces, obtaining in effect an extra pawn.

45 ♗f2! ♖a2 46 h3

A solid move, untieing the "hands" of the rook. An immediate 46 ♖b7 is not good because of 46...♘e3+ 47 ♔f3 ♘xg4.

46...♖b2

J.Fedorowicz apparently takes the firm decision "not to have anything to do with" the e4 pawn—46...♘d2!? 47 ♖a5 ♖c2 48 ♖a7 ♔e8.

47 ♖b7 ♔f6?!

Getting out of the pin, the king falls under the knight. After the simple 47...♘d6! Black gives his opponent the choice of a repetition of moves—48 ♖b6 ♘c4 49 ♖b7 ♘d6 or freeing himself from the pin by 48 ♖b8.

48 ♘d7+ ♔g6?

It was necessary to go back, 48...♔f7, intending 49 ♖c7 ♔e8.

In cruel modern play two mistakes in succession are punishable. The advantage finally passes to White.

49 ♖c7 ♘d6

Capturing the pawn, 49...♖xb4?, loses a piece—50 ♖xc4!.

50 ♘xe5+ ♔g7 51 ♘d3 ♖d2 52 ♖xe7+ ♔f6 53 ♖d7 ♘xe4 54 ♔f3 ♘xf2 55 ♔e3 Black resigned.

After 55...♖xd3+ 56 ♖xd3 ♘xd3 57 ♔xd3 ♔e5 58 ♔c4 ♔d6 59 ♔d4, the pawn ending is hopeless.

And, in conclusion, a memorable episode from my youth.

Sherwin - Gufeld
Helsinki 1961

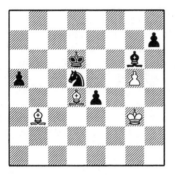

Black has two extra pawns, and for victory it is necessary to promote, if only one of them. But how can he do this for sure?

31...♗h5

All the spectators for this game were disappointed: why did I reject the simple 31...e3 ? You see, after 32 ♗xd5 ♔xd5 33 ♗xe3 a4 34 ♗c1 ♔c4 35 ♔f3 ♔b3 36 ♔e2 a3 37 ♗f4 a2 38 ♗e5 ♔c2 and 39...♔b1, Black wins. But, afterwards, when I showed the acknowledged endgame expert, grandmaster Y.Averbakh, well able to appreciate chess beauty, that upon calculating the variation I had discovered the move 33 ♗b6!!, he no longer felt so bad! Indicative was also the reaction of the then schoolboy champion of the USSR, A.Khalifman (FIDE world champion 1999): "This is a superhuman move!"

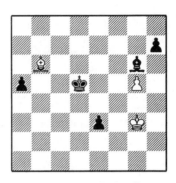

The bishop "urges on" the a-pawn—move forward, my friend! But, if it does so, there is a highly important role for the white king. After 33...a4 34 ♔f3 a3 35 ♔xe3 ♔c4 36 ♗d4! ♔b3 37 ♔d2, the game is a draw: White's king reaches d2 just in time (37...♔a2 38 ♔c1). Hence 31...e3? is a mistake, throwing away the win. But the winning idea had been found—it was important only to formulate it in the appropriate way.

The game ended:

32 ♔f2 ♔e6 33 ♔g3 ♗e2! 34 ♔h4 ♔d6 35 ♔g3 ♗b5! 36 ♗c2 ♗d3 37 ♗b3 e3!

Now this sacrifice quickly leads to the objective.

38 ♗xd5 ♔xd5 39 ♗xe3

Here 39 ♗b6 no longer works: 39...a4 40 ♔f3 e2.

39...a4 40 ♗c1 ♔c4 41 ♔f2 ♔b3 42 ♗f4 a3 43 ♔e3 a2 44 ♗e5 ♔c2 45 ♔f4 ♗g6 46 ♗d4 ♔b1 White resigned.

2 The game ends in a draw

Does the reader recognise that frequently played game at the end of which comes the laconic, "Draw?" Apparently not. Indeed, even commentators usually prefer to recount games with results. And to some extent this is right. Chess, above all, is a struggle, and in it a winner is determined. But what if there are two winners, if attack and defence are worthy of one another, and a fine plan of attack is parried by a no less fine defensive rejoinder? Then the game ends in a draw, in a win...for chess! In short, a drawn result of the game—is also a result.

Of course we do not include those games that not infrequently finish in draws when one inaccurate move has let slip the fruits of many hours' work. Chessplayers of every rank know the situation well. Examples of this are looked at in the previous chapters, they will also be looked at in the following chapters. Here we will stick to the accepted methods of study and examine examples of defence from the side having the "pawn minus", with material equality of other pieces. Other examples are looked at in the following chapters.

Above we saw a form of brilliant defence in the game Beliavsky-Polugaevsky, Moscow 1979, which (if it were not for the mistake 62...♘h4?) by right should be studied at this point in the book; we look also at other forms of active defence a pawn down.

Smyslov - Hübner
Candidates match, Velden 1983

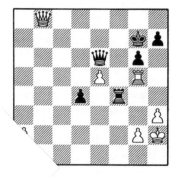

Apart from the pawn deficit, the black king is less secure than its opposite number. He cannot restore material equality by 42...♕xa2 because of 43 e6! with an attack on the rook and the threat 44 e7. Therefore his task is to render harmless the e-pawn, not forgetting at the same time about the preservation of his own, no less dangerous, passed d-pawn.

42...♔h6!

Driving away the rook—defender of the e5 pawn—and removing his king from attack along the seventh rank. Just how easily it is to "slip" in such virtually equal positions, can be seen by the sample variation: 42...♖f1 (42...♖f7 43 ♕d6) 43 ♕a7+ ♔h6 44 ♕xd4! ♔xg5 45 ♕e3+ ♖f4 46 ♔g3 ♕f5 47 h4+ or 42...d3 43 ♖g3 ♕d5 44 e6 and Black cannot hold back the e-pawn.

43 ♖g3

Also after 43 ♕d8 ♖e4! 44 ♕d6 ♕f7 45 ♖g3 ♕f4 the principal enemy—the e-pawn—lands in a siege.

43...♕f5!

The threat 44...d3! obliges White to force events. The alternative was 43...♖f5 44 ♖d3 ♕xe5+ 45 ♕xe5 ♖xe5 46 ♖xd4 ♖e2 with a theoretical draw.

44 e6 ♖e4!

Avoiding the last reef, 44...♖f1? 45 e7 ♕f2 46 ♖xg6+! hxg6 47 ♕h8+ ♔g5 48 ♕e5+ ♔h6 49 e8=♕ ♕g1+ 50 ♔g3 ♕f2+ 51 ♔g4 ♕xg2+ 52 ♕g3 and the checks are at an end.

45 ♕d6

To the same result would lead 45 ♖f3 ♕xe6 46 ♕f8+ ♔g5 (but not 46...♔h5? because of 47 g4+ ♔g5 48 h4+) 47 ♖g3+ ♔h5.

45...♕xe6 46 ♕xe6 ♖xe6 47 ♖d3 Draw.

The slogan for this ending is "Activity and still more activity!". It should be mentioned that in the first game of this same Candidates match V.Smyslov also played under the same motto, saving an ending the exchange down (given in Chapter 7).

One can also hardly remain indifferent to the following example of active defence a pawn down.

Spassky - Fischer
World Championship,
Reykjavik 1972

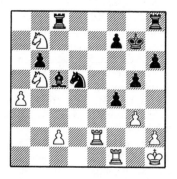

R.Fischer has, for a long time, conducted the game excellently. Beating off the opponent's attack in the opening, he counted on realising his material advantage without particular hindrance, but somehow he weakened, and...

32 c4!

This pawn is offered as a sacrifice; in return White takes out the dangerous wedge on f4.

32...②e3 33 ②f3 ②xc4 34 gxf4 g4

Possibly better was 34...②he8, but also the move in the game seems quite logical.

35 ②d3 h5 36 h3! ②a5

On 36...②a8 could follow 37 ②xc5 bxc5 38 ②c3.

37 ②7d6

The knight comes to life. From a long way away, White begins to prepare threats against the black king.

37...②xd6 38 ②xd6 ②c1+ 39 ②g2 ②c4 40 ②e8+!

No exchanges at all, only forward!

40...②g6

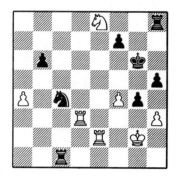

41 h4!

The sealed move at the adjournment of the game, over which B.Spassky thought for 45 minutes. Considerably weaker was the obvious 41 ②d5 f6 42 h4 (better is 42 ②e6 ②f7 43 f5 ②xe8 44 ②d7+ ②f8 45 ②xf6+, J.Timman) 42...②c3! 43 f5 ②h6 and White has serious difficulties in connection with the threat of ...②e3+ (N.Krogius).

41...f6

There was the threat of 42 ②d5 and 43 f5+, while in the event of 41...②f5 it is possible to repeat the position by 42 ②g7+ ②g6 43 ②e8.

42 ②e6! ②c2+ 43 ②g1

Weaker is 43 ②g3 ②f8 and the threat is 44...②d2 and 45...②f1.

43...②f5

The last chance was 43...②xe8!? 44 ②xe8 ②d2 45 ②e2 ②f3+ 46 ②f2 ②c4, but, by playing 47 ②xf3! gxf3 48 ②xf3 ②xa4 49 ②b2, White probably holds.

44 ②g7+! ②xf4

After 44...♔g6? 45 f5+! he might even lose: 45...♔xg7 46 ♖d7+ ♔f8 47 ♖d8+.

45 ♖d4+ ♔g3 46 ♘f5+ ♔f3 47 ♖ee4

White, from a position of strength, (he threatens 48 ♖f4 mate) obliges the opponent to force perpetual check.

There is no echo-mate after 47 ♖e1 ♖g2+ 48 ♔h1 g3! or 47 ♖d3+ ♔f4 48 ♘g3 ♖c1+ 49 ♔f2 ♖c2+ 50 ♔e1 ♖c1+ 51 ♔e2 ♖c2+ 52 ♔d1 ♖d2+! and an exchange of rooks is forced.

47...♖c1+ 48 ♔h2 ♖c2+ 49 ♔g1 Draw.

Kramnik - Kasparov
Wijk aan Zee 2000

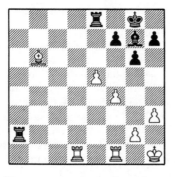

The pawns on both sides are placed on the same flank, which makes it difficult to realise the extra pawn. However, if Black does not succeed in carrying out the break ...f7-f6, it is not easy for him to achieve a draw.

25 ♗d8?!

Clever, but insufficient, since the bishop cannot be maintained on the d8-f6 diagonal. Stronger was 25 ♖d6! g5 26 g3 h5 27 h4 and for the ⸴ being he does not manage to ⸴ut the break ...f7-f6.

⸴6! 26 ♗c7

White suddenly thinks, and prevents 26...f6? by 27 ♖d6 ♖a7 28 ♗b6, but it is already too late. If 26 ♗h4 f6, then 27 ♖d6 is not dangerous: 27...♖xd6 28 exd6 ♖d8 29 ♖d1 ♔f7 30 ♗f2 ♔e6 31 ♗c5 ♗f8 and Black stands firm.

26...♖ae6 27 g4 g5!?

A counter-blow, characteristic for the energetic style of G.Kasparov. But also possible was 27...f6 28 f5 ♖c6 29 ♗d6 ♖d8!, but not 29...fxe5? because of 30 f6.

28 f5

White achieves nothing after 28 fxg5 ♗xe5 29 ♗xe5 ♖xe5 30 ♖d7 ♖xg5 31 ♖fxf7 h5.

28...♖c6 29 ♖d7

White counts on retaining the initiative in the rook ending, since, after 29 ♗d8 ♗xe5 30 ♗xg5, good is 30...♖c3 31 ♔g2 ♖g3+ and Black has sufficient counterplay.

29...♗xe5 30 ♖e1 f6 31 ♗xe5 ♖xe5 32 ♖xe5 fxe5 33 ♖e7 h5 34 ♔g2 hxg4

After the hasty 34...♖c2+ 35 ♔f3 ♖c3+ 36 ♔e4 ♖xh3 Black might lose: 37 f6 hxg4 38 ♔f5 and the king is effectively included in the attack.

35 hxg4 ♖c4 36 ♔f3 ♖f4+ 37 ♔g3 e4 Draw.

White does not hurry to take the pawn on g5—38 ♖e6 ♔f7 39 ♖g6 ♖f3+ 40 ♔g2 ♖f4 41 ♖xg5 e3, not giving up the g4 pawn.

Kamsky - Karpov
FIDE World Championship,
Elista 1996

At first sight, the extra b3 pawn has no significance—White's two bishops control the situation and moreover he has his own passed f-pawn, which White intends to reinforce with the advance g4-g5.

However G.Kamsky finds a way to breathe life into the passed b3 pawn.

47...g5+! 48 hxg5 hxg5+ 49 ♔g3

Upon the capture 49 ♔xg5?, the b3 pawn will cost a bishop: 49...♘f3+ 50 ♔f4 ♘xd4 51 exd4 ♔xf6 52 g5+ ♔g7 with ...♗e8-g6 to follow. On 49 ♔e5 he has to reckon with 49...♘f3+ 50 ♔d6 e5!.

49...b2! 50 ♗xb2 ♘b3 51 ♗c2

White strives to open the position, in order to exploit the strength of his two bishops, but it is also possible to retain the c5 pawn—51 ♗a3! (of course not 51 ♗d4? because of 51...♘xd4 52 exd4 ♔xf6 and ...e6-e5) 51...e5 52 ♗b4 d4! (after 52...♔xf6? the knight is lost: 53 ♗c2 ♘c1 54 ♗d2 ♘e2+ 55 ♔f3 ♘g1+ 56 ♔f2) 53 ♗c4+ ♗e6 54 ♗xb3 ♗xb3 55 exd4 exd4 56 ♗a5 ♔xf6. Finally Black takes the f6 pawn, but at the cost of allowing opposite-coloured bishops, which reduces his chances of a win.

51...♘xc5 52 e4

More accurate is 52 ♔f3 ♗c8 53 e4 dxe4+ (after 53...♗a6 54 e5 White defends the f6 pawn, making it difficult for Black to realise his advantage) 54 ♗xe4 ♗b7 55 ♗e5 ♘d7 56 ♗c3.

52...dxe4 53 ♔f2

After 53 ♗d4 ♘d3 54 ♗xd3 exd3 55 ♔f3 e5 56 ♗xe5 ♗xg4+! the

opposite-coloured bishops do not guarantee a draw.

53...♗c8 54 ♔e3 ♘d7 55 ♗xe4 c5

Both sides realise their plans: Black has an extra pawn, White has an active bishop and then also the potential to transfer to a satisfactory opposite-coloured bishops ending.

56 ♗f3 ♗a6 57 ♗a3 ♗b5

Premature is 57...♔xf6 because of 58 ♗c6 with the threat of exchanging knights.

58 ♔f2 ♗c4 59 ♗c6 ♘e5 60 ♗f3 ♗d5 61 ♗e2

The c5 pawn is invulnerable: 61 ♗xd5? exd5 62 ♗xc5?? ♘d3+.

61...♘d7 62 ♔e3 ♗c6 63 ♗d3 ♔xf6 64 ♔e2

64...♔f7?!

Black already has two extra pawns. It is possible to win also a third: 64...♘e5 65 ♗b2! ♗f3+ 66 ♔e3 ♗xg4, but how to free himself from the pin? Apparently A.Karpov was not attracted to the idea of winning the g4 pawn and moves away the king.

But, you know, one of the main maxims in the ending is to centralise the king. As shown by M.Gurevich, Black obtains real chances of a win by 64...♔e5! 65 ♗c1 ♔d5 66 ♔f1 (it is not easy even after 66 ♗xg5 ♘e5 67 ♗c2 ♗b5+ 68 ♔e3 ♘xg4+

or 66 ♔e3 ♘f6) 66...♘e5 67 ♗e2
♘f7 68 ♗d3 and now there is a
choice of 68...♔d4 or 68...c4 69
♗g6 ♘e5.

65 ♗c1 ♘e5 66 ♗xg5 ♘xg4 67
♔d2 ♗d5 68 ♔c3 e5 69 ♗f5 ♘f6
70 ♗h4 ♘e8 71 ♗f2 ♘d6 72 ♗d3

An apotheosis of the bishops!
Despite his two extra pawns,
G.Kamsky is not able to extract
anything real from the position. The
bishops cut off the king from the
pawns and without advancing them
he can't get round (72...♘b7 73
♗a6), but then the dark squares are
also weakened, and so also is the
role of the dark-squared bishop.

72...c4 73 ♗h7!

Preventing the transfer of the king
to the centre: 73...♔f6 74 ♗h4+ or
73...♔e6 74 ♗g8+, while on
73...♗e4 there is 74 ♗c5!
(74...♘b5+ 75 ♔xc4).

73...♔g7 74 ♗c2 ♔f6 75 ♔b4!
Yet another consequence of the
move ...c5-c4—the king's sphere of
influence is increased (useless is 75
♗h4+ ♔e6).

75... ♔e6 76 ♗c5!
White encircles the c4 pawn—the
threat is ♗d1-e2 and ♗c5xd6.

76...♘b7 77 ♗f2 ♘d6 78 ♗c5
♘f7 79 ♗e3 ♔f6 80 ♗d1 e4
Advancing the second pawn,
Black effectively acknowledges his
own fiasco. But he cannot achieve
anything even after 80...♘d6 81
♗e2 ♔f5 82 ♗c5 ♘e4 83 ♗a7 c3
(83...♘d2 84 ♗e3) 84 ♗d3.

81 ♗e2 ♘e5 82 ♔c5 ♗f7 83 ♔d4
♔f5 84 ♔c3 ♗d5 85 ♔d4 ♔e6 86
♔c3 ♔f5 87 ♔d4 ♗f7 88 ♔c3 ♘g4
89 ♗xg4+
Here we see the advantage of the
two bishops—at an appropriate
moment one of them can be
exchanged.

89...♔xg4 90 ♔d2 **Draw**.

5 Strengths and Weaknesses of Opposite-Coloured Bishops

The drawing tendencies of opposite-coloured bishops are generally well known, therefore their presence is often considered to herald a draw. This is in fact right when the bishops are the only remaining pieces, and the peculiarities of the pawn structure do not guarantee a win. However, the presence of other pieces can significantly alter the assessment of the position in favour of the side holding the initiative. This is determined by the fact that the bishop participating in an attack actually has no opponent on the diagonal of its own colour and the attack is conducted, as it were, with an extra piece.

In our presentation of the theme of small advantage, we give our main attention to looking at endings in which the opposite-coloured bishops join the heavy pieces. Their presence allows the creation of mating threats, which enables the struggle to assume elements of the middlegame.

Nimzowitsch - Wolf
Karlsbad 1923

Despite the material quality, White's position can be preferred. Let us turn our attention to the difference in strength of the bishops:

White's dark-squared bishop attacks Black's "Achilles heel"—the g7 pawn, whereas Black's light-squared bishop only performs the passive function of cover.

33 ♕g4 ♗f5 34 ♕g2 h6

Worth considering is 34...♗d3!? 35 c5 ♗g6, avoiding the weakening of the king's cover.

35 ♖g3 ♔h7 36 d5!

For the disturbance of the temporary balance, new resources are needed. Therefore, he undertakes activity on the queenside with the aim of diverting defence from the king's flank.

36...♖f7

Cramped positions are more difficult to defend. More logical looks 36...exd5!? 37 cxd5 g6, not fearing the invasion of the rook: 38 ♖c3 ♕d8 39 d6 b5 40 ♖c7 ♖xc7 41 dxc7 ♕d3.

37 d6 g6

And here also is a consequence of the advance of the d-pawn: a general exchange of pieces on g7 is threatened.

38 c5 ♕c8 39 ♖c3

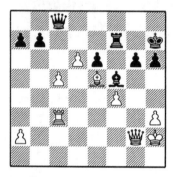

39...♕c6?

Avoiding a break on the c-file, Black gives his opponent the b-file. He should reconcile himself to the threat of c5-c6: (39...♖d7 40 c6 bxc6 41 ♖xc6 ♕b7! (not 41...♕a8 42 ♖c7), since in the event of 42 ♖c7 ♕xg2+ 43 ♔xg2 ♖xc7 44 dxc7, it is easier to defend himself in the bishop ending: 44...♗e4+ 45 ♔f2 ♗b7 46 ♔e3 ♔g8 and the king goes over to help the bishop.

40 ♕xc6 bxc6 41 h4 ♔g8

The strength of the d6 pawn shows in the fact that 41...♖b7 is impossible because of 42 ♖b3!.

42 ♖b3 ♖d7 43 ♖b8+ ♔f7 44 ♖c8 ♗e4 45 ♔g3 h5

The b-file, as before, is inaccessible to Black—45...♖b7? 46 ♖c7+.

46 ♔f2 ♗d5 47 ♔e3 ♗g2 48 ♔d4 ♗f3 49 ♗h8 e5+

After 49...♗d5 50 ♔e5 ♗f3 51 ♗g7!, full paralysis is imminent. 51...♔xg7 is impossible because of 52 ♖c7, and White, in time, constructs the mating formation, ♗h6 and ♖f8.

50 ♔xe5 ♗d5 51 ♗f6 ♗f3 52 ♗g5 ♔g7 53 f5!

A breakthrough on the theme of obstructing the diagonal to the c8 square (the threat is 56 ♖c7).

53...♗g4 54 f6+ ♔f7 55 ♖xc6 Black resigned.

Karpov - Kasparov
World Championship,
Moscow 1985

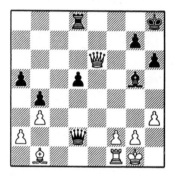

The position bears a double-edged character, but White's chances are preferable, since Black's rear is open to invasion along the light diagonal, which allows White to organise an attack.

44 ♗f5!

Mobilisation of the bishop, in conjunction with prophylaxis against counterplay along the f-file.

44...♕c3 45 ♕g6 ♔g8 46 ♗e6+ ♔h8 47 ♗f5 ♔g8 48 g3

A characteristic method, to which it is useful to direct our attention. Before going over to resolute action, White improves the position of his pieces to the maximum.

48...♔f8 49 ♔g2 ♕f6 50 ♕h7 ♕f7 51 h4 ♗d2?!

On 51...♗e7 would have followed 52 ♖e1, with the threat of 53 ♗e6 or 53 ♗g6. But worth considering is 51...♗f6!?, intending, on 52 ♖e1 ♕g8 53 ♕g6 ♕f7 54 ♕g4 d4, and Black has to reckon with the passed pawn. For example, not good is 55

♗e6?! because of 55...♕b7+ 56 ♔h2 d3, while on 55 ♗d3 possible is 55...♕d5+.

52 ♖d1 ♗c3 53 ♖d3 ♖d6 54 ♖f3!

White deploys his pieces on light squares, incidentally avoiding the little trap, 54 ♖e3 g5, exchanging the queens.

54...♔e7

Black renews the above-mentioned threat, whereas 54...♖f6?! already allows 55 ♖e3! to be played when 55...♖xf5 leads to the loss of the queen: 56 ♕h8+ ♕g8 57 ♖e8+ ♔xe8 58 ♕xg8+ ♔e7 59 f4 with advantage to White.

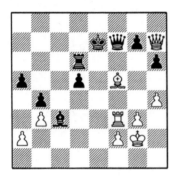

55 ♕h8!

With a beautiful queen manoeuvre, A.Karpov detains the king in the centre, threatening to drive it into "space" after 56 ♖e3+ ♔f6 57 ♗h3. The direct 55 ♖e3+ ♔d8 56 ♕h8+ ♔c7 57 ♕c8+ ♔b6 allows the king to get over to the other flank.

55...d4

Defending against 56 ♖e3+, Black dooms himself to playing a bishop down, but also 55...♗e5 does not save him: 56 ♗h3 ♖f6 57 ♖e3! ♖xf2+ 58 ♔g1.

56 ♕c8 ♖f6 57 ♕c5+ ♔e8 58 ♖f4 ♕b7+ 59 ♖e4+ ♔f7

The attempt to divert the bishop by 59...♖e6 leads to the loss of the queen after 60 ♕c4! ♖xe4 61 ♕g8.

60 ♕c4+ ♔f8 61 ♗h7!

The cooperation of the white pieces makes an aesthetic impression, each of his moves carries the threat of mate.

61...♖f7 62 ♕e6 ♕d7 63 ♕e5!

Black resigned.

There is no defence: 63...♕d8 64 ♕c5+ ♖e7 65 ♖f4+ ♔e8 66 ♕c6+ ♕d7 67 ♗g6+.

Even with the absence of other pieces, the presence of queens, together with opposite-coloured bishops, allows the development of an attack.

Reshevsky - Bronstein
Candidates tournament,
Zürich 1953

A characteristic feature of this position is the threat of penetrating with the black king to b2. But since this cannot be achieved without an exchange of queens, White does not risk losing: upon the loss of the a2 pawn he will stalemate the black king by ♔c2. Therefore Black's calculation can only be linked with the potential possibility of creating a passed g-pawn. This is achieved by the method of zugzwang.

50...♗c7 51 ♕f3 ♕b2+ 52 ♕e2 ♕d4 53 ♔f3 h5

After putting right as far as possible the coordination of his pieces, he creates a passed pawn.

54 ♔g2

More accurate is 54 ♕h2+ ♔b6 55 ♕e2.

54...g5 55 ♔g3 ♕f4+ 56 ♔g2 g4 57 hxg4 hxg4 58 ♔h1 ♔b6

More resolute is 58...♕d4! 59 ♕h2+ (59 ♕g2? ♗d6 60 ♕g1 ♕h8+ leads to mate) 59...♗d6 60 ♕h7+ ♔b6.

59 ♔g2 ♔c7 60 ♔h1 ♗d6 61 ♔g1 ♔b6

Zugzwang! White is forced to upset the coordination of his queen and bishop, since it is not possible to repeat by 62 ♔h1? because of 62...♕h6+ 63 ♔g1 ♗c5+ 64 ♔g2 ♕h3 mate. Also 62 ♗g2? does not work because of 62...♗c5+ 63 ♔h1 ♕h6+.

62 ♕g2 ♗c5+ 63 ♔h1 ♕h6+

Clearer is 63...♗f2! 64 ♗d3 ♕h6+ 65 ♕h2 ♕d2.

64 ♕h2 ♕e3!

Playing along the dark squares, D.Bronstein takes away from the opponent also the light ones. There remains only the final creation of the zugzwang theme by ...g4-g3 and the white queen cannot defend at the same time both the g1 and h6 squares.

65 b4 ♗d4 White resigned.

After 66 c5+ ♔a7 67 ♕g2 g3 he has the choice between the mates: 68 ♕c2 ♕g1 mate or 68 ♗e2 ♕h6+ 69 ♕h3 ♕xh3 mate.

Adams - Anand
Dortmund 1998

Despite the extra pawn, the position appears drawn. But White finds a way to breathe life into his distant passed pawn.

28 c5! dxc5 29 a5 ♗b2 30 a6 ♗d4 31 ♗f1 c4!

In accordance with the proverb: "one good turn deserves another", Black returns the pawn, striving for a coordination of his pieces. Otherwise, on passive play by Black, White lines up the "battery" ♕a2-♗c4 along the a2-g8 diagonal and, after ♔g1-g2, sets about the attack f2-f4-f5.

32 ♕xc4 ♕b2 33 ♕e2 ♕c3

Black refrains from the exchange of queens, apparently having doubts about the possibilities of saving himself in the minor piece ending with a distant passed pawn.

34 ♔g2 ♗b6 35 ♕a2 ♕d4 36 ♕c2 e6 37 ♗b5 h6 38 ♕e2 ♕c5?!

He should not give up the long a1-h8 diagonal "free of charge".

After 38...h5 Black can fully hold the position.

39 ♕b2 g5?!

On 39...e5 Black did not like 40 h4, but the idea of fixing the fianchetto formation is likewise poor, since Black creates weak pawns for himself. More logical is 39...h5.

40 ♗d3 g4?! 41 ♕f6 h5 42 ♕f4 ♔f8 43 e5 ♕d5+ 44 ♗e4 ♕d4?

Necessary was 44...♕c4.

45 ♕h6+ ♔e7 46 ♕f6+ ♔f8 47 ♗c6 ♔g8

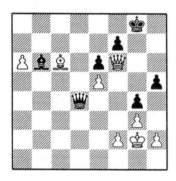

48 h4!

With the threat of 49 ♗e8; if played at once this move is no good because of ♕e4+.

48...gxh3+?

This leads to the loss of the h5 pawn. Correct was 48...♕c5 and though, after 49 ♗e8 ♕c7 50 ♔h2 ♗a7 or 49 ♗e4 ♗a7!, White has the preferable position, Black has counterplay against the f2 and e5 pawns.

49 ♔xh3 ♕a1

Upon the exchange of queens, 49...♕xf2 50 ♕xf2 (50 ♕g5+ ♔f8 51 ♕h6+ ♔e7) 50...♗xf2 51 ♔h4 ♔g7 52 ♔xh5 f6 53 exf6+ ♔xf6 54 g4, he cannot cope with the pawn "storm". Nevertheless he should keep the queen close at hand— 49...♕g4+.

50 ♔g2 ♕c1 51 ♗f3!

With the acquisition of a second pawn, the struggle is predetermined.

51...h4 52 gxh4 ♕c5 53 ♗h5 ♕c6+ 54 ♕f3 ♕c7 55 ♕b7 ♕xb7+ 56 axb7 ♗c7 57 f4 Black resigned.

We certainly also come across positions where an initiative, based on opposite-coloured bishops, proves insufficient and a player has to agree to a bishop ending. From examples on this theme in the treasure-house of endings comes the following.

Kotov - Botvinnik
Moscow 1955

In this position, White does not manage to retain material parity: he is constrained by the defence of the g2 pawn and therefore the a2 pawn is doomed. However, Black also has to reckon with the threat of 44 ♗xf6, since, after the direct 43...♔f7, White "comes alive" with 44 f5! ♗xf5 45 ♕f3! ♗e4 46 ♕xh5+ ♔e7 47 ♕g4 g5 48 h4, with sufficient counterplay. Therefore M.Botvinnik makes the decision to transfer to an ending with opposite-coloured bishops, despite its drawing tendencies.

43...♕xa2 44 ♗xf6 ♕xg2+ 45 ♕xg2 ♗xg2 46 ♗d4

On 46 ♗e7 would have followed 46...b3.

46...♗e4 47 ♔g3 ♔f7 48 h4 g6 49 ♔f2 ♔e6 50 ♔e2 ♔f5 51 ♔d2 ♔g4 52 ♗f6 ♔g3 53 ♗e7 ♔h3!

As M.Botvinnik himself acknowledged, upon accurate defence Black's extra pawn is still not enough for victory. But White continues the struggle with maximum energy, gradually creating new problems for the opponent. For example, the win of one of the passed pawns, 54 ♗xb4?, leads to the appearance of another, even more dangerous, one—54...♔xh4.

54 ♗f6 ♔g4 55 ♗e7 ♗f5!

The bishop transfers to e6, in order to support indirectly the b-pawn.

56 ♗f6 ♔f3! 57 ♗e7 b3 58 ♔c3 ♗e6!

Indirectly defending the b4 pawn. The win of a second pawn, 58...♔xe3 59 ♔xb3 ♔xf4 60 ♔c3 ♔e3 61 ♗g5+ ♔e4 62 ♔d2, proves insufficient for victory, since the bishop and king easily blockade the pawn formation, close by.

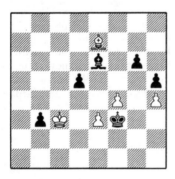

59 ♗c5?

Why do you think that White made this losing move? He was under the illusion that the bishop, not burdened with worries about the h4 pawn, might allow itself a certain freedom of movement. Moving away from the e7 square, the bishop allows a study-like solution to the

ending, though to predict Black's reply is practically impossible. To a draw leads 59 ♔d2! b2 60 ♔c2 ♔xe3 61 ♔xb2 ♔xf4 62 ♔c3.

59...g5!! 60 fxg5

As M.Botvinnik put it: Capturing with the h-pawn loses "prosaically": 60 hxg5 h4 61 f5 (61 ♗d6 ♗f5 62 g6 ♗xg6 63 f5 ♗xf5 64 ♔xb3 ♔g2) 61...♗xf5 62 ♔xb3 h3 63 ♗d6 ♔xe3; but after the decision taken by Kotov the ending becomes "poetic"!

60...d4+!! 61 exd4

White also loses after 61 ♗xd4 ♔g3 62 g6 ♔xh4 63 ♔d2 ♔h3! 64 ♗f6 h4 65 ♔e2 ♔g2.

61...♔g3!

It was still possible to "run into" a draw—61...♔g4? 62 d5 ♗xd5 63 ♗f2.

62 ♗a3 ♔xh4 63 ♔d3 ♔xg5 64 ♔e4 h4 65 ♔f3

On 65 d5 would equally follow 65...♗xd5+.

65...♗d5+ White resigned.

It is well-known that a bishop and rook, geometric in their action, complement one another excellently, and therefore it is always important to put right the coordination of their activity.

Bogoljubow - Kostić
Göteborg 1920

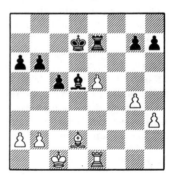

Black has a small advantage on account of his better pawn structure. He has two pawn islands against White's three which, moreover, require continual defence. Here, and on the following move, White does not go for the pawn sacrifice e5-e6, in order to activate his bishop, and wrongly. Black quickly puts right the coordination of his pieces and increases his advantage.

31 a3 ♖f7 32 h4

White endeavours to exchange the weak pawns, whereas an advance on the other flank, 32 b4 ♖f3 33 bxc5 bxc5 34 ♖e3 ♖f1+ 35 ♔c2 ♔e6, leads only to an increased number of pawn weaknesses.

32...♔e6 33 h5 ♖f2

Also worth considering is 33...♗f3!?.

34 h6 gxh6 35 ♗xh6 ♖g2!

It is important to provoke the advance of the g-pawn in order to restrict the mobility of the dark-squared bishop.

36 g5 ♗b3!

Closing the king in a cage. On 37 ♖e3 follows 37...♖c2+ 38 ♔b1 c4 with the threat of 39 ♖d2, and White's rook is forced to go back.

37 ♖h1 ♗c2

Also good is 37...♔xe5.

38 ♗g7 ♗d3!

A fine manoeuvre, underlining the difference in the load carried by the bishops. The white bishop in fact has no influence on events while Black's covers the d-file (39 ♖d1 c4) and takes part in an attack on the b-pawn.

39 ♖h3 c4 40 b3 b5 41 bxc4 bxc4 42 ♗h8

On 42 ♗f6 would follow 42...♖c2+ 43 ♔d1 ♖a2.

The principal result of the manoeuvre of the black bishop is the formation of a passed pawn. It is now possible to start generating threats.

42...♖xg5 43 ♔d2 ♔d5 44 ♔c3 a5 45 ♖h2

Repulsing the threat of 45...♖g2. But now all Black's pieces pounce on the king.

45...♖g3 46 ♖d2 ♔c5 47 e6 ♗f5+ 48 ♔b2 ♖b3+ 49 ♔a2 ♗xe6 50 ♗d4+ ♔c6 51 ♔a1 ♖xa3+ 52 ♔b2 ♖b3+ 53 ♔a1 c3 White resigned.

Karpov - Portisch
Milan 1975

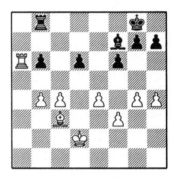

White's advantage is determined not so much by the extra pawn as the presence on the board of opposite-coloured bishops. The fact of the matter is that Black's pawns are placed mainly on dark squares, and so can become a convenient target for the opponent. A.Karpov realises the advantage of his position with filigree technique.

42 ♔d3 h5 43 b5!

Fixing the weak pawn.

43...hxg4 44 fxg4 ♖c8 45 ♖a4!

No way will the black pawns "run away".

45...♗e6 46 g5 f5

An attempt to remove the blockade—the only chance of saving himself. After 46...fxg5 47 hxg5 ♔f7 48 ♗d4, the b6 pawn is lost.

47 exf5 ♗xf5+ 48 ♔d4 ♔f7 49 ♗b4 ♔e6 50 ♖a6 ♖b8 51 h5 ♗g4 52 h6 gxh6 53 gxh6 ♗f5 54 ♗d2!

The h6 pawn diverts the black bishop, his rook is forced to defend the b6 pawn, and the king—the d6 pawn. The black pieces have a thankless task in prospect.

54...♖g8 55 ♗f4!

Allowing no counterplay at all, which Black could have obtained after 55 ♖xb6 ♖g4+ 56 ♔c3 ♖g3+ 57 ♔b4 ♖g4.

55...♖b8 56 ♖a7 ♔f6 57 ♖g7 ♗e6 58 ♖c7

The d6 pawn is "poisoned"—58 ♗xd6? ♖d8.

58...♖h8 59 ♖c6 ♖g8

Also no help is 59...♖c8 60 ♖xc8 ♗xc8 61 ♗xd6 ♔g6 62 ♗c7 and White wins.

60 ♖xd6 ♔f5 61 ♖xb6 ♖g4 62 ♖e6! ♔xe6 63 ♔e4 ♖g8 64 b6 Black resigned.

Ribli - Grunfeld
Interzonal tournament,
Riga 1979

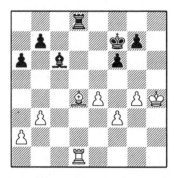

A classic position for the study of the theme of realising an extra pawn in the present type of ending. The winning plan consists of three stages: first, the advance of the f3 pawn to f5, then the carrying out of the advance e4-e5 or g4-g5, and,

after an exchange of pawns (otherwise it advances further), an attack on the g7 pawn.

39 ♔g3 a5 40 ♔f4 a4

In his turn, Black strives to create his own object of attack. He can anticipate the advance of the f-pawn by the cardinal 40...g5+, but in this case the f6 pawn becomes weak. A possible continuation: 41 ♔e3 a4 42 ♖h1 axb3 43 axb3 ♔g6 44 ♖c1 ♖a8 45 ♖c5 ♖a3 46 ♖f5 ♖xb3+ 47 ♔d2, winning the f6 and g5 pawns.

41 b4 ♗b5

On 41...a3 would have followed 42 ♔e3 ♗b5 43 ♖c1.

42 ♔e3 ♗c4 43 a3 b5 44 ♖h1!

Before setting about the intended f3-f4-f5, White improves the position of his rook.

44...♖c8

It seems he should decide on 44...g5!? broadening the defensive bridge-head and, though White has an obvious advantage, he will hardly manage to exploit the weakness of the f6 pawn without exchanging pawns, since he cannot do without e4-e5. Here are some sample variations.

a) 45. ♖h6 ♖d6 46 e5 ♖e6 and here 47 ♖xf6+ ♖xf6 48 exf6 leads to an endgame with opposite-coloured bishops, which is not winning.

b) 45 ♖h7+ ♔g6 46 ♖c7 (or 46 ♖b7 ♖d6 47 ♖c7 ♗b3 and on 48 ♗c5 there is 48...♖d1) 46...♖d6 47 ♖c5 ♔f7 48 ♖f5 ♖e6. If now, to carry out e4-e5, White attempts to leave the e-file, he encounters opposition from the rook: 49 ♔d2 ♖d6 50 ♔c3 ♖c6, and, upon the transfer of the king to c5, he must reckon with the possibility of attack on the f5-rook by the bishop: 49 ♗b2 ♔g6 50 ♔d4 ♖d6+ 51 ♔c5 ♖e6 52 ♗d4 ♗d3 with an "X-Ray" on the rook.

45 ♖h5 ♗f1 46 ♖d5

It was also possible to play 46 g5 ♔g6 47 ♖h1 ♗c4 48 gxf6 gxf6 with an attack against the f6 weakness —49 f4 ♖d8 50 f5+ ♔g7 51 ♖g1+ ♔f7 52 ♖g6.

46...♖c7 47 ♖d8 ♔e6

Also upon the active 47...♖c2 48 ♖d7+ ♔g6 49 f4 ♖a2 50 f5+ ♔h6 51 e5 ♖xa3+ 52 ♔f2 (52 ♔f4? leads to a draw by 52...g5+! 53 fxg6 fxe5+ 54 ♗xe5 ♔xg6) 52...♗h3 53 ♗e3+, White should win.

48 f4 ♗c4

After 48...♖d7 49 f5+ ♔e7 50 ♖h8 ♔f7 51 ♗c5!, Black is forced into the weakening 51...g5, which after 52 ♗d4 ♔g7 53 ♖h5 leads to material losses.

49 ♗c5 ♔f7 50 ♖f8+ ♔e6 51 f5+ ♔d7 52 g5! ♖c6

On 52...fxg5, the advance 53 e5 is decisive.

53 g6 ♖c7 54 ♖f7+ ♔c6 55 ♖xc7+ ♔xc7 56 ♗f8 Black resigned.

Seirawan - Yusupov
Indonesia 1983

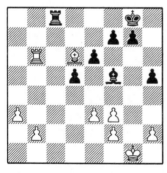

While White's passed pawns are presently situated on the distant boundary, Black can hurry to put right the coordination of his pieces.

And it is not surprising that A.Yusupov strives for active play.

He organises a siege of the enemy king, refusing to transfer from a position of strength to an ending with opposite-coloured bishops—22...♗h3 23 ♖b8 ♖xb8 24 ♗xb8 ♔f8— the prospects in which, with White having a distant passed pawn, look highly obscure.

22...♖c1+ 23 ♔g2 h4 24 h3

White repels the threat of a mating attack by 24...h3+ 25 ♔g3 g5. But now the king is restricted by the pawn corset, and Black, by organising the cooperation of his rook and bishop, prevents White from advancing the queenside pawns.

24...♗d3 25 ♖b8+ ♔h7 26 ♗e7

Striving to free himself from the yoke of the h4 pawn, White prevents the drawing mechanism, 26...♗f1+ 27 ♔h2 ♗e2 28 ♔g2 ♗f1.

26...f6 27 ♖b4

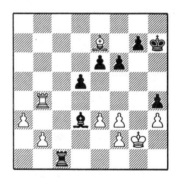

27...♗f1+?!

An at first sight insignificant transposition of the moves ...♗f1 and ...g5 which might have led to lamentable consequences. Correct is 27...g5! 28 f4 ♔g6 29 fxg5 fxg5 30 ♖g4 ♗e4+ 31 f3 ♖c2+ 32 ♔g1 ♖c1+ 33 ♔f2 ♖c2+ and Black forces a draw.

28 ♔h2 g5 29 ♗xf6

With an automatic capture of the pawn, White misses a chance which has arisen to free his king by 29 f4!. Now, after the possible continuation 29...♔g6 30 fxg5 fxg5 31 ♖g4 ♖c2 32 b4 ♖xf2+ 33 ♔g1, White obtains the advantage. But even upon the game continuation all is still not lost.

29...♔g6 30 ♗d8 ♖c8

On 30...♖c2 strong is 31 f4! (after 31 ♖g4 ♖xf2+ 32 ♔g1 ♖xf3 33 ♖xg5+ ♔f7, Black successfully defends himself) 31...♖xf2+ 32 ♔g1 ♖f3 33 fxg5 ♗xh3 34 ♖xh4 ♖xe3 35 ♖h6+ with advantage to White.

31 ♗b6 e5 32 ♗a5 ♗e2 33 ♖b6+ ♔f5 34 ♔g2 ♖c1

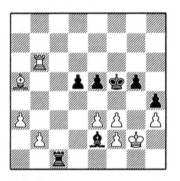

35 ♗d2?!

White falls into a drawing mechanism. Winning chances are retained by 35 ♖b8!, though the king gets out of the cage after 35...e4 36 fxe4+ dxe4 37 ♖f8+ ♔e6 38 a4 at the cost of an exchange sacrifice:

a) 38...♗f1+ 39 ♔h2 ♗e2 40 ♗d8 ♗f3 41 ♖xf3 exf3 42 ♗xg5.

b) 38...♗f3+ 39 ♖xf3 exf3+ 40 ♔xf3 ♖a1 41 b3 ♖a3 42 ♗d8.

35...♖d1 36 ♗c3

With the move 36 ♖d6!?, White can set a cunning trap: 36...♖xd2? 37 e4+! ♔f4 38 ♖f6 mate, but Black would be forced into a draw— 36...♗f1+.

36...♗f1+ 37 ♔h2 ♗e2 38 ♔g2 ♗f1+ 39 ♔h2 Draw.

Shipov - Goldin
St Petersburg 1998

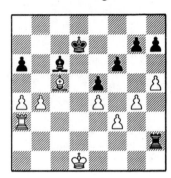

For the pawn, Black has sufficient compensation in the form of piece activity. However, White has the possibility of creating a distant passed pawn.

41 b5

The b-pawn is offered for sacrifice in order to provide transit for the a-pawn: its run to a7 is guaranteed. Another way, linked to 41 ♖d3+ ♔c8! 42 ♗f8 ♗xa4+ 43 ♔c1 g6 44 hxg6 hxg6 45 ♗g7, is less logical.

41...axb5 42 a5 ♖h1+

Black strives to put right the coordination of his pieces, preventing the possibility of invasion to his rear by the white rook via d3, which might occur on the hasty 42...g6? 43 hxg6 hxg6 44 ♖d3+.

43 ♔d2 ♖h2+ 44 ♔c3

After 44 ♔d3?! b4! 45 ♗xb4 ♗b5+ 46 ♔c3 (46 ♔e3?? ♖e2 mate) 46...♖f2, the coordination of forces is put right.

44...♖h1

Black intends 44...♖c1+.

45 ♗f8 g6 46 hxg6

Also worth considering is 46 h6!?, fixing the h7 pawn.

46...hxg6 47 a6 ♖c1+?!

Black carries out a manoeuvre, which has the ultimate object of exchanging rooks, but this brings him to a lost ending. He should hold up the white king by 47...♔e8! 48 ♗b4 (48 ♗d6 ♔d7) 48...♖f1 49 ♔c2 ♖f2+, retaining chances of a draw.

48 ♔b4 ♖c4+?

A direct realisation of the exchange of rooks leads to a lost ending. He should first drive away the bishop—48...♔e8!—and, depending on where it retreats, Black exchanges rooks in a more favourable situation:

a) 49 ♗h6 ♖c4+ 50 ♔a5 ♖a4+ 51 ♖xa4 bxa4 52 ♗c1 ♔b6.

b) 49 ♗d6 ♔d7 50 ♖d3 ♖c4+ 51 ♔a5 ♖d4.

49 ♔a5 ♖a4+ 50 ♔b6

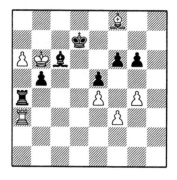

This is the whole point. The king occupies an active position and, with the creation of a second passed pawn, Black will not save himself.

50...♖xa3 51 ♗xa3 f5

There is nothing else, since the bishop gets to the f6 pawn anyway.

52 gxf5 gxf5 53 exf5 ♗xf3 54 ♗b2!

Black overlooked this in his calculations. Everything else leads to an elementary draw: 54 ♔xb5 ♔c7 55 ♗b2 ♔b8 56 ♗xe5+ ♔a8 or 54 a7 ♗a8 55 ♔xb5 e4.

54...b4

A very beautiful theme of overloading arises after 54...♔d6 55 f6 ♗d5 56 ♗xe5+!! ♔xe5 57 ♔c5!!, after which the bishop cannot cope and the game ends with queening: 57...b4 58 a7 b3 59 f7 b2 60 f8=♕ b1=♕ 61 ♕d6+ ♔f5 62 ♕xd5+ (S.Shipov).

55 ♗xe5 b3 56 a7 ♔c8 57 ♗d4 ♔d7 58 ♗g7 ♔d6 59 ♗c3 ♔d7 60 ♔c5 ♔c7 61 f6

Now, with the black king riveted to its pawns, its white counterpart completes its approach to the a7 pawn after first calling on the g5 square.

61...♔d7 62 ♔c4 Black resigned.

6 Rook versus Two Minor Pieces

This correlation of forces is quite often met in practice, since usually it is the consequence of an exchanging operation, where, with the presence even of mathematical material equality, the attacking side strives to determine an advantage.

What are the guiding principles in the struggle of rook against two minor pieces? This theme is hardly elucidated in capital essays on the endgame. According to the generally accepted opinion, in static situations with two minor pieces one can count on an advantage, however the rook also has its own chances, particularly when passed pawns are present.

But before going over to a study of positions of such a type, we turn our attention to the possibilities of the defensive side. As regards the resources of the defender—he should endeavour to exchange pawns, intending a transfer to a theoreticaly drawn ending, where the limited material is insufficient to play for a win. This is achieved with the help of a sacrifice: from the side possessing the rook—the exchange, from the side possessing the minor pieces—a sacrifice of one of them.

For example, in the last case this theme is beautifully illustrated by the tail-piece of the following study.

Zakhodyakhin, 1946

Draw

It is obvious that White cannot avoid the loss of a piece, but how can he capture the pawn in return for it?

1 &c3

White entices the king to the knight's sphere of activity in order to attack the pawn in a favourable situation.

1...&b3 2 &a1 &e1+ 3 &g2 &xa1 4 &c6

Now the pawn can be defended by the rook only from the e-file (alternatively 4...e6 5 &d4+ and 6 &xe6), where the rook is hampered in its activity.

4...&e1 5 &f2 &e4 6 &f3 &e1 7 &f2 Draw.

The rook cannot avoid being pursued by the king without loss of a pawn.

Let us look at a practical example of this same theme, but from the point of view of the side possessing the rook.

Gufeld - Mikhalchishin
Tbilisi 1979

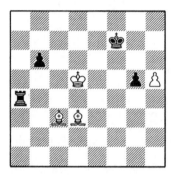

The h-pawn, with support of the bishop, intends to slip through to queen. Therefore the *leitmotiv* of Black's defence is to sacrifice the rook for the dark-squared bishop with a transfer of the king to the h8 square, which is not under the power of the light-squared bishop.

1... ♖a5+! 2 ♔d6

After 2 ♗xa5 bxa5, followed by 3...♔g7, arises a theoretically drawn position.

2... ♖a3 3 ♗g6+

Nor is the assessment of the position significantly changed by 3 ♗c4+ ♔f8.

3...♔g8 4 ♗d4 g4

This pawn eases Black's defence, since White is forced to keep an eye on it.

5 ♔e6

The b6 pawn is also inviolable, since after 5 ♗xb6 White achieves his objective with the help of a pin: 5...♖a6 6 ♔c5 ♖xb6 7 ♔xb6 g3 etc.

5...♖a4!

Not a second's peace for the bishop! Black loses spectacularly after 5...♖f3—6 h6 ♖h3 7 ♗g7 g3 8 ♔f6 g2 9 h7+! ♖xh7 10 ♗f7 mate. This rare mating finish deserves a diagram.

But to return to the game.
6 ♗e5 ♖a5! 7 ♗d4 ♖a4 8 ♗f6 ♖a2

There was also another round-about manoeuvre: 8...♖f4 9 ♗f5 (or 9 h6 ♖xf6+) 9...♖c4 10 ♗e5 ♖c6+.

9 h6 ♖e2+ 10 ♔d6 ♖h2 11 h7+ Draw.

Now we transfer to a more complicated situation. To start, we look at the possibilities of the rook, when it supports its own passed pawn. The specifics of play in such a cooperation of forces are characterised by the lengthening of communications. The outcome of the struggle in great part depends on deployment—the number of pawns and which is more compact, their placement, the communication of the rooks and their coordination, to best serve their capabilities. The presence of a distant passed pawn increases the chances of a long-range rook in the struggle against the less mobile minor pieces and even allows thoughts of playing for a win. You see, whereas minor pieces are usually attached to the blockade of a passed pawn, the rook can be utilised also on the other flank to create new objects of attack.

To counter the rook, it is important for the side having the minor pieces to put right the coordination between them, whilst controlling the passed pawn.

The defensive possibilities and technique to realise a weakening of a position with the presence of a distant passed pawn are well demonstrated by the following classical example.

Razuvaev - Kirov
Sofia 1981

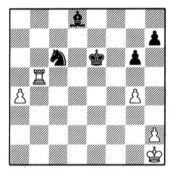

With such a specific arrangement of pawns on the kingside, even upon a transfer to an ending with an extra exchange for White, the bishop can resist the rook. Therefore to achieve a draw it is enough for Black to sacrifice his knight for the a-pawn. For the present, his pieces cooperate well: he prevents the advance of the passed pawn, and, if the opportunity arises, he is ready to transfer to the kingside. It is important only not to create new objects of attack for White.

However, surprisingly, there followed...

39...h6?

Again and again we draw attention to the care required with this

sort of move. Its drawbacks are shown not only in the middlegame but also in the ending.

Black needlessly weakens his kingside, which creates an object of attack for White—the h6 pawn. It is possible to get at it through the invasion square on f5, which is created after the g6 pawn is undermined by h2-h4-h5.

After 39...♔d6 40 h3, Black defends successfully. He has even got two possible plans of defence.

a) An active plan: 40...♘a5 (the knight transfers to c5 to attack the a-pawn) 41 ♔g2 ♔c6 42 ♖e5 ♘b7 43 ♖e8 ♔c5 44 ♖h8 ♔b4 45 ♖xh7 ♘c5 46 h4 ♔xa4 47 h5 gxh5 48 gxh5 ♗g5 and Black, by giving up the bishop for the a-pawn, obtains a theoretically drawn ending—rook against knight.

b) A passive plan: 40...♔e6 (Black sticks to waiting tactics) 41 ♔g2 ♔d6 42 ♔g3 ♔e6 43 h4 ♔d6 44 h5 (up to this advance White was forced to control the fifth rank with the rook, in order to prevent the move ...h7-h5, exchanging a pair of pawns) 44...♔e6 45 ♖b7 ♗e7 46 ♔f4 ♔d6 47 ♔e4 ♔e6. Now the king cannot break through to the c4 square without loss: 48 ♔d3 ♘e5+ 49 ♔c3 ♘xg4 50 ♔c4 (or 50 a5 ♘e5 51 a6 ♘c6) 50...♘e5 51 ♔b5 ♗d8, and, upon the attempt to go to c4 via the b3 square, he has to reckon with the threat ♘a5+. The attempt to penetrate with the rook to the eighth rank by 48 ♖c7 ♔d6 49 ♖c8? ♗d8 ends in its capture, nor is there anything in 48 ♖b5 ♗d8.

But we return to the game.

40 ♔g2 ♔f6?.

As before, Black does not sense the danger and upsets the coordination between his pieces, since now the position of the bishop is hampered by the blockading function of the knight. Better was 40...♔d6 41 ♖b7 ♗c7 with the idea of ...♘c6-a5.

41 ♖c5 ♘a5 42 ♔f3 ♔e6 43 ♔e4 ♗b6 44 ♖c8 ♔f6 45 h4! ♔e6

46 h5!

It is important to fix the weak pawn. Premature is 46 ♖h8 ♘b7 47 ♖xh6 ♘c5+ 48 ♔f3 ♔f7 49 h5 gxh5 50 ♖xh6 hxg4+ 51 ♔xg4 ♘xa4 with a drawn ending. Now, however, after 46...gxh5, 47 ♖h8 is unpleasant.

46...♔f7 47 ♔d5 gxh5 48 gxh5 ♔f6 49 ♖b8 ♗e3 50 ♔e4! ♗d2 51 ♖b2 ♗e1 52 ♖e2 ♗b4 53 ♖g2 ♔f7

The weakness of the h6 pawn lets itself be known. By combining an attack on it with an attack on the knight, White upsets the coordination of the opponent's pieces. On 53...♗f8 he should play 54 ♖g6+ ♔f7 55 ♖a6 and the a-pawn gets moving.

54 ♖g6 ♗d2 55 ♖d6! ♗g5 56 ♖d5!

An ideal square for the rook from where it prevents the coordination of pieces.

56...♘c6 57 a5 ♔e6 58 a6 ♗e3

Black tries to blockade the a-pawn on the last frontier but the mechanism of breaking the coordination of pieces again swings into action.

59 ♖b5 ♗g1 60 ♖b1 ♗f2 61 ♖b2 ♗c5 62 ♖b7 ♘a7 63 ♖h7

White wins the h6 pawn and the game.

63...♔f6 64 ♔f4 ♗d6+ 65 ♔g4 ♗c5 66 ♖xh6+ ♔e5 67 ♖g6 Black resigned.

A very fine ending!

And here is an example from the practice of champions, where, apart from small nuances, attack and defence are at a height.

Karpov - Kasparov
World Championship,
Moscow 1985

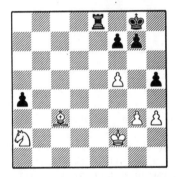

Also in this position Black has a distant passed pawn, the advance of which controls the white pieces. However, they will not allow the rook to get behind them via the queenside, as they block the lines of invasion (♗b4 or ♗c3), whereas the central files are covered by the king.

48...♖b8 49 ♗b4 ♖d8 50 ♔e2 a3?!

While no extra objects of attack have been created on the kingside, the advance of the pawn to a vulnerable square is premature. It was necessary to increase the communication of the rook's sphere of activity with an exchange of the f-pawn by 51...g6, which forces the white king to situate itself further from his pieces.

51 ♗c3 f6

Also here, stronger is 51...g6. For study of the further play we make use of the comments of G.Kasparov in his book *Two Matches*.

52 ♗b4

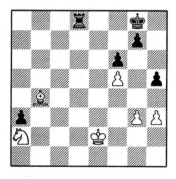

52...♔f7?!

Here the king does nothing: you see, there are no prospects of him coming out to the centre. Much more accurate was 52...♔h7. In this case, the method of defence, applied by Karpov in the game, places White under threat of defeat. For example, 53 ♗c3 ♖b8 54 ♗b4? ♖b5! 55 g4 ♖b8, and a zugzwang position is reached and White is forced to allow the rook into his camp: 56 ♔d3 ♖d8+ 57 ♔c2 hxg4 58 hxg4 ♖d4 59 ♗a3 ♖a4 60 ♔b3 ♖xg4 61 ♗c1 ♖g3+ 62 ♘c3 ♖f3 63 ♔c2 ♖xf5 64 ♔d3. A simple assessment of such an ending is not possible, but in practice Black would have excellent chances. However, after 54 ♘b4!, Black holds on: 54...♖b5 55 g4 ♖b8 56 ♔d3! ♖a8 57 ♘a2 ♖a4 58 ♗b4 ♔h6 59 ♗d2+, and he will not succeed in taking the fortress.

53 ♘c3 ♖b8 54 ♘a2 ♖b5 55 g4 ♖b8 56 ♔d3 ♖d8+ 57 ♔c4 ♖d1 58 ♗xa3 ♖a1 59 ♔b3 ♖h1 60 gxh5 ♖xh3+ 61 ♘c3

This is where the position of the black king tells (in comparison with the previous note)—after 61...♖xh5 62 ♘e4, the f5 pawn is untouchable.

61...♖f3 62 ♗c1! ♖xf5 63 h6

For a draw, it remains to sacrifice a piece for two pawns.

63...g6

On 63...g5 White achieves his aim by 64 ♘e4 ♔g6 65 h7 ♖f3+ (65...♔h7 66 ♘xf6+) 66 ♔c4 ♖h3 67 ♘xf6!.

64 ♘e4 ♖h5 65 ♗b2 Draw.

The f6 pawn is lost, since on 65...f5 follows 66 h7.

Beliavsky - Dolmatov
Minsk 1979

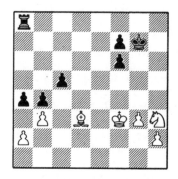

It is hard to believe in this position, where the material advantage is on White's side, that Black has sufficient basis to play for a win. It all comes down to the fact that White's pieces are separated and badly coordinated and Black can count on the creation of a distant passed a-pawn. But how to achieve this? You see it remains for White only to bring the knight to the centre of events, in order to put right the coordination of his pieces. Sergei Dolmatov finds a study-like solution.

38...c4!! 39 ♗xc4

After 39 bxc4 ♖b8 Black organises a dangerous passed b-pawn: 40 ♘f2 b3 41 a3 (losing quickly is 41 axb3 a3 42 ♗b1 ♖xb3+) 41...b2 42 ♗b1 ♖b3+ 43 ♔e2 ♖c3 44 ♘e4 ♖xc4 45 ♘d2 ♖c1 etc.

39...♖c8!

Threatening an exchange sacrifice.

40 ♗d3 a3!

An important moment. Black fixes a potential object of attack—the a2 pawn.

41 ♔e3

The king hurries to help the bishop. An attempt to include the knight in the defence loses quickly:

a) 41 ♘f2 ♖c1 42 h4 ♖a1 43 ♗c4 ♖xa2 44 ♘d3 ♖f2+! 45 ♔xf2 a2.

b) 41 ♘f4 ♖c3 42 ♔e2 ♖xb3 43 ♗c4 ♖b2+ 44 ♔d3 b3.

41...♖c1

Stronger than 41...♖c3 42 ♘f2!.

42 ♘f4 ♖a1 43 ♘d5 ♖xa2 44 ♘xb4 ♖xh2

The aim of the break on the 39th move is achieved: Black has a distant passed pawn.

45 ♗e2 ♖h3 46 ♔f2

Not allowing the rook to collaborate in the advance of the a-pawn, which moves off after 46 ♔f3 ♖h1 47 ♗c4 ♖a1 48 ♘c2 ♖a2 49 ♘b4 ♖b2 etc.

46...f5!

After 46...♖h1 White hurries to limit the rook's sphere of activity: 47 ♗f1 ♖h2+ 48 ♗g2 ♖h8 49 ♘a2 ♖c8 50 ♗e4. Now, however, in connection with the threat of the break ...f5-f4, the manoeuvre 47 ♗f1 ♖h2+ 48 ♗g2 is not effective because of 48...♖h8 and the rook breaks through the queenside.

47 ♘a2 f4 48 gxf4 ♖xb3 49 ♗c4 ♖h3!

50 ♗f1

Up to now, attack and defence have been worthy of both rivals. And it is only here that A.Beliavsky misses the opportunity to put right the coordination of his pieces and control the passed pawn. This is achieved by the manoeuvre 50 ♔e2! ♔f6 51 ♘b4 and, if now Black tries to remove the f7 pawn from attack by 51...♔e7 52 ♔d2 f6, then follows 53 ♘d5+, while after 52...f5 53 ♗d3 White again attacks the pawn and resists the rook: 53...♖h2+ 54 ♔c3 ♔f6 55 ♗c2.

50...♖h2+ 51 ♗g2 ♔f6 52 ♔g3 ♖h5!

The shortest path to the key b2 and c2 squares, at the same time preventing the coordination of the minor pieces.

53 ♗f1 ♖c5! 54 ♗d3 ♖d5 55 ♗a6 ♖d2 56 ♗c4 ♖d4 White resigned.

If, with rooks on the board, there is no passed pawn, then roles are reversed. All that remains for the rook is to counter the opponent's attempt to create his own passed pawn. Nevertheless the defensive resources of the rook are sufficiently great. That it is not easy to find the best way in positions with a non-typical alignment of forces is characterised by the following example.

Short - Kasparov
Belgrade 1989

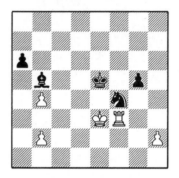

In this position, Black's chances can only be linked to the organisation of a passed g-pawn. Therefore he strives to win the h2 pawn. However, for this it is necessary to break through the demarcation line—the third rank, which the rook is prepared to leave only "by exchanging" it for a counterattack from the rear. It is not easy to do this. Let us look at the possibilities of the sides based on an analysis by G.Kasparov.

53 ♖g3 ♘d5+ 54 ♔f2 ♔f5 55 ♖f3+ ♔g4 56 ♖g3+ ♔h4 57 ♔f3

White strives to activate his king, since upon the passive 57 ♖b3 ♘f4, in connection with the threat of ♘d3, he will not hold out. Now, however, after 57...♘xb4 58 ♔e4 ♗d7 59 ♔e5 the centralised king prevents Black putting right the coordination of his forces and, if the opportunity arises, White will manage to exchange pawns on the kingside.

57...♘f6?!

Stronger is 57...♗d7!, keeping under attack the b4 pawn, while on 58 ♔e4 the knight hurries to attack the h2 pawn: 58...♘f6+! 59 ♔e5

♘g4+ 60 ♔d6 ♗b5 61 ♖g2 ♘e3 and the black king draws close to the h2 pawn.

58 ♔g2 ♘h5 59 ♖e3 ♘f4+ 60 ♔g1 ♔g4

Now, with the white king driven back, Black puts right the coordination of his king and pieces.

61 ♖g3+ ♔f5 62 ♖f3 g4

Not letting out the king, since after 64...♔e4 65 ♔f2 ♘d3+ 66 ♔g3 ♘xb4 67 ♖f8, White again activates his forces.

63 ♖e3 ♘d5!

Again insufficient is 63...♘d3 because of the activating of the rook, 64 ♖e7! ♘xb2 65 ♖f7+! ♔g6 66 ♖f8 ♘d3 67 ♔g2 ♘xb4 68 ♖f4.

64 ♖b3 ♔f4 65 ♔f2 ♘f6 66 ♖a3 ♘e4+

Now follows an encirclement of the king.

67 ♔g2 ♗e2

The manoeuvre, 67...♘d2 68 ♖c3 ♘c4 69 ♖c1! ♘xb2 70 ♖c8, allows the rook to break out to freedom.

68 ♖b3 ♗f1+ 69 ♔g1 ♗c4 70 ♖a3 ♘g5 71 ♖c3 ♗d5 72 ♖a3 ♗e4?!

The a6 pawn is indirectly defended (73 ♖xa6?? ♘h3+ 74 ♔f1 ♗d3+), but this move loses time, allowing the rook again to break free. Stronger was 72...♘f3+ 73 ♔g2 ♘e5+ 74 ♔f2 ♗c4.

73 ♔f2! ♗b7

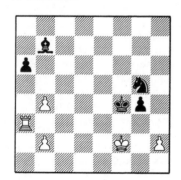

74 ♖d3?!

White misses the chance to activate the rook by 74 ♖a5!, threatening, with tempo, to exchange the b-pawn: 74...♘e4+ 75 ♔g1 ♘d6 76 ♖c5, holding the balance.

74...♘h3+ 75 ♔e1?.

After moving away the king from the h2 pawn the game already cannot be saved, since now Black cuts off the king from this pawn. Necessary was 75 ♔f1 ♗c6 76 ♖c3.

75...♗c6! 76 ♖d4+ ♔f3 77 ♖d3+ ♔e4 78 ♖g3 ♔f4 79 ♖a3?

More stubborn was 79 ♖c3 ♗b5 80 ♖c8, although after 80...♔f3 81 ♖f8+ ♔g2 82 ♖g8 ♘f2! White likewise loses the h2 pawn.

79...♗b5 80 ♖c3 ♘g5! 81 ♖c8 ♔e3! 82 ♖h8 ♘f3+ 83 ♔d1 ♗e2+ 84 ♔c2 ♘xh2! 85 ♖xh2 g3 and **Black won.**

The presence of an extra pair of rooks also gives extra chances to the side having the minor pieces, since playing for the realisation of a material advantage might be accompanied by an attack on the king. In this case the defending side must strive for maximum activity of the rooks. The attempt at passive defence is practically doomed. In any case the struggle usually assumes a protracted character.

Stetsko - Gipslis
Moscow 1975

In this position, if White succeeds in exchanging a pair of rooks, then the chances will turn out rather on his side, as he has a distant passed pawn. However, with rooks on, the assessment swings in Black's favour, since the b-pawn becomes an object of attack.

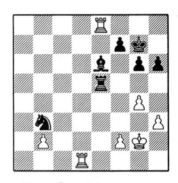

32 ♖dd8 ♘c1 33 f4

It is worth exploiting the chance to activate the b-pawn: 33 b4, intending on 33...♖b5 to play 34 ♖b8.

33... ♖b5 34 ♖b8 ♖c5! 35 ♔f3

Also here it was still not too late for 35 b4!? ♖c2+ 36 ♔f3! (dangerous is 36 ♔g3 ♖c3+ 37 ♔h4? because of 37...♘d3 with the threats of 38...♘xf4 and 38...♘f2) 36...♖c3+ 37 ♔e4! ♖xh3 38 g5 and now, on 38...♗f5+, possible is 39 ♔d5 ♖d3+ 40 ♔c5 ♘b3+ 41 ♔b6.

35...♔f6 36 ♖h8?!

He should not reduce the activity of the rook for the sake of a dubious chase after a pawn. Stronger was 36 ♖b6! ♖c4 (on 36...♖c2?! follows the same reply) 37 h4 ♘d3 38 g5+ hxg5 39 hxg5+ ♔f5 40 ♖b5+ (weaker is 40 ♖bxe6?! ♖xf4+ 41 ♔e3 fxe6 42 ♔xd3 42...e5 with advantage to Black) 40...♖c5 41 ♖xc5+ ♘xc5 42 ♔e3 and, after the exchange of a pair of rooks, White is not worse.

36...h5! 37 gxh5?!

White is captivated by the false idea of winning the h-pawn. It was necessary to decide on 37 g5+ ♔f5 38 ♖hd8.

37... gxh5 38 ♖h6+ ♔g7 39 ♖bh8 ♘b3 40 ♖6h7+ ♔f6 41 ♖h6+ ♔e7 42 ♖xh5 ♘d4+ 43 ♔e4 ♘f5 44 ♔d3

Despite the approximate material equality and reduction to the minimum of the number of pawns, White's position is very difficult in view of the poor position of the rook. White decides to retain, if only, the b-pawn since 44 ♖g5 is quite unpromising: 44...♖c4+ 45 ♔f3 ♖b4 46 h4 ♖b3+ 47 ♔e2 ♖xb2+ 48 ♔d3 ♖b4 49 h5 ♖d4+ 50 ♔e2 ♖xf4 51 h6 ♖h4 etc.

44...♖b5 45 ♔c2 ♖b4 46 ♖g5 ♖xf4 47 ♖gg8 ♖f2+ 48 ♔c3 ♖f3+ 49 ♔d2 ♘d6

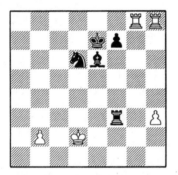

The material alignment has not changed, but the a- and h-pawns do not have any significance. Without difficulty, Black organises an attack on the king.

50 h4 ♘e4+ 51 ♔e2 ♖h3 52 b4

There is no change in the situation by 52 ♖e8+ ♔f6 53 b4 (53 ♔e1 ♔f5) 53...♗c4+.

52...♗c4+ 53 ♔d1 ♖h1+ 54 ♔c2 ♖h2+ 55 ♔c1 ♘c3 56 ♖c8 ♘a2+ 57 ♔d1 ♗b3+ 58 ♔e1 ♘xb4 And White's position is hopeless. He only managed to gain moral consolation by resisting until the 90th move.

In the following example, the defending side deploys his forces far more actively, but this does not ease the problems of defence.

Panchenko - Vaisser
Sochi 1983

Black has two passed pawns. But both are firmly blockaded and the single c-pawn, supported by his pieces, is enough for White to play for a win. He must only watch carefully for exceptional possibilities of sacrificing one of the rooks for a minor piece and pawn with a transfer to a theoretically drawn ending.

53 ♘c2 ♖g8

Black chooses a plan of attack on the c-pawn, but it leads to a dead end. Another possible plan begins with the move 53...♖g4, attempting to stop the king going to the fourth rank and from where the rook will also indirectly support the d-pawn. After 54 ♘b4 ♖h4 White is at a crossroads. It is obvious that then 55 c6? does not work because of the possibility of the sacrifice 55...♖xb4 56 ♔xb4 ♖xc6 with a draw. However White has two ways to oust the active rook.

a) 55 ♘a6 ♖c8 56 ♖a2 ♖h3 57 ♖e2+ ♔f6 58 ♖g2 ♖h6 59 ♖g4 ♖c6 60 ♔d4 and the king is activated.

b) 55 ♗a6 ♖h3+ 56 ♘d3+ ♔e4 57 ♖a4+ ♔e3 58 ♖d4 ♖h5 59 ♗b5 and Black again lands in a dead end.

54 ♘b4 ♖gc8

Also here, apparently insufficient is 54...♖g4 55 c6. For example:

55...♔e6 56 ♖c5 ♖g5 57 ♘a6 ♖c8 58 c7 etc.

55 ♘a6! ♖c6 56 ♗e2 ♖h6

It is worth stopping at the active 56...♔e4!? 57 ♔b4 (57 ♗d3+ ♔e5) 57...d4, though after 58 ♖a3 this pawn is blockaded on the next line.

57 ♘b4 ♖h4 58 ♗a6!

Ousting the rook with tempo, and then also the king to a more modest position.

58...♖c7 59 ♘d3+ ♔e6 60 ♗b5 ♖b7 61 ♖a6+!

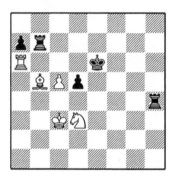

It is interesting that, after all White's pieces have in turn visited the a6 square, the fall of the d5-pawn proves decisive.

61...♔e7 62 ♖a4! ♖h3

After the exchange of rooks, 62...♖xa4 63 ♗xa4 ♔e6 64 ♔d4 ♖g7 65 ♗d1! (not 65 ♗b3? because of 65... ♖g4+) 65...♖g1 66 ♗f3, does not ease Black's lot.

63 ♗c6 ♖c7 64 ♖a6 ♔d8 65 ♔d4 ♖h4+ 66 ♔xd5 ♖g7 67 ♗b5 ♖h5+ 68 ♔c4 ♖g4+ 69 ♔c3 ♖g3 70 ♖d6+ ♔c7 71 ♔b4 ♖g1

The alternative, 71...♖g7!? 72 ♘f4 a5+ 73 ♔c4 ♖h4, after 74 ♖d4 ♖gg4 75 ♘e6+ ♔b7 76 ♖xg4 ♖xg4+ 77 ♔d5, leads to the exchange of a pair of rooks, but not to the saving of the game.

72 ♖d7+ ♔c8 73 ♖d4

Simpler is 73 ♖xa7 ♖b1+ 74 ♔a5, but White counts on exploiting this rook for an attack on the king.

73...♖b1+ 74 ♔c4 a5 75 ♗a4 ♔c7 76 ♗c2 ♖b8 77 ♖g4 ♖h7 78 ♖g6

After 78 ♘f4 the black rook, surprisingly, becomes aggressive: 78...♖b4+ 79 ♔d5 (79 ♔c3 ♖h3+! 80 ♘xh3 ♖xg4) 79... ♖h5+! 80 ♘xh5 ♖xg4 and the passed pawn shows its teeth.

78...♖h4+ 79 ♔c3 ♖b5 80 ♖f6 ♔b8

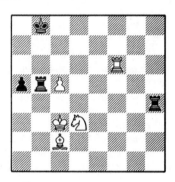

81 ♖f1!

Now, in turn, tackling the a-pawn.

81...♔a7 82 ♖a1 ♖h3 83 ♔c4 ♔a6 84 ♗a4 ♖b8 85 ♗d7 ♖h4+ 86 ♔d5 ♖h5+ 87 ♔c4

On 87 ♘e5 follows 87...♖b2!.

87...♖h4+ 88 ♔c3 ♖d8

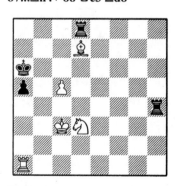

89 ♗e6

After 89 c6 ♔b6 the black king comes to life. For example: 90 ♖b1+ ♔c7 91 ♖b7+ ♔d6 92 ♘b2 a4 93 ♘c4+ ♔c5 94 ♖b5+ ♔xb5 95 c7+ ♖xd7 96 c8=♕ ♖h3+ and Black saves himself.

89...♔b5 90 ♖b1+ ♖b4!

A clever defence. After 91 ♘xb4? axb4+ 92 ♖xb4+ ♔xc5 arises a theoretically drawn endgame.

91 ♗c4+ ♔c6 92 ♖a1!

Again the rook is untouchable: 92 ♖xb4? axb4+ 93 ♔xb4 ♖b8+ 94 ♔c3 ♖d8! and the c5 pawn is lost.

92...♖bb8

He has to retreat, since 92...♖xd3+? 93 ♗xd3 ♔xc5 leads to the loss of a piece by 94 ♖xa5+.

93 ♖xa5 ♖a8 94 ♘b4+ ♔c7 95 ♘a6+!

Repeating, but by now without the black pawn. White sets about constructing a mating net.

95...♔c6 96 ♗b5+ ♔b7 97 ♖a1 ♖d5 98 ♔c4 ♖g5 99 ♖e1 ♖g4+ 100 ♔c3 ♖g3+ 101 ♔b4 ♖g7 102 ♖e6 ♖h8 103 ♔a5 ♖c8 104 ♖d6 ♔a8 105 ♗d7 ♖h8 106 ♔b6 ♖xd7 107 ♖xd7 ♖h6+ 108 ♔a5 ♖c6 109 ♖d6 Black resigned.

Rublevsky - P.Nikolić
Polanica Zdroj 1996

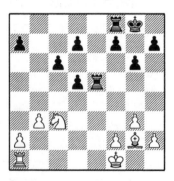

Black has a small material advantage, which might tell in case of an exchange of rooks. White should take this into account.

19 ♘a4 ♖b8 20 ♖c1 ♔f8 21 ♘c5 ♖e7

Also not bad is 21...♔e8, freeing the rook for more active play.

22 ♘d3 a5

Also worth considering is 22...h5 with the idea of ...h5-h4.

23 ♖c5 ♖a8 24 h4 h6 25 ♘f4 ♔g7 26 ♗h3 ♖a7

More energetic is 26...a4!? 27 b4 g5 28 ♘d3 gxh4 29 gxh4 a3 with approximately equal chances.

27 h5 ♖e5 28 ♗g4

White plans to oust the rook and obtain an active position. He intends to exchange on g6 and withdraw the knight, ♘f4-d3, so as, after f2-f4, to transfer it to e5.

28...a4 29 b4 ♖e4 30 a3 g5?!

Played, apparently, after taking into account the previous note. But from such small concessions are also formed real advantages. He should not needlessly weaken the f5 square. From the point of view of general considerations it would be useful to exchange a pair of rooks by 30...♖c4.

31 ♗f3 ♖d4

The transfer to a rook ending, after 31...gxf4 32 ♗xe4 dxe4 33 gxf4, is in White's favour.

32 ♘e2 ♖d3 33 ♖c3

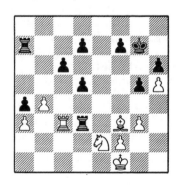

33...♖d1+

Also worth considering is activating the idle pieces, though psychologically it is difficult to voluntarily part with a pawn: 33...♖xc3 34 ♘xc3 ♔f6 35 ♗d1 ♔e5 36 ♘xa4 ♔d4 37 ♔e2 f5 38 ♔d2 d6.

34 ♔g2 f5

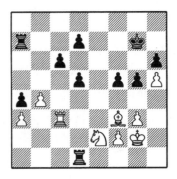

35 g4!

S.Rublevsky immediately reveals the weakness of the f5 square, since 35...f4 does not work because of 36 ♘xf4, while on 35...d4 follows 36 ♘g3! and now 36...fxg4 37 ♗xd1 dxc3 38 ♘e4 leads to the loss of a pawn.

35...fxg4 36 ♗xg4 ♖d2 37 ♘g3 d4 38 ♘f5+ ♔h7 39 ♖c4 ♖d3 40 ♖xd4 ♖xa3

Black succeeds in organising a passed pawn but his king falls under attack by the white pieces.

41 ♖d6 ♖b3 42 ♖xh6+ ♔g8 43 ♖g6+ ♔f8 44 ♖f6+ ♔g8 45 ♘e7+ ♔g7 46 ♖g6+

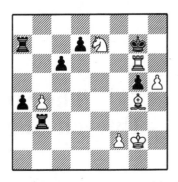

46...♔f7?

Up to here Black has quite successfully repulsed the threats, but with this retreat he overlooks the possibility of an intermediate check on g7. Necessary was 46...♔f8! and if White follows the same path as in the game, 47 h6 ♖xb4 48 ♖g7, then there is a defence for Black: 48...♖xg4+ 49 ♔f1 ♖b7. Here, for example, a possible, though not exactly a forced development of events, is 50 ♘g6+ ♔e8 51 h7 ♖b1+ 52 ♔e2 ♖h1 53 h8=♕+ ♖xh8 54 ♘xh8 a3 and White has to return the knight with a pawn deficit (55 ♖g8+ ♔e7 56 ♖a8 ♔f6 57 ♖xa3 ♔g7).

White achieves nothing of significance after 47 ♘c8 ♖c7 48 ♘b6 d5.

47 h6 ♖xb4 48 ♖g7+ ♔f6 49 ♘g8+ ♔e5 50 ♖xg5+ Black resigned.

The continuation 50...♔f4 51 h7 ♔xg5 52 h8=♕ ♖xg4+ 53 ♔f3 ♖f4+ 54 ♔e3 ♖f7 55 f4+ only drags out the inevitable end.

7 The Struggle with an Uneven Alignment of Forces

In the Introduction we mentioned that there are positional, material and psychological advantages. But we come across quite a few positions where the struggle features various pieces. This, for example, includes situations where one of the opponents has an extra exchange, while the other has in return compensation in the shape of one or two pawns. We not infrequently come across positions where the queen is struggling against rook and minor piece, in various combinations. Also frequently occurring is a rook fighting against a pair of minor pieces.

This theme is quite complex and it is not easy to give a ready recipe for playing positions with non-typical alignments of forces. Detailed expositions of these also do not enter into our work and it is possible only to recommend general directions of play. Certain positions with a small alignment of forces can be studied in individual text books on the endgame. Therefore, in our work, we look at more complicated situations, which are distinct by their original solutions and paradoxical moves, in other words, all those things which make us love our art of chess.

1 The Queen in the struggle against weaker pieces

Fragments from the following games are shining illustrations of the struggle in irrational positions where the queen appears both as a hero, and, alas, also as a sacrifice. We start with positions where the queen has to prove its obvious superiority.

Chiburdanidze - Akmilovskaya
Tallinn 1977

It is no accident that this position is included in a book about small advantages. Black has built a fortress, which is very difficult to take by storm. Most surprisingly, in its structure, it resembles a position, with transposition of colours, analysed in detail by M.Botvinnik in his comments to a game against

Troianescu, Budapest 1952. The only difference is the placement of the black rook on d5, while the white queen stands on b6 and the pawn on h3. It was established that the winning method in such positions lies in the sacrifice of queen for rook with transposition to a favourable pawn ending. Analysis of the ending from this time has occupied a firm place in endgame manuals. The study of it is a necessary element of chess culture.

We mention that the position in the diagram after 43...♜d5 44 h3 ♚g8 45 ♚e4 ♚g7 46 g4 could transpose "to Botvinnik" in conditions more favourable for White: he is already set to sacrifice his queen on d5. Let us look at the position: with the exchange on g4 and without the exchange of pawns.

a) 46 g4 hxg4 47 hxg4 ♚g8 48 ♕xd5!! exd5+ (after 48...f5+ White gains victory by 49 ♚e5! exd5 50 g5) 49 ♚xd5 ♚f8 (there is also no saving himself by 49...♚h7 50 ♚d6 ♚g7 51 ♚d7, after 51...♚h7 52 ♚d8 ♚h8 53 f5! or 51...♚f6 52 ♚e8 ♚e6 53 ♚f8 ♚f6 54 g5+ ♚e6 55 ♚g7 White wins) 50 ♚d6 ♚e8 51 f5! g5 52 ♚c7 ♚e7 53 ♚c8! ♚d6 54 ♚d8 with a decisive march of the king around to the enemy's rear.

b) 46...♚g8 47 ♕xd5 exd5+ 48 ♚xd5 ♞f8 49 gxh5 gxh5 50 ♚e5 ♞g7 51 ♚f5 (but not 51 h4? ♚g6 with a draw) 51...h4 52 ♚g5 f6+ 53 ♚h5! (53 ♚xh4 would be a mistake, since after 53...♚g6 54 ♚g4 f5+ there arises a drawn ending) 53...♚h7 54 f5 and White wins.

Now it is clear that White wins the pawn ending because of the distance of the black king. But, possibly, the black king should come closer to the centre?

c) 46...hxg4 47 hxg4 ♚f8. Now the pawn ending promises nothing, for example: 48 ♕xd5 exd5+ 49 ♚xd5 ♚e7. But there is another plan, 48 ♕a4!, playing for zugzwang! Let us look at the possible replies:

c1) 48...♚g7 49 ♕a1+ ♚h7 (49...♚g8 is not possible because of 50 ♕a8+ ♚g7 51 ♕xd5) 50 ♕a8!. Now White either takes on d5, or plays 51 ♕f8, destroying the fortress and quickly achieving success.

c2) 48...♚e7 49 ♕a3+ ♚e8 (49...♚f6 50 ♕f8!) 50 ♕b4! ♜d7 51 ♚e5, and the march of the king to f6 quickly decides.

c3) 48...♜d2 49 ♕a8+ ♚g7 50 ♕a1+ ♚g8 51 ♚e5! ♚g7 52 f5! exf5 53 gxf5 gxf5 54 ♚xf5 ♚g8 55 ♕g1+ ♚f8 56 ♕c5+ ♚g8 57 ♚f6, and White wins.

With an analysis of this ending we are continually reminded of positions in which the queen does not win against rook and pawn. By way of an example, if in the last variation Black places the rook on e6 with the pawn on f7, then a drawn position is reached.

Akhmilovskaya rejected this classical fortress in favour of **43...g5**, which allowed White to utilise the g-pawn as a battering ram.

44 fxg5 ♜xg5 45 h3 ♚h7 46 ♚e4 ♜d5 47 ♕b8 ♚g7 48 ♕b2+ ♚h7

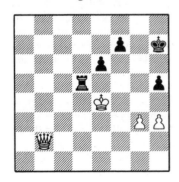

49 ♕b1

After 49 ♕f6 ♖f5 50 ♕xf5+? exf5+ 51 ♔xf5 arises a pawn ending, which at first sight might be shown as winning for White, but Black manages to save himself: 51...h4! 52 g4 ♔g7 53 ♔g5 f6+ 54 ♔xh4 ♔g6 55 ♔g3 f5 and the draw is inevitable.

But possible was 49 g4 hxg4 50 hxg4 ♖g5 51 ♔f4 ♖g6 (there is no salvation in 51...♔g6 52 ♕h8 e5+ 53 ♔f3 e4+ 54 ♔f4! ♖c5 55 ♕g8+ ♔f6 56 g5+ ♔e7 57 g6 and Black's defence is broken) 52 ♕e5! ♔g8 53 g5 and now it is obvious that the rook is tied to the g5 pawn, which means that it cannot prevent the white king from breaking through to its rear.

49...♔g7 50 ♕a1+ ♔g6

On 50...♔h7 good is 51 g4, endeavouring to carry out the plan pointed out in the previous note.

51 ♕a8 ♖g5 52 ♕g8+ ♔f6 53 ♕d8+ ♔g6 54 ♕f8!

Exploiting the fact that the g3 pawn is indirectly defended (54...♖xg3? 55 ♕g8+), White deprives Black of the possibility of playing 54...♔f6?, which would lead to the loss of the h5 pawn: 55 ♕h6+ ♖g6 56 ♕xh5.

54...♖f5 55 g4 hxg4 56 hxg4 ♖d5 57 ♕g8+ ♔f6 58 ♕h8+ ♔g6 59 ♔f4 ♖c5 60 ♕g8+ ♔f6 61 g5+ ♔e7 62 g6

Forcing an exchange, after which arises a position with pawns on the sixth rank where there is no fortress.

62...♖f5+ 63 ♔e4 fxg6 64 ♕xg6 Black resigned.

The queen can be presented with more problems by a pair of bishops. And yet, all the same, we have an example of a siege similar to a "fortress"—a particular case. In practice we have the most varied alignments of forces and play assumes a more lively character.

Here, of decisive importance for organisation of opposition to the queen by the pieces is the coordination of their activity. The following study is indicative of this aspect.

O.Pervakov, 2001

Draw

In order to hold the position, White has to put right the coordination of his minor pieces and hold up the d6 pawn. It is obvious that the key point must become the d5 square. The coordination of forces is achieved thanks to the position of the black king and with help of the theme of distraction.

1 ♘e7 ♕f7!

On 1...♕b1 the knight immediately occupies the d5 square—2 ♗e2+ ♔g5 3 ♘d5! ♕e1+ 4 ♔d3 and it remains for Black to be content with a perpetual check: 4...♕b1+ 5 ♔c3 ♕a1+ 6 ♔b3.

After 1...♕g5 the knight penetrates to d5 via the square of deflection, f4—2 ♗e2+ ♔h4 3 ♘f4! and the knight consolidates itself on d5.

1...♕e6 does not work because of 2 ♗d7!.

2 ♘d5!

A false trail is 2 ♗e2+? ♔g5 3 ♘c6 ♕c7 4 ♗f3 d5!.

2...♕f3+

On 2...♔xh5 there is the deflection 4 ♗e8+!.

3 ♔b4! ♕e4+

Now on 3...♔xh5 a deflection is carried out on the other side—4 ♗e2!.

4 ♔a3! ♕f3+ 5 ♔b4 Draw.

Stetsko - Nokin
Moscow 1979

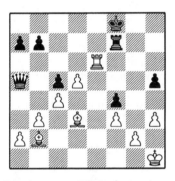

For the queen White has only two bishops, but all his pieces control the main arteries of the board and cooperate excellently against the "bare king".

41 ♗f6!

White not only limits to the maximum the mobility of the rear defenders but also prepares the advance of the d-pawn. It becomes clear that the strength of the queen can perhaps only be exploited in a quest for perpetual check.

41...♕xa2?

Black does not sense the danger. He could still save himself by 41...♔g8! 42 d6 ♖xf6 43 ♖xf6 ♕e1+ and Black gives perpetual check.

42 d6 ♕xb3

Here already there is no salvation in 42...♖xf6 43 ♖xf6+ ♔g7, since after 44 ♖e6! White takes under

control the e1 square and Black cannot prevent the move 45 ♗f5 with the threat of d6-d7 and ♖e6-e8, after which the pawn promotes.

43 ♗e7+ ♔e8 44 ♗g6 ♕b4 45 ♖e4 h4 46 ♗g5+ ♔d7 47 ♗xf7 ♔xd6 48 ♗e8 ♔c7 49 ♗xf4+ ♔b6 50 ♗g5 a5 51 ♗d8+ ♔a7 52 ♗b5 and White wins easily.

In the annals of the Spanish Game, in one of the lines of the Open variation there is a queen sacrifice for a rook and two bishops: **1 e4 e5 2 ♘f3 ♘c6 3 ♗b5 a6 4 ♗a4 ♘f6 5 0-0 ♘xe4 6 d4 b5 7 ♗b3 d5 8 dxe5 ♗e6 9 c3 ♗c5 10 ♘bd2 0-0 11 ♗c2 f5 12 ♘b3 ♗a7 13 ♘fd4 ♘xd4 14 ♘xd4 ♗xd4 15 cxd4 f4 16 f3 ♘g3 17 hxg3 fxg3 18 ♕d3 ♗f5 19 ♕xf5 ♖xf5 20 ♗xf5 ♕h4 21 ♗h3 ♕xd4+ 22 ♔h1 ♕xe5 23 ♗d2 ♕xb2 24 ♗f4**, first encountered in the game Smyslov-Reshevsky, USSR v USA 1946, where after 24...c5? 25 ♗e6+ ♔h8 26 ♗xd5, Smyslov gained victory.

For the following half century Black's hopes were associated only with **24...d4**, however the desire to play this position, as before, is small. It is clear that only individual dare-devils will take it on: what is more real: an attack on the king or the strength of the passed pawn? Here is one modern example from the practice of a famous grandmaster.

Tiviakov - I.Sokolov
Groningen 1994

For the present, theory does not give an accurate evaluation of this position, which in our view can be assessed as one of dynamic balance. Therefore the price of a move here is very great, since any inaccuracy can pass the initiative into the hands of the opponent.

25 ♗xg3

The capture 25 ♗xc7 is not considered dangerous: 25...d3 26 ♗e6+ ♔h8 27 ♗xg3 d2 etc.

25...c5 26 ♗e5!?

Up to this game was played only 26 ♖ae1 d3 with not bad prospects for Black.

26...♖e8 27 f4 ♕e2 28 ♖ae1 ♕h5

Interesting is 28...♕xa2!?, not fearing 29 ♗d6?! in view of the possibility of the attack 29...♖e3! 30 ♗xc5 ♖xh3+!.

29 ♖c1! d3 30 ♖xc5 ♕e2 31 ♖g1 ♖d8 32 ♖c7 ♔f8! 33 ♗xg7+ ♔e8

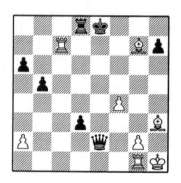

At this critical moment of the struggle, S.Tiviakov plays poorly.

34 ♗g4? ♕xg4 35 ♖e1+ ♕e2 36 ♖xe2+?

White finally gets confused. It was still possible to save himself by 36 ♗c3! ♕xe1+ 37 ♗xe1 d2 38 ♗xd2 ♖xd2 39 a4! bxa4 40 ♖c6.

36...dxe2 37 ♗c3 ♖d1+ 38 ♔h2 ♖c1! and the e-pawn cannot be held.

Meanwhile, Andre Lilienthal, who, incidentally has met all the world champions of the 20th century, demonstrated in an excellent analysis that in the diagram position White could aspire for more:

I. 34 f5!!

The threat to advance this pawn forces Black to attend to defence, since 34...d2? 35 f6 loses quickly.

34...♖d7 35 ♖c8+

Now, for a draw, it is sufficient to repeat the position by 35...♖d8 36 ♖c7, but why not try to find a win?

35...♔f7 36 ♗h6!

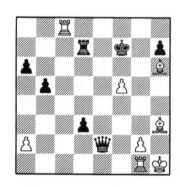

After this move it becomes clear that Black is losing. Let us turn to the role of the dark-squared bishop: it is the main director of the harmonious orchestra of white pieces.

a) 36...♔f6? 37 ♖f8+ ♖f7 38 ♖a8 ♕xa2 39 ♖e8! ♖d7 40 ♖e6+ ♔f7 41 ♗g4 and there is no defence against mate.

b) 36...♖d6 37 ♖f8+ ♔e7 38 ♗g7 d2 39 f6+ ♖xf6 40 ♖xf6 d1=♕ 41 ♖xd1 ♕xd1+ 42 ♔h2. A temporary respite, but can't Black save himself? Here is one of the benefits of his waiting: 42...♕a4 43 ♖f5 ♕xa2? 44 ♗f8+ ♔d8 45 ♗d6 and White wins.

c) 36...d2 37 ♖f8+ ♔e7 38 f6+ ♔d6 39 ♗f4+

c1) 39...♔c5 40 ♖c8+ ♔b4! 41 ♗xd2+ ♕xd2 42 ♗xd7 ♕h6+ (after 42...♕xd7 the f6 pawn "stays alive": 43 ♖cc1! ♕d2 44 ♖b1+! ♔a3 45 ♖gf1 ♕h6+ 46 ♔g1 ♕e3+ 47 ♖f2, which is irresistible) 43 ♗h3 ♕xf6 44 ♖b1+ and White's chances of a win are quite considerable. On 44...♔a3, good is 45 ♖c2 when Black can play neither 45...b4 nor 45...a5 because of 46 ♖b3+. In the event of 44...♔a5, White transfers the rook to attack the a6 pawn: 45 ♖e1! ♕f2 46 ♖e6 ♕f1+ 47 ♔h2 ♕f4+ 48 g3 ♕f2+ 49 ♗g2 and 50 ♖cc6.

c2) 39...♔c6 40 ♖c8+ ♔b7 41 ♗xd7 ♕h5+ 42 ♗h3 d1=♕ 43 ♖xd1 ♕xd1+ 44 ♔h2 ♕d4! 45 ♗g5!! (the officer is ready to give up his life for a modest soldier!) 45...♕e5+ 46 g3 ♕e2+ (after 46...♕xg5 47 f7 the pawn cannot be stopped) 47 ♗g2+ (now already the light-squared bishop takes charge of the orchestra) 47...♔xc8 48 f7! ♕f2 49 ♗f4 ♕c5 50 ♗h6! (it is as if the bishop has cosmic energy!) 50...♕h5+ 51 ♗h3+ ♔b7 52 f8=♕ and "*finita la comedia*"!

II. 34 ♗f6!? (this is sufficient only for a draw) **34...d2** (the threat was 35 ♖e7+ or 35 ♗xd8 and therefore Black has no choice) **35 ♗xd8 d1=♕ 36 ♖xd1** (on 36 ♗h4!? Black defends by 36...♕d6 37 ♖gc1 ♕xf4 38 ♖c8+ ♔f7 39 ♖8c7+! ♔g8 40 ♖c8+ with a draw) **36...♕xd1+ 37 ♔h2 ♔xd8 38 ♖c8+ ♔e7 39 ♖c7+ ♔f6 40 ♖c6+ ♔g7 41 ♖c7+ ♔h6 42 ♖c6+ ♔g7** (not possible is

42...♔h5?? 43 g4+) **43 ♖c7+** with a draw.

But far more often we encounter situations where the queen is compensated by a rook and minor piece and the chances of the sides in great part depend on the possibility of constructing a fortress. Upon the presence of a pair of rooks it is more difficult to hold.

Kamsky - Karpov
FIDE World Championship,
Elista 1996

In the preceding struggle A.Karpov was forced to give up his queen for rook and bishop, reckoning on "sitting it out" in the fortress. This would be quite realistic in case of an exchange of a pair of rooks and a substantial pawn structure—then the rook could hold the defence along the 6th rank. An exchange of rooks is sufficient after 24...♖fe8 and, on any retreat of the queen, Black hurries to include the intermediate move 25...♗g4, forcing also an exchange of a pair of minor pieces: 25 ♕d2 ♗g4! 26 ♖xe8+ ♖xe8 27 h3 ♗xf3 28 gxf3 a6 or 25 ♕d3 ♗g4! 26 h3 ♗xf3 27 ♖xe8+ ♖xe8 28 ♕xf3 ♘xa5. In both cases White's advantage might be assessed as small.

However A.Karpov transposes moves and White succeeds in retaining his rook which, in turn, increases his chances because of the possibility of organising an attack on the king.

24...♗g4?!

Not for the first time, we have the opportunity to convince ourselves that the cost of a move may be higher than a measure of advantage. Now White's initiative already increases and Kamsky's technique in exploiting it is very instructive.

25 a6!

The a-pawn gives itself up in order to destabilise the black position. Losing its most secure guard, the knight on c6 will be in permanent trouble.

25...bxa6 26 ♕e4 ♗xf3 27 ♕xf3 ♖fe8

28 ♖a1!

A brilliant move! I think that 28 ♖f1 would have done just as well, but moving the rook to the d-, c-, or b-files would have given Black the chance again to offer an exchange of rooks. By keeping the rooks on the board, White reduces Black's chances of building a fortress. White is technically winning.

28...♖e6 29 h3 ♖d8 30 ♕c3 ♖dd6 31 ♖b1 ♖d7 32 ♕c4 a5 33 ♖b5 ♖d1+ 34 ♔h2 ♖d2 35 ♖f5

♖d4 36 ♕c3 ♖dd6 37 ♖c5 ♖f6 38 ♖c4 ♖fe6 39 ♖c5 ♖f6 40 ♕e3 ♖fe6 41 ♕g3 ♖g6 42 ♕b3 ♖gf6 43 ♕b7 ♖fe6 44 ♕c7 ♖f6 45 f4!

After protracted manoeuvring, White activates the heavy pieces and commences a pawn storm. Black's reply is forced.

45...g6

After 45...♖fe6?! White breaks up the defence with a single pawn: 46 f5 ♖f6 47 g4 g5 48 h4!

46 f5! gxf5 47 ♖xf5

With the opening of lines, this rook creates much disquiet to the enemy king. At the present moment Black cannot exchange it since after 47...♖xf5 48 ♕xd6 ♘e5 49 g4 it can no longer be called a fortress, while from now on White does not give such chances.

47...♖de6 48 ♖h5 ♖h6 49 ♕g3+ ♔f8 50 ♖d5 ♖hg6 51 ♕f2 ♖gf6 52 ♕b2 ♔e7 53 ♖h5 ♖h6 54 ♖b5 ♖hf6 55 ♕c3 ♔f8 56 ♖h5 ♖h6 57 ♖f5 ♖hg6 58 ♕f3

The result of the second cycle of prolonged manoeuvring—pressure on the weak point in Black's position, the f7 pawn. Black is forced to remove one of his rooks from the 6th rank.

58...♖g7

More stubborn was 58...♖e7, though even this, after 59 ♕f4 ♔e8

60 h4, ought to lead to further retreats.

59 ♕f4 ♔g8 60 ♕c7 ♔f8 61 ♕c8+ ♔e7

The king is forced to go under cover of the rook.

62 ♖d5 ♔f6

And so the king falls under a deadly pin but the choice is not great. Also losing is 62...♖h7 63 ♕c7+ ♔f6 64 ♖d6 and 62...♖gg6 63 ♖d7+ ♔f6 64 ♕h8+.

63 ♕h8! ♖e4 64 ♖h5 ♘e7

On 64...♘e5, decisive is 65 ♖h6+ ♘g6 66 g4 ♖e5 67 h4.

65 ♖h7 Black resigned.

There are also exceptions, when the queen assumes the role of a defender.

Ivanchuk - Short
Riga 1995

From the arithmetical standpoint White has a material advantage, having an extra, albeit doubled pawn. Moreover, Black's position is worse, but in order to reveal its defects White must demonstrate filigree technique.

40...♔g8 41 f5 ♔f7 42 ♖g3 ♕h1 43 h3 ♕e4?!

From such small mistakes are created new problems. He should

prevent the advance of the h-pawn by 43...♔f6.

44 ♖g4! ♕h1 45 h4 ♕h2

The activation of the king by 45...♔f6 46 ♖b4 ♔e5 doesn't look bad.

46 ♘f1!

Transferring to the theme of a vertical pin, White moves the knight out of the danger zone.

46...♕e5 47 ♔f3 ♕d5+ 48 ♖e4 ♕d1+?!

48...♕d3+ would force the knight to return to e3.

49 ♔g2 ♕d5 50 ♘g3! ♕c6?!

White completes the regrouping of forces and now, next in turn, comes the activating of the king. For the present it was possible to prevent this by 50...♕d2 51 h5 (or 51 ♔f3 ♕d1+ 52 ♖e2 ♕d4 53 ♘e4 ♕d1) 51...♕d5+ 52 ♔h3 ♕d2 53 f3 ♕g5.

51 ♔h3! ♕c2 52 f3 ♕d1 53 ♔g4

The king goes into the attack under the considerate cover of his small army.

53...♕g1 54 ♖e6 ♕d4+?!

Simplifying White's task. The only possibility was 54...♕g2, though even here after a regrouping of the white army by 55 ♖e2 ♕g1 56 ♖c2 ♔e7 (or 56...♕d4+ 57 ♘e4 ♕g1+ 58 ♔f4) 57 ♔f4 ♕b6 58 ♘e4, Black, as before, is in a difficult position.

55 ♘e4 ♕d7 56 ♘g5+ ♔g8 57 ♔h5 ♕d8 58 ♔g6

The king is no weaker than a queen.

58...♕d7

On 58...♕f8 follows a decisive regrouping of forces—59 h5 ♔h8 60 ♘f7+ ♔g8 61 ♘d6.

59 h5! ♕b5 60 ♘e4 Black resigned.

2 The exchange ahead

With the modern style of conducting the chess struggle, the sacrifice of the exchange is one of the elements not only of tactics but also of strategy. Its aim is to obtain a non-typical situation with sufficient compensation thanks to the activity of the pieces. It goes without saying that it envisages also material compensation in the shape of one or two pawns. In our section on this theme let us look at examples with a small advantage for the side having the rook against minor piece and one pawn.

We start with a classic from the 19th century.

Chigorin - Steinitz
World Championship,
Havana 1889

The black pieces are placed so harmoniously that it is not apparent how White is to going to realise his small advantage. Black's position resembles a well-reinforced fortress where there are no real objects of attack. And yet M.Chigorin finds one—the f5 pawn. Let us see how he exploits, in virtuoso style, the tactical possibilities concealed in the position.

36 h5!

A fine move, placing Black in a dilemma: to worsen his pawn structure or give White a support point on g6, which will be useful for a rook invasion.

36...gxh5

He has to go for the positional concession, since, after 36...g5+ 37 ♔f3 ♖d7, Black cannot prevent the occupation of the e-file with the rook: 38 ♖e1 ♖e7 39 ♖xe7 ♔xe7 40 ♖e5+.

37 ♗c2 ♔e7 38 ♖e5+ ♔f8 39 ♖xf5+ ♔e7 40 ♖e5+ ♔d7 41 f3!

In the style of modern prophylaxis. After 41 ♖xh5 ♖f8+ White, of course, retains the f-pawn, but in a more complicated way: 42 ♗f5+ ♔c6 43 f3.

41...h4! 42 ♔g4 ♖g8+

The rook is an active piece. Thus it is not in its style to play 42...♖f8 after which follows 43 ♖h5 ♗e3 44 ♖xh4.

43 ♔xh4 ♖g2

Black loses a pawn, but he succeeds in activating his rook. Moreover the king's position is not very good.

44 ♗f5+ ♔c6 45 b3!

A profound decision: White prefers to retain compact pawns, defended by the bishop, reckoning on a future exploitation by the rook of the weakened black periphery.

45...♗f2+ 46 ♔h3 ♖g3+ 47 ♔h2 ♖xf3 48 ♔g2 ♖f4!

The endgame after 48...♖xf5 49 ♖xd6+ ♔xd6 50 ♖xf5 ♗e3 51 ♔f3 assumes a technical character: the win for White is only a matter of time.

49 ♗e6!

On 49 ♖f1 Black saves himself: 49...♘xf5! 50 ♖xf2! ♖xf2+ 51 ♔xf2 ♘d4 52 ♖e3 b5! 53 ♖d3 bxa4! 54 bxa4 ♔c5.

49...♗c5 50 ♗d5+ ♔d7 51 ♖e6 ♘f5 52 ♗c4+ ♔c7 53 ♖d3! h5 54 ♗b5 ♖g4+

More cunning is 54...♖f2+ 55 ♔h3 ♗d6 56 ♖e2 ♖f4 57 ♖c3+ ♗c5 with active play, but it seems that W.Steinitz was happy with his choice in the game.

55 ♔h2 ♖h4+ 56 ♖h3 ♗d6+ 57 ♔g2 ♖g4+ 58 ♔f1

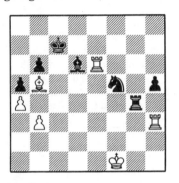

58...♘g3+

Black continues mechanically with the realisation of his plan to advance the h-pawn. Actually the rook on h3 is cramped and it is not easy to bring it into play, but during the course of further play it becomes clear that M.Chigorin has assessed the position more deeply. Meanwhile Black's pieces cooperate more harmoniously after 58...♖f4+!? 59 ♔e1 (59 ♔g2 ♖g4+ 60 ♔f2 ♖f4+) 59...♗b4+ 60 ♔d1 ♘d4 61 ♖h6 ♖e4. It is obvious that Black has active counterplay.

59 ♔f2 h4 60 ♖h6! ♖f4+ 61 ♔g2 ♗e7 62 ♖c6+ ♔b7 63 ♖c4 ♖f8

This retreat allows the white rook to penetrate behind enemy lines with unpleasant threats. It is possible that the sufficient mobility of the black king was enough reason for an exchange of a pair of rooks: 63...♖xc4!? 64 ♗xc4 ♔c6 65 ♔f3 ♔c5. For example: 66 ♔e3 ♗g5+

67 ♔d3 ♘f5 68 ♖f3 ♘d6 69 ♗e6 ♗e7 and Black holds the defence.

64 ♖d4 ♔c8 65 ♖d7 ♗d8 66 ♖h2! ♘e4 67 ♖g7 ♘c5

Here the exchange of rooks by 67...♖f2+ 68 ♔g1 ♖xh2 69 ♔xh2 will already come about in a far worse situation, since the black king is out of play.

68 ♖h3 ♗f6 69 ♖g6 ♗d8 70 ♗c4 ♖f4 71 ♖f3! ♖d4 72 ♖g7 ♔b8 73 ♖ff7.

At last White succeeds in putting right the coordination of his pieces, and with decisive effect. It remains only to include the bishop in the attack.

73...♖d6 74 ♔h3 ♖d2 75 ♖h7 ♖d6 76 ♗f1!

The bishop transfers to g2, after which the manoeuvre ♖f7-a7 will already threaten a linear mate.

76...♘e6 77 ♖d7!

A prosaic offer to exchange rooks, whereas after the automatic 77 ♖b7+? ♔c8 Black surprisingly saves himself.

77...♖c6

It is obvious that, on a rook exchange 77...♘g5+ 78 ♔g4 ♘xh7 79 ♖xd6, the endgame is lost. For example: 79...♔c7 80 ♖h6 ♘f6+ 81 ♔f5 ♘d7 82 ♗b5 ♘c5 83 ♔e5 ♘xb3 84 ♖h7+ ♔b8 85 ♔d6 etc.

78 ♔g4 ♖c7 79 ♗c4! ♖xc4+ 80 bxc4 ♔c8 81 ♖d6 ♘c5 82 ♖c6+ ♔b8 83 ♖h8 Black resigned.

Khalifman - Leko
Budapest 2000

Here, Black's passed pawn is some sort of guarantee of counterplay, but for the present his pieces are insufficiently coordinated. The first impression is that it is necessary first to take care of the king, which P.Leko does.

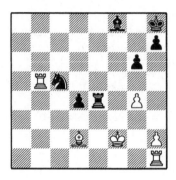

31...Re8

He should exploit the chance that has turned up to simplify the position by taking the pawn, 31...Rxg4. But, it goes without saying, this requires accurate calculation for which there is not always time in a time-trouble situation. For the sake of truth we continue the variation: 32 Rb8 ☗g7 33 Rxf8 ♘e4+ 34 ☗f3 ♘xd2+ 35 ☗xg4 ☗xf8 36 Rd1 and, though White captures the d4 pawn, he will hardly succeed in realising the extra exchange.

32 ☗f3 ♘d3 33 Rd5

It is worth bringing into play the second rook: 33 Rd1 ♘e5+ 34 ☗g3 and now on 34...♗g7 unpleasant is 35 Re1. If 34...♘b4 35 ♗f4 ♗g7 36 h4 ♘e3 37 Rdb1 ☗g8 38 Rb8 ☗f7 39 Rxe8 ☗xe8 40 Rb7 White exchanges rooks in a favourable situation.

33...♗g7 34 Rf1

34 Rb1!? promised more practical chances. Now Black carries out the virtually forced manoeuvre...

34...♘e5+ 35 ☗g3 ♘c4 36 Re1 ♘e3 37 ♗xe3 dxe3 38 ☗f3 ♗h6 39 g5 ♗g7 40 Rxe3 Rxe3+ 41 ☗xe3 ☗g8 42 Rd8+ ☗f7 43 Rd7+ ☗g8 44 h4 ♗b2 45 ☗f3 ♗g7 46 ☗f4 ♗f8, assuming that this was a theoretically drawn position.

And in fact after **47 h5?** P.Leko managed to "keep standing". The game continued **47...gxh5 48 ☗g3 h6 49 g6 ♗a3 50 ☗h4 ♗c1 51 ☗xh5 ♗g5 52 ☗g4 ♗c1 53 ☗f5 ♗g5 54 ☗e6 ♗h4 55 Rh7 ♗g5**

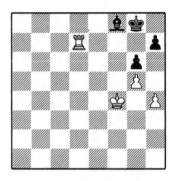

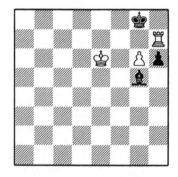

Here followed a gentlemen's exchange of "courtesies" leading to a trade of the remaining pawns: **56 g7! h5! 57 Rxh5 ♗f6!! 58 Rh3 ♗xg7 Draw.**

But all is not so clear. We return to the position after Black's 46th move. As A.Khalifman claimed after the game, 47 Ra7 led to a win but he did not confirm this with analysis.

On the other hand, an analysis in *64—Chess Review* (no.1, 2000) was published by S.Shipov, who demonstrated his own winning plan, which we reproduce here: 47 ☗g4 h5+ 48

♞f3! (leading to a draw is 48 gxh6 ♝xh6 49 h5 gxh5+ 50 ♞xh5 ♝c1 51 ♞g6 ♞f8) 48...♝b4! (losing are both 48...♝a3 49 ♜b7 ♝d6 50 ♜b6 and also 48...♝g7 49 ♜xg7+! ♞xg7 50 ♞e4 ♞f7 51 ♞d5) 49 ♜c7 ♝e1 50 ♜c4 ♞g7 51 ♞e3 ♞f7 52 ♞d3 ♞g7 53 ♜e4 ♝g3 54 ♞c4 ♞f7 55 ♞d5 ♞g7 56 ♞e6 ♝f2 57 ♜b4 ♝g3 58 ♜b7+ ♞g8 59 ♞f6 and White wins.

In the previous examples the rook demonstrated its superiority over the minor pieces. But at times a position occurs where an extra exchange does not produce victory. It goes without saying that here energetic play is required from the defending side.

Reshevsky - Fischer
Los Angeles 1961

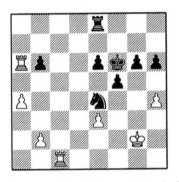

Upon passive defence it is obvious that Black's position will become hopeless. The only chance to save himself is by activating his pieces to the maximum with the idea of exploiting his pawn majority on the king's flank.

32...♜d8! 33 ♜c2

Necessary. He cannot give Black the opportunity to put right the co-ordination of his rook and knight. As shown by R.Fischer, after 33 ♜xb6 ♜d2+ 34 ♞g1 g5 35 hxg5+ hxg5 36 ♜cc6 g4 37 ♜xe6+ ♞g5 38 ♜h6 f4, Black has good counterplay.

33...♜d3 34 ♜xb6

34 ♜e2 is not dangerous for Black in view of 34...♜b3.

34...♜xe3 35 a5 f4

In advancing his pawns Black incidentally creates threats against the opponent's king. This is of no little significance. In such positions each gain of tempo might prove decisive.

36 ♜f2?

Psychologically it is not difficult to understand S.Reshevsky. It seems to him, after an exchange of the passive rook for an active knight, that his connected passed pawns will guarantee him a draw, while also leaving him chances of victory. He took this decision in his traditional time trouble—which often gives rise to bad advice. The principled 36 a6 would lead to a position of dynamic equality, in which the most probable outcome would be a draw. Here is a characteristic variation: 36...f3+ 37 ♞f1 ♜d3 38 ♞e1 ♜e3+ 39 ♞f1 ♜d3. Now, however, with a fine manoeuvre, R.Fischer manages to take over the initiative and obtain a decisive advantage.

36...♞xf2 37 ♞xf2 ♜e4! 38 b4 ♜e3!

Black, as it were, "urges on" the opponent's pawn with the idea of attacking it with his rook from the rear.

39 a6 ♜a3 40 ♜c6 g5 41 hxg5+ hxg5 42 b5 g4 43 ♜c8

43 ♜c7 would only lead to a little longer resistance.

43...♞f5 44 b6 g3+ 45 ♞e1

Also after 45 ♞g2 the king falls into a mating net: 45...♜a2+ 46 ♞f1 f3.

45...♜a1+ 46 ♞e2 g2 47 ♜f8+ ♞e4 48 ♜xf4+

Clever, but insufficient—there will be no perpetual check.

48...♔xf4 49 b7 g1=♕

More effective was the thematic 49...♔e4! 50 b8=♕ ♖a2+ 51 ♔d1 g1=♕ mate.

50 b8=♕+ ♔f5 51 ♕f8+ ♔e4 52 ♕a8+ ♔d4 53 ♕d8+ ♔c4 54 ♕d3+ ♔c5 55 ♕c3+ ♔d6 56 ♕d2+ ♔e5 57 ♕b2+ ♔f5! White resigned.

Suba - Chiburdanidze
Dortmund 1983

White has a clear extra exchange, but Black's forces have their own compact and resolute character.

87...f4!

Black decisively thrusts herself into the attack, ignoring, it seems, the obvious regrouping of the knight from its flank position to a central one: 87...♘g3 88 ♖a1 ♘e4. But with the material deficit it becomes a slow death. White hurries to regroup and forces Black to transfer to defence: 89 ♖b6! ♖c8 90 ♖aa6 ♖g8 The further course of this play takes place in the "goal-mouth": 91 g3 ♖g7 92 ♔g2 ♘c5 93 h4+ ♔h5 94 ♖a5 ♖c7 95 ♔f3 ♘e4 96 ♖a8 etc.

88 ♖2a3 ♖c1 89 ♖a1

Fortune favours the brave! White is bothered by the energy of the black pieces and strives to exchange

the rook, but nudges it to a more active square, whereas he could have gone over to a counterattack: 89 ♖3a5+! ♔h6 90 h4 ♘g3 (passive is 90...♔g7 91 ♖g5 ♘f6 92 h5 and the support pawn on g6 is exchanged) 91 ♔h3 ♖c3 92 ♔g4 ♘e2 93 ♖a3 ♖c5 94 ♖e6 with a decisive advantage for White.

89...♖c2

Now she has to reckon on the threat of f4-f3.

90 ♖1a5+ ♔h6 91 ♖a2 ♖c1 92 h4 ♘g3 93 ♖a1

In case of 93 ♔h3 the attacking mechanism, pointed out in the note to White's 89th move, does not achieve harmony in work, since the "lower" rook is placed more passively (on a2, and not on a5) and Black swaps a pair of pawns: 93...♖h1+ 94 ♔g4 ♘f5! 95 ♔xf4 ♖xh4+.

93...♖xa1 94 ♖xa1 ♔h5!

Not a second's respite! Now the natural 95 ♔h3, after 95...♘e4, allows Black to exchange a pair of pawns, even despite the check—96 ♖a5+ g5! and on 97 hxg5 ♘xg5+ 98 ♔h2 ♔g4 there is nothing concrete. However after 97 g4+ Black realises her cherished dream—the exchange of all the pawns: 97...fxg3 98 ♖e5 g2 99 ♔xg2 ♘d6! 100 hxg5 ♘f7.

95 ♖a4

A move of an experienced practical player; after the exchange of a pair of pawns, 95 ♖a6 ♔xh4 96 ♖xg6, the small but strong cluster of black pieces proves unassailable: 96...♘e4 97 ♔g1 ♘g5 98 ♔f2 ♔g4 etc.

95...♔g4 96 ♔g1 ♘f5 97 ♔f2 ♘g3

Avoiding a little trap: 97... ♘xh4? 98 g3!.

98 ♖b4

98 ♖a6 g5 99 hxg5 ♘e4+ 100 ♔e2 ♘xg5 leads to a fortress already well known to us.

On the board is an original mini-fortress, it is necessary only to take the h4 pawn at an appropriate moment. As pointed out by M.Chiburdanidze, this is achieved by means of a knight manoeuvre: 98...♘h1+! 99 ♔e1 ♘g3 100 ♖b6 (but how to strengthen the position further?) 100...♔xh4 101 ♖xg6 ♘e4 102 ♔e2 ♘g5 and the fortress, as before, is unassailable.

Unfortunately Black was tempted by **98...♘f5?** 99 ♖e4 g5 (quite bad is 99...♘g3? 100 ♖e6 g5 101 hxg5 ♔xg5 102 ♔f3 etc.) **100 hxg5 ♔xg5 101 ♖e5 ♔g4 102 ♖e8 ♘h4?** (one mistake often leads to another, it was necessary to retreat to a new line 102...♘d4!, counting on the manoeuvre ...♘d4-e6-d5) **103 ♖g8+ ♔f5 104 ♔e2 ♔e4 105 g3! ♘f3 106 ♖g4 ♘d4+ 107 ♔f2 ♘e6 108 gxf4 ♘d4 109 f5+ Black resigned.**

In the following example the chances are equalised not by exchanging (or threatening to exchange) all the pawns, but by serious counterplay. Remember the motto: "Activity and still more activity".

Hübner - Smyslov
Candidates match,
Velden 1983

The hopes of the ex-world champion were linked to the excellent coordination of all his pieces and the passed d-pawn. But in order to get this moving, he has to reconcile himself to the loss of another fighting unit of Black's scant army, the c5 pawn.

41...♖c1! 42 ♖a5

In case of 42 ♖a7 the c-pawn comes into play: 42...♖f1+ 43 ♔g3 c4! 44 bxc4 dxc4 45 a4 c3 46 ♖d7+ ♔e2! 47 ♖xc3 ♖f3+ with a draw.

42...♖f1+ 43 ♔g3 ♔e2!

Making way for the foot-soldier! Very modest, but he becomes a general...

44 ♖axc5 ♖f3+! 45 ♔h4 d4 46 ♖d8 d3 47 a4 d2 48 a5 d1=♕ 49 ♖xd1 ♘xd1

The newly promoted general costs White a whole rook. The game did not continue much longer.

50 ♖b5 ♘c3 51 ♖b7 ♔d3 52 a6 ♖f6 53 a7 ♖a6 54 ♔g5 ♘d5 55 ♔f5 ♔c3 Draw.

Topalov - Kasparov
Linares 1999

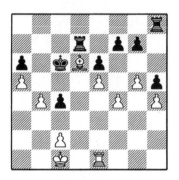

White has "classical" compensation for the exchange in the shape of bishop and pawn. But is this sufficient to save the game? The closed character of the position, with the active bishop on d6, gives White cause for optimism.

33...f6 34 gxf6?
A serious strategical mistake, opening the g-file, on which White can perhaps then exchange rooks. It is worth striving to give the position a closed character—34 g6! ♖h6 35 ♖g1 ♔d5 (or 35...c3?! 36 ♖g3 ♔d5 37 ♖xc3 ♖xg6 38 ♖c5+ ♔e4 39 ♖c6 with an excellent game for White) 36 ♔b2 ♔e4 37 ♔c3 and 37...♔xf4? is not possible because of 38 exf6+! ♖xd6 39 fxg7 ♖d8 40 ♖f1+ ♔e5 41 ♖f8 and White wins.

34...gxf6 35 ♖g1 f5
Wisely not broadening the sphere of activity of the bishop by 35...fxe5?! 36 ♗xe5.

36 ♔d2 ♔d5 37 ♔e3
A gesture would be 37 ♔c3!?, attacking the c4 pawn, since dangerous for Black is 37...♔e4 38 ♔xc4 ♔xf4 39 ♖g6. Black would apparently have to play as in the game, 37...♖hh7 38 ♗f8 ♔e4 39 ♖g6 when he probably can't strengthen his position.

37...♖hh7! 38 ♗f8
Preventing ...♖h7-g7.
38...♖hf7
38...♖df7? loses after 39 ♖d1+ ♔c6 40 ♖d6+ ♔c7 41 ♖xa6!.
39 ♗h6 ♖h7
To gain time on the clock in time-trouble. 39...♔c6 40 ♖g6 ♖fe7 (Black's pieces are too passive after 42...♖de7 43 ♔d4 ♔b5 44 ♔c3) 41 ♗f8 changes little. It is also not easy to assess the consequences of 39...c3 40 ♔d3 ♖c7 41 ♖g8 ♖fd7 42 ♖b8 ♖c4 43 ♖b6.
40 ♖g6?
The decisive mistake, now Black wins in great tactical style. White shouldn't avoid repetition. It seems that V.Topalov overestimated his chances, otherwise in time trouble he would have repeated the position —40 ♗f8 ♖hf7 41 ♗h6.
Better than the text was even the tactical 40 ♖g8!? ♖b7! (losing is 40...♖xh6?? 41 ♖c8) 41 ♖c8 ♖hc7 42 ♖a8 ♖xb4 43 ♖xa6 ♖d7, after which Black's chances are still preferable.
40...♖b7! 41 ♗f8 ♖hf7 42 ♗d6
He has to return to base, since losing is 42 ♖f6 ♖bd7! 43 c3 ♖xf6 44 exf6 e5 etc. But now Black wins the struggle for the g-file.
42...♖g7 43 ♖g5
The last frontier of defence.
43...♖bf7 44 c3
Opening the d3 and b3 squares for the black pieces, but this position is an original zugzwang. Everything is bad: 44 ♗c5 ♖xg5 45 hxg5 h4; 44 ♔f3 ♔d4 45 ♖xh5 ♖h7!; 44 ♖xh5 ♖g3+ (or 44...♖h7).
44...♔c6 45 ♔f3 ♔b5 46 ♗c5
There is also no joy in 46 ♖xh5 ♖h7.
46...♔a4 47 ♗d4 ♖d7!

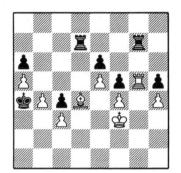

Preparing the removal of White's key defensive piece.

48 ♔e3

He has to defend the bishop. On 48 ♖xh5 would have followed 48...♖xd4! 49 cxd4 c3 50 ♔e2 c2 51 ♔d2 ♔b3 52 ♖g5 ♖xg5 53 fxg5 ♔b2 and Black queens.

48...♔b3 49 ♔e2 ♖xg5!

Accurately calculating the approaching queen ending.

50 fxg5

After 50 hxg5 h4 he has to reckon with the passed h-pawn—51 ♔f3 h3 52 g6 ♖g7 53 ♔g3 ♖xg6+ 54 ♔xh3 ♔c2 loses even more quickly.

50...♖xd4

It was possible to proceed even without the exchange sacrifice— 50...f4 51 b5 (what else?) 51...axb5 52 a6 b4 53 a7 ♖d8.

51 cxd4 c3 52 g6 c2 53 g7 c1=♕ 54 g8=♕ ♕c4+ 55 ♔e3 ♔c3!

A beautiful example proving positional factors and piece coordination can outweigh material even in a queen ending

56 ♕d8 ♕d3+ 57 ♔f4

Or 57 ♔f2 f4! 58 ♕g5 ♕xd4+ 59 ♔e2 ♕d2+ 60 ♔f1 ♔e3.

57...♕d2+ 58 ♔f3 ♕d1+ 59 ♔e3

There is no saving himself by 59 ♔f2 f4 60 ♕c8+ ♔d2.

59...♕g1+ 60 ♔e2 ♕g2+ 61 ♔e3 f4+ White resigned.

After 62 ♔xf4 ♔d3 63 ♕g5 ♕f2 is mate.

And in the concluding section we look at an ending which has theoretical significance for the study of methods of resistance by bishop against rook.

Gufeld - Bagirov
Leningrad 1963

With the move 56...♖e1! Black would easily achieve victory, as the rook cuts off the enemy king two files away from the passed c-pawn: 57 ♗c3 ♖e6 58 ♔f4 (or 58 ♗d2 c4 59 ♗e3 c3 60 ♔e2 ♖d6) 58...c4 59 ♔f5 ♔e7 60 f4 ♖e3, and the pawn slips by to queen. But in the diagram position it is *White's* move and this allows him to draw his king closer to the black pawns, which proves to be a highly significant factor.

56 ♔e4 ♖d1

If 56...♔d7, then 57 ♔d5! ♖c1 58 f4 c4 59 ♗e5 c3 60 ♔c4 c2 61 ♔c3, with a draw.

57 ♗f8! c4 58 ♗b4 ♔d7 59 f4

59...Rc1

It would be more difficult to defend after 59...Rd3!. The bishop does not have the right to abandon the e1-a5 diagonal, while the king is riveted to the e4 square. We can convince ourselves of this: 60 Bc5? Rh3! 61 Be3 c3 62 Bc1 c2 and 63...Rh1 or 60 Ke5? c3, and Black wins. So White should play 60 f5!, placing his hopes on the pawns as diversionary bait. Let us look at two possible plans for Black to play for the win.

1) The king goes to the kingside: 60...Ke8 61 Ba5 Kf7 62 Be1 Kg7 63 Ba5 Kf6 64 Be1 Kg5 65 Bb4 (further progress of the black king by 65...Kg4 is contra-indicated because of 66 f6 with an easy draw) 65...Rh3 (65...Rd7 66 Bc3) 66 Kd4! (mistaken would be 66 Be7+? Kh5, and Black wins) 66...Rh4+ 67 Kc5! (paradoxical, but the white king should hold against the enemy pawns, from the rear; losing is 67 Kc3? Kxf5 68 Bc5 Ke6 69 Bd4 Kd5) 67...Kxf5 68 Bc3, with a draw, since Black is in no position to avert the manoeuvre Bc3-d4 and Kc5xc4.

2) The king goes to the queenside: 60...Kd8! (Black's objective is to obtain a position with the king on d7 and the bishop on b4, with White to move; 60...Kc6 does not work

because of 61 f6; now, however, on 61 f6?, follows 61...Ke8 and 62...Kf7, winning the white pawn) 61 Be1 Ke7 62 Ba5 Kd6 63 Bb4+ Kd7 64 Ba5 Kc6 65 Be1 (it becomes clear that there is nothing in 65...Kb5 66 f6! or 65...Kc5 66 Bf2+) 65...Rh3 (Black's last try) 66 f6!. Draw! On 66...Kd6 White replies 67 Kd4, while in the event of 66...c3 there are two possibilities: 67 Bxc3! and 67 f7.

All this analaysis remains behind the scenes. We return to the game continuation after Black's move 59...Rc1.

60 Kd4 Kc6 61 Bc3 Kb5 62 f5 Rd1+ 63 Ke4 Kc5 64 f6 Kd6 65 Be5+ Ke6 66 Bc3 Rd3

In the end, Black goes for the plan we have looked at, but also here it does not bring success. It was necessary to identify an important nuance: the bishop can occupy only two squares along the long diagonal, a1 and b2, and in neither case is it possible to retreat it to the d4 and e5 squares in view of Rd3-h3.

67 Ba1 Kf7 68 Bb2 Kg8 69 Ba1 Kf8 70 Bb2 Ke8

The game continued to the 116th move and ended in a draw after vain attempts by Black. White's method of defence has been visually demonstrated and therefore here we can put a full stop.

After I had adjourned this ending, Geller and Spassky at some point asked me: "Eddy, you are dragging it out, why don't you resign?" And I bet the pair of them ten shashliks, that the position on the board was drawn. In reply the grandmasters made a laughing stock of me. Naturally, the shashliks, which they treated me to after I had concluded peace with Bagirov, seemed unusually tasty. Is it possible that there is an echo of these ten shashliks in the surplus weight I carry around nowadays?

3 An extra piece

Not infrequently, sharp play is echoed in the ending, where, for a piece, the opposing side has two or three pawns. If these are connected and sufficiently far away from the centre, they can serve as sufficient compensation for the piece.

Gufeld - Smyslov
Riga 1975

White has for the piece just two pawns, but this does not guarantee Black a quiet life, since the pawns may quickly gain victory in the future.

44 a5!
At first sight, White can capture the last pawn, 44 ♖xa7, but then after 44...♖c5 45 ♔c3 ♘f4! the black knight arrives in time on the queenside.

But also in chess applies the proverb: fools rush in... Activity of the rook is more important than a pawn.

44...♖f4
It becomes clear why White did not hurry to dispatch the rook on a mission to a7. Now, on 44...♖c5,

follows 45 ♖e2! with an attack on both knights.

In the meantime, however, the impression seems to be that the pawns are held up. The threat is 45...♖xc4, and if 45 b6, then 45...axb6 46 axb6 ♘e4+ 47 ♔d3 ♘c5+. And yet....

45 c5!!
White gives up not a pawn, but the exchange. Now already the active pawns are worth more than a rook.

45...♘e4+ 46 ♖xe4! ♖xe4
Black has an extra rook, but the white pawn has advanced further. Is it enough for a win? As before, it seems, it is not. By way of example, 47 ♘xa7 ♔e6, and the black king step by step has time to get to the queenside.

47 b6!!
Time is more important than a pawn! If 47...axb6, then 48 cxb6! (in the endgame it is necessary to try and take the pawn not towards the centre, but away from it—the further away, the more dangerous) 48...♘e3 49 b7 ♖e8 50 a6 ♘c4+ 51 ♔d3 ♘d6 52 b8=♕ ♖xb8 53 ♘xb8 and the ending is winning for White. For example: 53...♘c8 54 ♔c4 ♔e7 55 ♔c5 ♔d8 56 ♔c6 ♘e7+ 57 ♔b7 ♘c8 58 ♘c6+ ♔d7 59 ♘e5+ ♔d8 60 ♔b8 ♘b6 61 a7 ♘a8 62 ♔b7 (62 ♔xa8 ♔c7!—

draw) 62...♘c7 63 ♘c4 ♘a8 64 ♘e3 ♘c7 65 ♘d5 ♘a8 66 ♔c6, achieving, as say the study composers, domination of the knight over the knight! But for Black, it would seem, there is a sufficient defence.

47...♖e8

Now, on 48 bxa7, Black is ready to reply 48...♖a8, while on 48 b7— 48...♔e6, and the king gets over in time.

48 ♘xa7!

Again a pawn is more important than a rook. Now the black king already does not get over: 48...♔e6 49 b7 ♔d7 50 a6 ♘e3 51 ♘c8! ♔c7 52 ♘d6 with the double threat 53 ♘xe8 and 53 a7 or 50...♔c7 51 ♘b5+ ♔c6 52 ♘d6 ♖d8 53 a7, and the pawn promotes to a queen.

But, is it possible to get over with the knight? Alas, no! On 48...♘f4 with the idea, if the opportunity arises, to exploit the move ...♖e2+ there would follow 49 a6! ♔e6 50 ♘c8!! ♔d7 51 a7 and White wins. The following variation also says much about the "underwater reefs": 50 b7 ♔d7 51 c6+ ♔c7 52 ♘c8 ♖e2+! 53 ♔c3 ♖a2 54 a7 ♖xa7 55 ♘xa7 ♘d5+ 56 ♔c4 ♘e7 57 ♘b5+ ♔b8 58 ♔c5 ♘xc6! with a draw. Possibly, this is why Black decides to take the knight along the other route.

48...♘e3 49 a6 ♘c4+

A little more tenacious was 49...♔e6! (with the little trap 50 ♔xe3 ♔d5+), coming closer to the pawns and knight and king, to take the opportunity to meet direct play 50 c6? ♘c4+ or 50 b7 ♔d7. The way to victory lies in the sacrifice of the last piece: 50 ♘c8!! ♘c4+ 51 ♔c3 ♘a5 (or 51... ♘xb6 52 ♘xb6 ♖e7 53 ♔c4 ♖a7 54 ♔b5 ♖c7 55 c6 ♔d6 56 ♘c4+ ♔d5 57 ♘a5, with the decisive threat of a king

invasion on b6) 52 b7 ♘c6 53 a7 ♘xa7 54 b8=♕ ♘xc8, and the queen and pawn should overcome rook and knight.

50 ♔c3 ♘e5 51 b7 ♔e6 52 c6 ♔d5 53 c7 Black resigned.

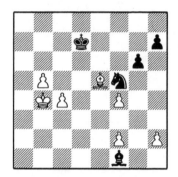

Here the pair of passed pawns are not so mobile as in the previous example. Black has everything ready to blockade them. However, due to the fact that his king has been forced considerably far away from his pawns, it is not easy to gain victory and the further course of the struggle is not short of fine points.

41...♘d6!

A move which decides the fate of the pawn-pair. Black is faced with the alternatives of losing a pawn or exchanging the last piece. He prefers a temporary initiative to the inevitable paralysis after 42 ♗xd6 ♔xd6 43 c5+ ♔d5 44 c6 ♔d6 45 ♔a5 ♔c7! (after 45...♔c5?? 46 f5! he might even lose, since the promotion square of the c-pawn is recovered) 46 ♔a6 h5 and, after all the pawns are blockaded, Black sacrifices the bishop for the queenside pawns and obtains a winning pawn ending: 47 ♔a5 h4 48 ♔a6 h3 49 ♔a5 ♗g2 50 ♔a6 ♗xc6 51 bxc6

&xc6 52 &a5 &c5 or 47 h4 &e2 48 &a5 &f3 49 &a6 &xc6! 50 bxc6 &xc6 51 f3 &d6.

42 b6 ♘xc4 43 b7

Together with the b7 pawn, White has at least a chance of breaking through with his king to his opponent's pawns.

43...♘xe5 44 fxe5 &c7 45 &c5 &xb7 46 &d6 &c8 47 &e7

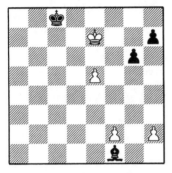

If he manages to win the h7 pawn, then in turn will also come the g6 pawn. For example, in the event of 47...&d3, after 48 e6 he has to play 48...&c4 49 &f7 &d8 50 &g7 and White has achieved his objective. However, a surprise awaits White.

47...g5!!

Black is ready to part with one of his pawns and even splits the f-pawns for the sake of a firm block-ade formed by the pawn phalanx along the b1-h7 diagonal.

48 &f6 g4 49 &g5 &h3!

49...&e2 leads only to a draw: 50 &h6 &d7 51 &xh7 &e6 52 &g6 &xe5 53 &g5 &f3 54 &h4 and White exchanges the last pawn.

50 &f6 &d8 51 &f7 &f1 52 e6 &c4 53 &g7 &e7 54 &xh7 &xe6 55 &g6 &e5 56 &g5 &e6

Now after 57 &g6 &f5+ 58 &g5 &d7 he has to allow the opposition. Therefore **White resigned**.

Situations also occur, when all the remaining forces are to be found on a single flank. In this case the defending side is obliged to avoid an exchange of pieces, since with pawns only he will hardly manage to put up resistance. Chances of defence are usually increased with the reduction of pawn material. However, with the presence of queens, the defending side is denied the possibility of advancing pawns since his king might fall under attack. However, as shown by the following example, "staying put" also does not secure a quiet life.

Gufeld - Damjanović
Skopje 1971

Despite the fact that the pawn chain is fixed, Black has a difficult position since he has to reckon with the possibility of an attack on the king.

46 ♕b2!

Above all to centralise the queen, with its sights set on the weak f6 square.

46...♕c5 47 &e4 ♕e7 48 ♕e5

Already 49 ♕xh5+ is threatened.

48...&g8 49 ♕g5! ♕e8

He has to go back.

50 ♕f6 &h7 51 g4

After the queen has been chained to the king there begins a pawn attack.

51...hxg4 52 h5 ⌂h6 53 hxg6 fxg6 54 ⌂g3!

The start of a victorious raid with the king, which is included in an attack on its counterpart.

54...⌂h7 55 ⌂xg4 ⌂h6 56 f4 ⌂h7 57 ⌂g5 ♕b5+ 58 f5! exf5 59 ♕f7+ ⌂h8 60 ⌂h6 Black resigned.

With the presence of rooks the defending side gets the chance to advance pawns with the aim of provoking their exchange. Therefore realising a material advantage sometimes requires considerable effort.

Honfi - Gufeld
Kislovodsk 1968

In this rare endgame position the game was adjourned. Home analysis showed that the win is far from easy. Exchanging pawns is contra-indicated; the h1 square is light, while the bishop is dark-squared, this is also something to discuss. I intended this plan: to pile up on the f2 pawn (the root of the pawn tree f2-g3-h4) and, above all, to force White to advance one of his pawns. To talk is easy—to do, considerably more difficult.

41 ⌷e2 ⌷b3 42 ⌷e8

The threat is 42...⌷b2, but it is necessary for White to retain the rooks.

42...⌷b2 43 ⌷f8 ⌂e4 44 ⌷e8+ ⌂d5 45 ⌷e3 ⌴d4 46 ⌷f3

The pile-up is complete, how to proceed further? The manoeuvre ⌷b2-b6-f6 does not achieve its objective: 46...⌷b6 47 ⌷a3! ⌷f6 48 ⌷a2, and nothing has changed.

46...⌷a2 47 ⌷f5+ ⌂c4 48 ⌷f7

In this position the only way to victory. Now he should play 48...⌷a7 49 ⌷f8 ⌷a6 50 ⌷e8 ⌂d3 etc., which happens only after ten moves.

48...⌂d3 49 ⌷f3+ ⌂e2 50 ⌷f4 ⌷d2 51 ⌷e4+ ⌂d1 52 ⌷f4

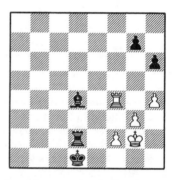

At this moment I already wrote down the move 52...g5 on my score-sheet. There remained only to reproduce it on the board, but then something caused me to have doubts about the pawn advance—though, going into the adjournment, I was vowing not to change it. Again I looked at the variation 52...g5 53 hxg5 hxg5 54 ⌷f5 g4 55 ⌷f4 ⌷xf2+ (it was precisely this possibility that tempted me: 56 ⌷xf2 ⌴xf2 57 ⌂xf2 ⌂d2, and I win, but...) 56 ⌂h1!! (seeing this move, I sweated profusely) 56...⌷xf4 57 gxf4 ⌂e2 58 ⌂g2 ⌴f2 59 f5 ⌂e3 60 f6, and a draw (later it became clear that the same theme also occurs after 55 ♖g5! ♖xf2+ 56 ♔h1!!). I crossed out the move 52...g5??.

52...♔e2 53 ♖e4+ ♔d3 54 ♖f4 ♖a2 55 ♖f3+ ♔c4

Stronger is 55...♔e2 56 ♖f4 ♖d2 57 ♖e4+ ♔d1 58 ♖f4 g6! and White is in zugzwang. For example: 59 ♖f7 ♔e1 60 ♖e7+ ♖e2 or 59 ♔f1 g5 60 hxg5 hxg5 61 ♖f5 g4 62 ♖f4 ♖xf2+ 63 ♖xf2 ♗xf2 64 ♔xf2 ♔d2.

56 ♖f7

After having had a "cold shower" on the 52nd move, I happily returned to the position reached after White's 48th move.

56...♖a7! 57 ♖f8 ♖a6 58 ♖e8

No help is 58 ♔h3 ♖f6 59 ♖xf6 ♗xf6 60 ♔g4 ♗d4 61 f4 ♗f2 62 ♔f5 ♗xg3 63 ♔g6 ♗xf4 64 ♔xg7 ♔d5 65 ♔g6 ♔e4 66 ♔h5 ♔f3 and Black wins.

58...♔d3!

Now White's rook cannot go to the second rank to defend the f2 pawn.

59 ♖e7 ♖f6 60 f3

The crowning of Black's plan: the advance of the white pawn has been provoked, obtaining an important square for invasion into the enemy camp. The rest is simple.

60...♖f5 61 ♖d7 ♖b5 62 ♖e7 ♖e5 63 ♖d7 ♖e2+ 64 ♔h3 ♔e3 65 h5 ♗c3 66 ♖f7 ♖f2 67 f4 ♔f3 68 ♖e7 ♖c2 69 ♖d7 ♖d2 70 ♖c7 ♗d4 71 ♖b7 ♖d1 72 ♖b3+ ♗e3 73 ♔h2 ♖e1 74 ♖b7 ♗f2 75 ♖xg7 ♗g1+ White resigned.

Gufeld - Ribli
Camaguey 1974

In order to set about the realisation of his material advantage it remains for White to gather his forces together into a "fist". Therefore Black should hurry to display maximum activity.

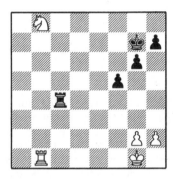

45...h5

Z.Ribli preoccupied himself with this, though, possibly on general considerations, he should play 45...♖c2. In this case, in order to free the king, White has to reply h2-h3, creating a lever for the black pawns, since after 46 ♖b7+ ♔h6 47 ♘d7 ♔g5 48 ♘f8, he has to reckon with 48...♖c1+ 49 ♔f2 ♖c2+. However this also does not save Black.

46 ♘d7 g5

Now, on 46...♖c2, possible is 47 ♘e5 ♔f6 48 ♘f3.

47 ♘e5 ♖a4

Worth considering is 47...♖c5 48 ♘f3 f4.

48 ♘f3 g4 49 ♖b7+ ♔h6 50 ♖b6+ ♔g7 51 ♖b7+ ♔h6 52 ♖b6+ ♔g7 53 ♘e1 h4 54 ♖c6 f4

And here more stubborn is 54...♖a2 55 ♖c2 ♖a3.

55 ♔f1 ♖e4 56 ♖d6 ♖a4 57 h3

Undermining is a characteristic method for breaking up a pawn phalanx. Now Black has a choice between 57...gxh3 58 gxh3 ♖a3 59 ♘d3 and 57...f3 58 gxf3 gxh3 59 ♖d2 ♔f6 60 ♔g1 ♖a1 61 ♖e2, which does not save him. Therefore he prefers to lay down his arms.

8 Psychological Advantage

It cannot be ruled out that this heading might prompt a sceptical smile from some of our readers. The fact that an advantage can be material, positional, or a combination of both, we know very well, but a psychological advantage...

We will not be jumping to conclusions, but better to let specialists in the area of psychological chess creativity have their say. Here are the words of Doctor of Psychological Science, N.Krogius: "In the chess struggle, as in other spheres of human activity, we have two sides —objective and subjective. These cannot oppose each other nor can chess just take the objective side, only scientific theory—laws and principles of theory are applied to the practice of living people, alike or different".

How often it happens that a position assumes a drawish character, but the defender must make "only" moves, whereas at the same time the opponent risks practically nothing. The probability of mistakes from the defending side in such situations considerably increases. Linked to these mistakes can be definite character traits. If a chessplayer is stubborn, strong-willed, calm and collected, then it is possible to hope for a successful defence. If he lacks one of these necessary components the ending might be lamentable.

There is one more and highly interesting detail. By not winning a won position, every chessplayer, of course, falls apart—it hurts to lose half a point. But even more grief is caused by an objectively drawn position. The loss is half a point in the first and second cases, equally, but is perceived as a painful and unquestionable defeat.

From the mathematical point of view all this looks paradoxical, illogical, but it is *people* that play chess, and not machines (we are not looking here at the fashionable trend of playing against computers). Sometimes emotion turns out to have a stronger influence on the psyche of a man than obvious factors. It is particularly difficult for him to cope when the game assumes a complicated character and one aspect of a formal advantage changes to another.

Here is an example from the practice of one of the leading specialists of the endgame in the 20th century, Akiba Rubinstein.

This example might also have been looked at, to the same extent, in chapter 5 under the theme of playing with opposite-coloured bishops. But, in the present case, there are also obvious psychological implications: Black is doomed to long-term waiting. Then again, to exploit his chances in full measure, Rubinstein has to look consistently at two types of endings: one with queens and one with only opposite-coloured bishops. White's manoeuvres are so deep that great accuracy in defence is required. And although, throughout, the struggle balances on the edge of a draw, Grünfeld cannot endure such a protracted trial.

Rubinstein - Grünfeld
Karlsbad 1929

White's small advantage lies in his more active bishop and better pawn structure. He might organise a complex attack on the c5 and f7 pawns by ♕e2-f2 or ♕e2-c4 (after a preliminary ♗c4-b3). But, as we know, upon the presence of opposite-coloured bishops, the win of a pawn does not always lead to victory, a more important factor is to maintain the initiative.

25 g3 ♔g7

The method of realising a small advantage, demonstrated by Rubinstein, is highly instructive. First he improves the position of his king, at the same time limiting the sphere of activity of the enemy bishop. Grünfeld does not immediately sense the danger, he believes in the inpenetrability of his position and sticks to waiting tactics. And wrongly! He should activate his

bishop by 25...♗g5. In this case, on 26 ♕f2, he could offer an exchange of queens by 26...♕f6 27 ♕xf6 ♗xf6 28 ♗a6 ♗g5 29 ♔e2! ♗c1 30 b3 ♔g7 31 ♗b7 with a transfer to an ending with opposite-coloured bishops (but what guarantee is there that it can be won?) or choose 25...♕e7!?, in a more favourable light in comparison to the game.

26 h4! ♕d7 27 ♔g2 ♕d6 28 ♗b3 ♕d7 29 ♕c4 ♕d2+

Upon passive defence, 29...♕e7, White moves the king over to e2, preventing a queen invasion on the d-file, and then rearranges his pieces: queen—on a6, bishop—on a4, to attack the c6 pawn.

30 ♔f3 ♔h6 31 ♕xc5

The only real way to maintain the initiative. After the exchange of queens, 31 ♕e2 ♕xe2+ 32 ♔xe2 ♔g7 33 ♗a4 ♗e7 34 ♗xc6 f5, chances of a draw appear for Black.

31...♕xb2

Exchanging queens would show more persistence: 31...♕d3+ 32 ♕e3+ (32 ♔f2 ♕d2+) 32...♕xe3+ 33 ♔xe3 g5 etc.

32 ♕e3+!

Very refined! The king is driven towards the f7 pawn, which in the future will be attacked with tempo.

32...♔g7 33 ♕xa7 ♕xc3+ 34 ♔g4 ♕d3! 35 ♕xf7+ ♔h6

Black cleverly defends with the king: on 36 ♕xf6 follows 36...♕xe4+ 37 ♔h3 ♕h1+ with perpetual check. However, wise Akiba has calculated everything...

36 ♕c4!

A worthy finale to the far-seeing raid of the queen along the route c4-c5-e3-a7-f7-c4. White offers an exchange of queens in a principally different situation: the distant passed a-pawn guarantees a win even with opposite-coloured bishops. Now already Black is forced to avoid an exchange of queens.

36...♕d2!

Beautiful harmony between attack and defence! White plays on the light squares, Black—on the dark. He creates the cunning masked threat of 37...♗xh4! (38 ♔xh4?? ♕h2+ 39 ♔g4 ♕h5 mate).

37 ♕f1 ♔g7 38 ♕d1 ♕g2 39 ♕f3 ♕d2

Encroaching on the monopoly of the light squares by the threat of 40...♕d7.

40 ♔h3 ♕d8

On 40...♕d4, also follows 41 g4 and he has to retreat.

41 ♕c3 ♕d6 42 g4!

An important moment. The further strengthening of the position is linked to the inclusion of extra resources. White prepares an attack on the king.

42...♗d8 43 g5 ♗b6 44 ♕f3!

The culmination of the manoeuvre, begun on the 32nd move. Black is forced to exchange queens, after which the distant passed a-pawn comes into play.

44...♕f8

On 44...♕e7 White would continue the attack: 45 h5! gxh5 (also losing is 45...♕xg5 46 ♕f7+ ♔h6 47 ♕f8+ ♔xh5 48 ♗d1+) 46 ♕xh5 and the black queen cannot at the

same time repulse the mating threats on the h6 and f7 squares.

45 ♕xf8+ ♔xf8

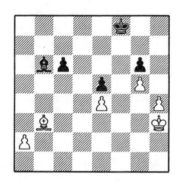

The second stage of realising the advantage: the ending with opposite-coloured bishops. Rubinstein also plays this in virtuoso style.

46 ♔g4 ♗e3 47 ♗a4! c5 48 ♗b3

The result of the manoeuvre ♗b3-a4-b3, "inviting" the pawn to c5. Now the blockaded c5 and e5 pawns will hamper the freedom of manoeuvre of his bishop.

48...♗d2 49 ♗c4! ♔g7 50 a4 ♔f8 51 ♔f3!

Now it becomes clear that the black bishop is limited to the short e1-a5 diagonal, since it is obliged to watch over the a-pawn. The black king is also limited in its movement —it has to reckon with the threat of the appearance of two passed pawns on the kingside.

51...♔e7 52 ♔e2 ♗a5 53 ♔d1 ♗b4 54 ♗e2 ♔d6 55 h5! gxh5 56 ♗xh5 ♔e7 57 ♔c2 c4 58 ♗e2 c3?

Exhausted by the protracted defence, Grünfeld makes a mistake. He should give up the c4 pawn. After 58...♔f7 59 ♗xc4+ ♔g6, Black captures the g5 pawn and has time to detain the a-pawn. For example: 60 ♔b3 ♗d2 61 ♗d5

♔xg5 62 ♔c4 ♔f6 63 ♔b5 ♔e7 64 a5 ♔d8 with a draw.

59 ♔b3 ♔f7 60 ♗d3 ♗a5 61 ♔c4 ♔g6 62 ♔b5

Also possible was 62 ♔d5 ♗c7 63 ♔c6 ♗d8 64 ♔d6, but Rubinstein shines with another beautiful idea. He undertakes a manoeuvre, the aim of which becomes clear after five moves.

62...♗d8 63 a5 ♗xg5 64 a6 ♗e3 65 ♔c6 ♔g5 66 ♔b7 ♔f4 67 ♗b1!!

White gains an important tempo, since the black bishop impedes its own king. An immediate win of the bishop, 67 a7?! ♗xa7 68 ♔xa7 ♔e3 69 ♗b1 ♔d2 70 ♔b6 ♔c1 71 ♗d3 ♔d2, would lead only to a draw.

67...♗d4 68 a7 ♗xa7 69 ♔xa7 ♔e3 70 ♔b6 Black resigned.

An amazing endgame, rich in ideas!

Whoever has had to defend a position with an isolated d5 pawn, will know the agony of trying to maintain equality. You see, with each exchange, hopes of counterplay run dry, while an unpleasant endgame becomes all the more real. There is no doubt about the psychological pressure on the opponent!

Ivanchuk - Korchnoi
Lvov 2000

An old story. Before you is the consequence of the Tarrasch variation of the French defence (1 e4 e6 2 d4 d5 3 ♘d2 c5 4 exd5 exd5), of which V.Korchnoi is a great specialist. But in this game he does not manage to cope with the problems posed by the white pieces rotating around the isolated pawn. Though these do not threaten much, they twist like a knife blade.

31...g5

By taking away his control of the f5 square, Black creates new weaknesses in his position. V.Korchnoi could hardly have forgotten Nimzowitsch's maxim about the need to create a second weakness in the opponent's position in order to realise a positional advantage. Rather this activity is the consequence of the exclusion of other candidate moves. Where can he move? The knight f6 is tied to the defence of the f7 pawn, but there is the threat to advance the g- and h-pawns and drive it away (31...h5? 32 g4). 31...b5? does not work because of 32 ♕xf6+! and 31...♕d6? because of 32 ♘xg6!. After 31...♕e7 32 ♕d4, Black cannot endure the pin on the long diagonal and has to return 32...♕c5. But the choice, as before for White, among others, is the need to accurately assess the consequences of the knight ending: 33 ♕xc5!? bxc5 34 b4 cxb4 35 cxb4 axb4 36 axb4, where the b-pawn easily breaks through to b6, diverting the knight away to stop it.

32 ♕d2 ♘e4 33 ♕e2 ♕d6 34 ♘g4 ♕e6 35 ♕d3 h5 36 ♕d4+ ♔g8 37 ♘e3 ♘f6 38 f3 ♔f8 39 ♔f2 ♔e8 40 b4!

And here is the consequence of the weakening of the f5 square. White will create a distant passed pawn. Black cannot prevent this: his queen is not in a position to control all the squares of invasion.

40...axb4 41 cxb4 ♔d7 42 a4 ♔c8 43 ♔e2 h4 44 ♔d2 ♔b7 45 ♔d3 ♔a8 46 ♔c3 ♕c6+ 47 ♔b3 ♕e6 48 ♔b2 ♔b7 49 ♔a3 ♕d6 50 ♔b3 ♕e6 51 a5 bxa5 52 bxa5 ♔a6 53 ♔b4 ♕d6+ 54 ♕c5

54...♕b8+?!

An obvious consequence of White's psychological advantage. V.Korchnoi loses his nerve and is "ruined" through activity. He should continue to control the b6 and f5 squares with his queen. More deserving of approval is 54...♕e6 as nothing significant is threatened. On 55 ♘c2 possible is 55...♔b7 and, after 56 ♘d4, activity by 56...♕e1+ is now appropriate.

55 ♔c3 ♕b1?

According to the proverb: "it never rains but it pours". But, you know, everything was still not lost and 55...♕e5+! 56 ♔c2 allows Black to hold the defence. True, already insufficient here is 56...♕e6?! in view of 57 ♔d2 ♘d7 (57... ♔b7? 58 ♕b5+ ♔a7 59 ♘c2) 58 ♕c8+ ♔xa5 59 ♕d8+ ♔b4 60 ♕xg5 d4 61 ♘c2+ ♔c4 62 ♕xh4 with advantage to White. But 56...♘d7!? allows him to defend: 57 ♕c6+ ♔xa5 58 ♕xd5+ ♕xd5 59 ♘xd5 ♔b5 60

♔d3 ♔c5 61 ♔e4 ♔d6 62 ♔d4 f5 and everything is in order for Black.

56 ♘c2 Black resigned.

In the ability to exploit the psychological elements in the chess struggle, Mikhail Botvinnik could join ranks with Emanuel Lasker.

Suetin - Botvinnik
Moscow 1952

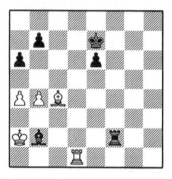

The position has assumed a drawish character, since Black's extra pawn presents not so much a material as a psychological advantage. Black does not risk losing, but can hope for an error from the opponent. Therefore a more collected game is required of Black: he should be attentive and observe a certain accuracy.

58...a5 59 bxa5 ♗c3+ 60 ♔b3 ♗xa5 61 ♗b5 b6 62 ♔c4 ♔f6 63 ♔d4 ♖f4+ 64 ♔e3 ♔e5 65 ♖h1 ♖e4+ 66 ♔d3 ♖g4 67 ♖h5+ ♔d6 68 ♖h8 ♔e5 69 ♖h5+ ♔f4

Black waits, striving to gain time before the next control.

70 ♖h3 ♖g8 71 ♖h4+ ♔e5 72 ♖h5+ ♔d6 73 ♖h4?!

"Lulled to sleep" in a simple position, White commits the first inaccuracy. It was necessary to defend the rook on the third rank—73 ♖h3. But could A.Suetin imagine that his king would land in a mating net in the very centre of the board?

73...罝g3+ 74 含e4?!

The king does nothing here; necessary was 74 含d4. However White is affected by a stereotyped optical illusion that his king will be safer on the white squares where things seem calmer...

74...皇d2

75 皇d3?

How strange that this natural move loses the game. It was still not too late to play 75 含d4 or 75 罝h5. White continues to "find" a whole series of mistakes...

75...皇g5! 76 罝h5?

White does not want to part with his a4 pawn, 76 罝h8 罝g4+ 77 含f3 罝f4+ 78 含e2 罝xa4, but overlooks a cunning mating net.

76...含c5! White resigned.

It was only possible to save himself from the mating net at the cost of transferring to a hopeless pawn ending: 77 含e5 罝xd3 78 罝xg5 罝d5+.

Gheorghiu - Beliavsky
Interzonal, Moscow 1982

This game was played in the last round of the interzonal tournament. F.Gheorghiu had no appetite for a

serious struggle and was happy to settle for a draw.

But for A.Beliavsky only a win would do: in this case he would qualify for the Candidates. The difference in motivation tells on the character of play: White is striving only to maintain equality, Black to get the better of it.

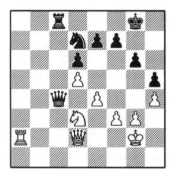

White has spent the whole game standing in a kind of "pit", and has only managed to hold his "ground" at the cost of weakening the periphery. Therefore the position in the diagram, though it looks roughly equal, is not drawn. And it is not surprising that F.Gheorghiu, exhausted by prolonged psychological pressure from A.Beliavsky, loses his nerve. In mutual time-trouble he "cuts loose" with activity, underestimating the fact that his exposed king might serve as an object of attack.

39 ②b4?

The knight transfers to the beautiful, but useless, c6 square, whereas it was necessary to cover the king by 39 ②f2, trying to prevent the penetration to his rear by the black pieces. Without delay, A.Beliavsky seizes his opportunity.

39...罝b8! 40 罝b2

An illusion, since now he will only manage to free himself from the pin at too high a price. He should return with 40 ♘d3 ♖b3 41 ♘c1 ♖b1 (after 41...♖c3 42 ♘e2 ♖d3 43 ♕c2 White defends himself) 42 ♖c2 ♕b5 43 ♕e2 ♕b6 44 ♕f2 ♘c5! and, though Black has achieved a great deal, White can hold on.

40...♘e5!

Zugzwang! On 41 ♔f2? winning is 41...♖xb4!. White has to go back with the knight to a distant area, from where it will not return.

41 ♘a2 ♖xb2 42 ♕xb2 ♕d3 43 ♕f2 ♕a3!

The threat is 44...♘f3 and so he has to weaken himself further.

44 f4 ♘g4 45 ♕d2?

Losing quickly. It was still possible to go with the flow by the further weakening, 45 ♕e2 ♘f6, with the threat to capture on e4.

45...♘e3+ 46 ♔f2

Or 46 ♔g1 ♘c4 47 ♕f2 ♕d3.

46...♘c4 47 ♕e2 ♘b2!

Knight traps knight! On 48 ♘c1 follows 48...♕c5+.

White resigned.

Gelfand - Topalov
Amsterdam 1996

Isn't it true that, in terms of the weakening of the white periphery, this position reminds us of the preceding example? And yet, with such limited material, it is hard to be certain that White will lose. The impression is such that he can simply stay put. But this is deceptive, as indicated by the assessment of B.Gelfand himself: "An unpleasant position. It is necessary to play very accurately, you see, the difference in the positions of the knights is significant: his is in the attack, mine in defence". Going deeper into the position, other features come to light. For example, The f2 and g3 squares are inaccessible to the white king because of a queen sacrifice on c3, followed by ...♘f6xe4+.

In short, Black's psychological advantage is obvious: he is not risking anything, whereas very careful play is required from White.

36...♕a3! 37 ♔g2 ♕b2+ 38 ♔g1

38 ♘e2 is not possible because of 38...♕c2.

38...♕c1+ 39 ♔g2 ♕d2+ 40 ♔f1 h6!

A knight transfer to g5 (after 41...♘h7) is threatened and, if White doesn't do anything, then he loses the e4 pawn.

41 ♘e2 ♕d1+ 42 ♔f2 ♕c2 43 ♔e3 ♕b1 44 ♘g3 ♕e1+ 45 ♔d3 ♕g1 46 h4?!

B.Gelfand cannot put up with the "sleepy" play and decides to threaten h4-h5, but he does not take into account that this weakens the g4 pawn. He should play 46 ♕e3.

46...♕b1+ 47 ♔e2?

But this is already serious. Necessary was 47 ♔d2, not allowing the queen to the c-file (47...♕b2+ 48 ♔d1).

47...♕c2+ 48 ♔f1

On 48 ♔e3 also follows 48...♕c8! and on 49 g5—49...hxg5 50 hxg5 ♕c1+ 51 ♔e2 ♕xg5.

48...♕c8! 49 h5

49 g5 loses a pawn along the lines of the preceding note.

49...♘xg4 50 ♕e2 ♕c1+ 51 ♔g2 ♕f4 52 hxg6 ♔xg6 53 ♕f3 ♔g5 54 ♘f5 ♕d2+ 55 ♔g1 h5 56 ♘g7

56 ♘xd6 ♕c1+ 57 ♔g2 ♕c2+ 58 ♔g1 ♕c5+ loses the knight.

56...♕c1+ 57 ♔g2 ♕b2+ 58 ♔g1 ♕a1+ 59 ♔g2 ♕a2+ **White resigned**.

Beliavsky - Ehlvest
Olympiad, Erevan 1996

Together with material equality, White has a positional advantage, though in view of the limited pawn material he is not guaranteed a win. But obviously White also has a psychological advantage: he dominates the position and all that remains for Black is to exercise patience.

White's hopes are linked to the win of kingside pawns, he needs only to "sell" the c5 pawn as dearly as possible. It is obvious that he can then guarantee his king a "pass" to the weakened kingside. First it is necessary to occupy himself with the f5 pawn: he wins, if he manages to place his bishop on e6, his king on d5 and his pawn on h3. The question is this, how to deflect the black king from the e6 square?

49 ♔c3!

"Such moves provide aesthetic satisfaction. It seems that the king

needs to go right, but it goes left (A.Beliavsky).

White sets about realising the first part of his plan—to strengthen the positions of his king and bishop to the maximum.

49...♔c6 50 ♔b4 ♔c7 51 h3!

Another important, imperceptible, finesse—it is important to take away the g4 square from the black bishop.

51...♔c6 52 ♗b3 ♔c7 53 ♗e6 ♔c6 54 ♔c4 ♔c7 55 ♔d5

Zugzwang. In order not to allow the further advance of the white king, Black has to give up the f5 pawn.

55...♗h5

After 55...♗h7 56 ♗f7 is again zugzwang.

56 ♗xf5 ♗f7+ 57 ♔d4

But now begins the realisation of the second part of the plan—the king heads for the h4 square to attack the kingside pawns.

57...♔c6 58 ♗e4+ ♔c7 59 ♔e3 ♗e6 60 ♗g2 ♗f7 61 ♔f2 ♗g6 62 ♔g3 ♔d7 63 ♗d5 ♔c7 64 ♔g4 ♔d7 65 ♔h4 ♔c7 66 ♗f3

66...♗f7?

No wonder, after such protracted manoeuvres, though not lacking fine points, he goes astray. It would be better for the bishop to stay on g6 and continue to move the king: 66...♔d8 (on 66...♔d7? there is the winning manoeuvre 67 ♗h5 ♗e4 68 ♗g4+ and the king proceeds to the h6 pawn) 67 ♗h5 ♗f5 68 ♗f7 ♔c7! (after 68...♔e7?! 69 ♗d5 ♗g6 70 ♔g4 ♔d7 71 f5! ♗e8 72 ♗g8 ♔c6 73 ♗h7 ♔c5 74 ♗g6 ♗d7 75 ♔h5 ♔d6 76 ♔xh6 ♔e5 77 h4 arises the losing position which occurs in the game) 69 ♔h5 ♗xh3 70 ♗d5 ♔d7 71 ♔xh6 ♔e7 72 ♔g6 ♗c8 73 ♗e4 ♗h3 74 c6 ♗f1 75 ♗f5 ♔d6 76 ♔f6 ♔c6 77 ♔e7 ♔c7 78 ♗e6 ♗d3 and Black achieves a draw. This analysis only demonstrates what sort of effort is required from J.Ehlvest to keep in check the psychological pressure from A.Belyavsky.

67 ♗h5 ♗c4 68 ♗g6 ♗e2 69 ♗f5 ♔c6 70 ♗g4 ♗d3 71 ♔h5 ♔xc5 72 ♔xh6 ♔d4 73 ♗d7!

The careless 73 f5? would lead to a draw as the black king has the time, step by step, to catch up with the h-pawn: 73...♔e5 74 ♔g6 ♗e4 75 h4 ♔f4 76 ♗h3 ♔g3 77 h5 ♔h3 78 h6 ♔g4.

73...♔e4 74 f5! ♔e5 75 h4! ♔d6

Upon 75...♗xf5 76 ♗xf5 ♔xf5 77 h5, the white passed pawn runs on.

76 ♗e6 ♔e7 77 ♔g7 ♗e2 78 ♗f7 Black resigned.

9 Seek and Ye Shall Find

Often in critical situations the fate of a position is decided by the one and only correct, quite often even study-like, move. Therefore, setting about illustrating this theme it is appropriate to quote the great Lasker: "To defence we apply the evangelical words: seek and ye shall find. Trust in principles, do not allow yourself to be blinded with real and imaginary threats, honestly investigate and zealously try all means to find the threatened dangers, and do not yield until the end of this task—this is the moral code of defence".

Let us add that the same approach is appropriate also for achievement of an advantage. If there is only the slightest chance, even if associated with with colossal difficulties—fight! It is important not to prematurely lose heart and not hastily resign even in the most desperate situations. The nature of chess is such that, thanks to its inexhaustible possibilities and imagination, it is possible for players to count even on miracles. I believed in this, even in the years of my chess youth, thanks to the example of the game Smyslov-Petrosian from the Candidates tournament 1953.

Smyslov - Petrosian
Candidates tournament,
Zürich 1953

In this position, V.Smyslov adjourned the game, giving his opponent the opportunity to convince himself of the futility of resistance. And, indeed, despite the material equality, Black's position looks quite hopeless since there is no apparent means of holding back the passed d-pawn. However, a miracle occurs...

41...♕a2+ 42 ♔g3 ♕d2 43 d6

After 43 ♕e6+ ♔h8 44 d6 there is a perpetual check—44...♘e2+ 45 ♔g4 ♕f4+ 46 ♔h5 ♕xh2+.

43...♕e1+ 44 ♔g4 ♘d3 45 ♕d5+

After 45 d7 h5+! 46 ♔xh5 ♕xe7 47 ♕d5+ ♔h7 48 d8=♕, White gets a new queen, but on the spot loses the old one—48...♘f4+!.

45...♔h7 46 d7

46...♕e5!!

Here is the wonderful resource found by Petrosian! Mate is threatened in two ways: 47...♘f2+ 48 ♔h4 ♕xh2 mate or 47...♕f4+ 48 ♔h5 g6 mate, while after 47 ♕d4 ♕xh2, perpetual check is inevitable.

It is astonishing that V.Smyslov, who in those years was the main pretender to the world championship, does not find anything better than to reconcile himself to a draw.

47 ♕xd3+ cxd3 48 d8=♕ Draw.

After 48...h5+ Black gives perpetual check: 49 ♔h3 (there is no changing matters by 49 ♔h4 ♕xh2+ 50 ♔g5 ♕e5+ 51 ♔h4 ♕h2+, provided Black does not want to achieve more — 50...♕xg2+!?) 49...♕f5+ 50 ♔g3 ♕e5+ 51 ♔h3 (losing is 51 ♔f2? ♕e2+ 52 ♔g3 d2) 51...♕f5+. And if Black attempts to play for a win, 48...♕e2 49 ♔h3 d2, White himself forces a draw: 50 ♕d7 d1=♕ 51 ♕f5+.

But the reader should not rush into putting a full stop. The worst is still not over. On returning home, Petrosian demonstrated this game to students of one of the Moscow Institutes, confidently beating off surprise attacks by his audience. But then suddenly came a timid questioner: "Tigran, what if 47 ♕d6 ?"

This time Petrosian was stumped—in short, the h2 pawn is "seen" through X-Ray by the queen on d6. Tigran helplessly spread out his arms and pronounced: "This, I didn't notice, nor did Smyslov". It becomes clear, that there is no saving the game—after 47...♘f2+ 48 ♔h4 g5+ 49 ♔h5 the king hides from the checks.

It remains to add that the name of the author of the move 47...♕d6!!, honoured trainer of Georgia R.Turkestanishvili, became well known only in 2000 (when he told this story in the Russian magazine *64—Chess Review*).

Remembering this story and basically hoping for a miracle, I once was in no hurry to resign four(!!) pawns down against M.Tal himself. In short, based on the "reverse"—also in a winning position one must be able to find the only move. And the miracle happened—Tal did not find "his" move...

Tal - Gufeld
Jurmala 1977

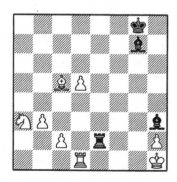

Of course, Black's initiative is not worth four pawns and, if M.Tal were not "greedy" and let go of part of his material by 34 ♘c4! ♖xc2 35 d6 ♗d7 36 ♗d4 ♗c6+ 37 ♔g1, then he would undoubtedly win. But what does not happen in chess? Even with the greats.

34 ♖d3?

Misha plays solid-like and Black's initiative becomes so effective that the improbable happens—White lets slip the win. The further play is reminiscent of an entertaining vaudeville, though without the traditional happy ending.

34...♖e1+ 35 ♗g1 ♗f5 36 ♖e3 ♖a1! 37 ♘c4 ♗d4 38 ♖g3+ ♔h7 39 h4 ♖c1! 40 ♘d2

On 40 ♔h2 he has the strong reply 40...♗e4! 41 ♖g2! ♗xg1+ (losing is 41...♗xg2? 42 ♗xd4 ♗xd5 43 ♘e3) 42 ♖xg1 ♖xc2+ 43 ♔g3 ♗xd5 44 ♘e3 ♖c3 45 ♔f4 ♗xb3, with a drawn ending.

40...♗xc2 41 d6 ♖d1!

The position already assumes a drawn character.

42 ♘c4 ♗f2!

42...♗xb3? 43 ♖xb3 ♗xg1 was mistaken because of 44 ♖b7+ ♔h6 45 ♔g2 and White has great chances of victory.

43 ♖g4

Also after 43 ♖g2 ♗e4 44 ♔h2 ♗xg2 45 ♗xf2 ♗d5 the game should end in a draw.

43...♗xb3 44 ♘b2

Also to a draw leads 44 ♔h2 ♗xg1+ 45 ♖xg1 ♖d4 46 ♘a5 ♗e6 47 ♘b7 ♗c8 48 ♖b1 ♔g6. After the text the draw is still there were it not for Black's forthcoming terrible mistake which is nothing short of masochism.

44...♗d5+ 45 ♔h2 ♗xg1+ 46 ♖xg1 ♖d2+ 47 ♔g3 ♖xb2??

Capitulating to matter over mind! Right up to now, I just don't understand: how could I fold up in this way? In short, Black "takes revenge" for 34 ♖d3?, forgetting the old truth—greed will be punished.

And good fortune was so close—47...♗b3 or 47...♗e6 and the draw is at hand.

Now, however, an endgame arises which is theoretically winning for White.

48 d7 ♖b8 49 ♖d1 ♖g8+ 50 ♔f4 ♗e6 51 d8=♕ ♖xd8 52 ♖xd8

Here the game was adjourned and adjudicated a win for White.

But this example is rather exceptional from the "negative" point of view. Not infrequently the search for achieving an advantage is crowned with finding a study-like solution.

Gufeld - Klovans
Moscow 1966

This game was played in the USSR Team Championship. Analysis of the adjourned position continued until deep in the night. The results of this were not comforting: despite White's material advantage, he did not manage to find an effective means of averting the threat of mate on g3. Therefore the decision was taken to force a draw by perpetual check.

But a miracle occurred! Dropping in to me in the morning, a smiling Efim Geller quietly made the move 43 ♗f4!! and...suddenly there was enlightenment. The bishop defends the g3 square and Black can resign. After 43...exf4 44 ℤd8+ ♚e7 45 ℤe8+ ♚d6 46 ℤd1+ ℤcd3 47 ℤxd3+ ℤxd3 48 ℤd8+ he is left a rook down, while 43...♝xg1 44 ℤf7+ ♚g8 45 ℤe7 leads to mate on e8.

When the move **43 ♝f4!!** was "shown" to Klovans, all the participants present gathered round. Janis went into deep thought for nearly an hour, but he could not find a way to save himself.

43...ℤhd3 44 ℤxd3 ℤxd3 45 ℤh1 ♚e7 46 ℤh8 Black resigned.

Dreev - Vaganian
Budapest 1996

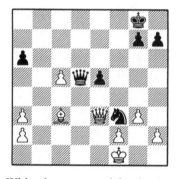

White has a material advantage, though his extra pawns are not felt: one of them is doubled, while the one on c5 requires defence. At the same time the black pieces are active, leaving only the knight to be reinforced by the pawn advance ...e5-e4, after which the threat ...♕d5-d1 might become unpleasant. What can White do? You see, he will not succeed in ousting the knight with the king from e2 because of a check on g1. And yet there is a resource!

34 ♚g2!!

"A move which wins the game", commented Alexéi Dreev. "I must say that, in playing this, I experienced great aesthetic satisfaction—it is not easy to put your king in the line of a discovered check. Now not only does it succeed in parrying Black's idea but also finishes the harvest with the knight".

34...♘d4+

The double check 34...♘e1+ is not terrible: 35 ♚h3 ♕e6+ 36 g4 h5 37 f3 and White wins the e5 pawn.

35 f3 ♕xa2+

After 35...♕xc5 36 ♝xd4 exd4 37 ♕e8+ ♕f8 38 ♕e6+ ♚h8 39 ♕xa6, White creates a dangerous distant passed a-pawn.

36 ♕d2 ♕xd2+

Objectively speaking, it is worth trying his luck in the queen ending: 36...♕d5 37 ♝xd4 exd4 38 c6 ♕xc6 39 ♕xd4. However, even in the minor piece ending, all is not lost.

37 ♝xd2 ♚f7 38 ♝c3

After 38 ♝e3 ♘c2 39 ♚f2 ♘xa3 Black is out of danger.

38...♘c6 39 ♚h3! g5

In the event of 39...♚e6 40 ♚g4 ♚d5 41 f4 exf4 42 ♚xf4 g6 43 ♚g5, the king breaks through Black's lines.

40 ♚g4 ♚g6 41 f4

After 41 h4 gxh4 42 ♚xh4 h5 there are inevitable further exchanges and moreover White has to reckon on the presence of the light-squared "drawing" corner for the a-pawn, with a dark-squared bishop.

41...h5+

Also on a passive stance after 41...exf4 42 gxf4 gxf4 43 ♚xf4 ♚f7, White should win—44 ♚f5 ♚e7 45 a4! ♚f7 46 ♝f6 ♘b4 47 ♝g5 etc.

42 ♚f3 exf4 43 gxf4 g4+ 44 ♚e4 h4 45 f5+ ♚g5 46 f6 ♚g6

On 46...♘d8 the second thrust, 47 c6, is decisive.

47 ♔f4 Black resigned.

Now we look at examples on the theme of miraculous salvation. In the previous game we have seen how hard it is to place one's own king in check! But this also happened in a duel between two world champions.

Xie Jun - Chiburdanidze
Olympiad, Moscow 1994

Black has an extra pawn, but the opponent's pieces are ideally placed. In view of this White has to reckon on Black's intention to oust the queen from its central position. White's reply, not giving up a pawn, suggests itself...

65 ♔h3?

Alas...the natural move turns out to be a mistake, now Black loses.

65...♕e5 66 ♕d7 (after 66 ♕c4 or 66 ♕b3 Black exchange queens— 66...♕c3+) **66...♕e3+ 67 ♔g2 ♕e2+ 68 ♔g1 ♕xg4+ 69 ♔f1 ♕f5+ 70 ♔g2 ♕e4+ 71 ♔f2 ♕a8 72 ♕c7 ♕d5 73 ♕c8+ ♔f7 74 ♘c7 ♕d2+ 75 ♔f1 ♕d1+ White resigned**.

Meanwhile there was a way to save the game! It is achieved by the paradoxical **65 ♔g1!!**—White gives up a pawn, and that even with check! After **65...♕xg4+ 66 ♔h1!**

White maintains the queen in an ideal position, where, in tandem with the knight, it works smoothly. But, on the move of the king, 66...♔h7??, White forces mate: 67 ♕d7+! ♔g6 68 ♘f8+ ♔h5 69 ♕e8+ etc. And in the event of 66...a5 there is a perpetual check: 67 ♕a8+! ♔f7 68 ♕f8+! ♔g6 69 ♕e8+ ♔f5 70 ♘g7+! ♗xg7 71 ♕d7+ ♔f4 72 ♕a4+ ♔f3 73 ♕d1+. An original square circle! It remains to add that, if the g4 pawn is declined, Black also cannot oust the queen— 65...♕e5 66 ♕c4.

But possibly Xie Jun would have found such an unusual king move if she had been familiar with the tail-piece of the following game.

Michalchishin - G.Garcia
Cienfuegos 1981

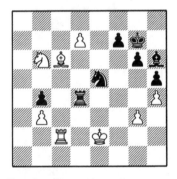

Despite the active placement of his pieces, Black's position looks suspect: he is tied down by the threat of the white pawn on d7 to promote to a queen. But how can he get at the pawn? No good is 43...♖d6, in view of 44 ♘c4! ♘xc4 45 bxc4! ♔f6 46 c5. On 43...♔f8 there is 44 ♗d5 ♔e7 45 ♖c8 and, for the d7 pawn, Black has to part with the exchange: 45...♖d2+ 46 ♔f1 ♖d1+ 47 ♔g2 ♖d2+ 48 ♔h3 ♘xd7 49 ♖c7 ♖xd5 50 ♘xd5+ ♔d6

51 ♖a7 ♔xd5 52 ♖xd7+ ♔e6 53 ♖d4, though there are still chances of a draw.

The decision of G.Garcia strikes one as paradoxical. There followed **43...♔h8!!** and, surprisingly, A.Michalchishin, bowing to the inevitable, offered a draw. Indeed White's pretensions can only be linked to **44 ♖c5**, but after **44...♖d2+ 45 ♔f1 ♖d1+ 46 ♔g2 ♖d2+ 47 ♔h3 ♘g4** he has to reconcile himself to a draw by perpetual check: **48 ♖c2 ♖xc2 49 d8=♕+ ♔h7 50 ♗g2 ♘f2+ 51 ♔h2 ♘g4+**.

Kir.Georgiev - Smagin
Yugoslavia 1995

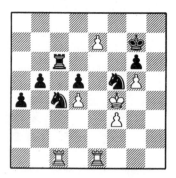

On the material plane Black has everything in order, though he will have to give up a knight for the e7 pawn. But in this case the activity of White's rooks can become dangerous. For example: 42...♘fd6 43 e8=♕ ♘xe8 44 ♖xe8 ♔f7 45 ♖ce1 ♖c7 46 ♖h8 etc. In short it needed thinking about. And a miracle occurred! In any case, even S.Smagin himself could not explain from where enlightenment suddenly came.

42...♘b2!!

The maximum accepted standard exclamation mark is clearly insufficient here. Not only is the rook under attack, the pawn can also be promoted to a queen: but one little observation—in this case White forces perpetual check: 43 e8=♕ ♘d3+ 44 ♔g4 ♘f2+ 45 ♔f4 ♘d3+, while on 43 ♖cd1 Black defends by 43...♖c8.

This jump of the knight so shocked the Bulgarian grandmaster, that he moved his king a little way away, **43 ♔g4**, and after **43...♘d3 44 e8=♕ ♘f2+** the game ended in a draw by perpetual check. It's funny, that after 44 ♖cd1 or 44 ♖xc6 the knight "works" from the other side: 44...♘f2+ 45 ♔f4 ♘d3+.

Meanwhile White could have set Black more complicated, possibly insurmountable, problems with the no less extravagant 43 ♖e3!. Black has to reconcile himself to the loss of a knight, hoping to mobilise his passed pawn pair, but, as shown by I.Zaitsev, this could prove insufficient to save himself.

a) 43...♘xe7 (the direct capture allows White to win the g6 pawn, obtaining his own passed pawn) 44 ♖xe7+ ♔f8 45 ♖xc6 ♔xe7 46 ♖xg6 a3 47 ♔f5! (combining an attack on the enemy king with surveillance of the passed pawn, White gets the g-pawn into action; after 47 ♖a6 ♘a4, Black is left with chances of saving himself) 47...a2 48 ♖e6+ ♔f8 49 ♖a6! ♘a4 50 ♔f6 ♔e8 51 ♖e6+! ♔d7 52 ♖e1 b4 53 g6 and White comes first in the pawn race.

b) 43...♖e6 (thanks to this roundabout manoeuvre Black retains the g6 pawn) 44 ♖c7 ♘d3+!? (it is important to divert the rook from the open file) 45 ♖xd3 ♖xe7 46 ♖xe7+ ♘xe7 47 ♖a3! (this is clearer than 47 ♖c3 b4 48 ♖c7 ♔f8, though even here winning is 49 ♖a7!—49...b3 50 ♖xa4 ♘c6 51 ♖a6 ♘xd4 52 ♖f6+! ♔g7 53 ♔e5 b2 54 ♖b6 ♘xf3+ 55

♔f4 etc. or 49...a3 50 ♖a8+ ♚g7 51 ♚e5 with a win) 47...♘c6 48 ♖c3 ♘xd4 49 ♚e5 and the king invades the enemy position.

But all this was revealed as a result of many hours' analysis, while, in the conditions of a real game, the draw achieved by S.Smagin came to be a worthy payment for the miraculous 42...♘b2!!

And, to conclude, "a miracle square" from a game by the world's greats.

Anand - Kasparov
Linares 1999

At first sight White's position is worse everywhere. Black has an extra exchange, a more active placement of pieces and visions of attack, while the previously intended 27 ♘f5+ ♚f7 28 ♕xd5+ ♗xd5 29 ♘d6+ etc., is ruined after 27...♕xf5! 28 gxf5 ♘b3+ 29 ♚d1 ♗f3+! 30 ♚e1 ♘xd2 31 ♚xd2 ♗g4, transferring to a technical endgame. Nevertheless fighting optimism triumphs—as in the proverb: "seek and ye shall find". And V.Anand does find!

27 ♘c3!!

He sacrifices a piece, transferring to an ending with definite practical chances for a draw. In order to realise the idea of exchanging queens, White places an extra barrier on the c-file.

27...bxc3 28 ♘f5+ ♚f7

Black can leave White not with a knight but a bishop—28...♚f8 29 ♗h6+ ♚e8 30 ♕xd5 ♗xd5 31 ♘d6+ ♚d7 32 ♘xc8 ♚xc8, but then White retains the g4 pawn.

29 ♕xd5+ ♗xd5 30 ♘d6+ ♚g6 31 ♘xc8 ♚xg5

Kasparov doesn't insert 31... cxb2+. It turns out that the doubled pawns rather get in White's way.

32 ♘b6 ♗e6! 33 bxc3 ♚xg4 34 ♚b2 ♚f4 35 ♚a3

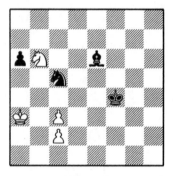

V.Anand had this position in mind when sacrificing the knight by 27 ♘c3!.

White's hope is to win the only black pawn on a6, keeping in mind also the a1 square and not allowing Black to exchange knights (the light-squared bishop!).

35...a5?!

The obvious (not allowing the king to b4!), but not the best move.

Circumstances have changed so much, that it must have affected even G.Kasparov. After 35...♚e5! 36 ♚b4 ♘b7 (or 36...♚d6 37 ♚a5 ♚c6) 37 c4 ♚d6 38 c5+ ♚c6, Black wins.

36 ♘a4 ♘e4?

As we have seen repeatedly, one mistake leads to another. And again Black misses a win. It is achieved, as pointed out by G.Kasparov himself, by means of 36...♘d7 37 ♘b2 ♘b6. Now on 38 ♘d3+ Black reforms by 38...♔e3 39 ♘c5 ♗f7 40 ♘b3 ♘c4+, and no good is 38 c4 ♗xc4 39 ♘xc4 ♘xc4+ 40 ♔b3 (or 40 ♔a4 ♔e4 41 ♔b5 ♔d4) 40...♘e5! 41 ♔a4 ♘c6.

37 ♘b2 ♘xc3 38 ♘d3+ ♔e3 39 ♘c5 ♗f5

To a draw leads 39...♗f7 40 ♘b3 ♗xb3 41 cxb3 ♔d4 42 b4 a4 43 b5! ♔c5 44 b6 ♔xb6 45 ♔b4.

40 ♔b2!

Losing is 40 ♘b3? a4 41 ♘c5 ♗xc2 42 ♔b2 ♔d2.

40...♘d5 41 ♘b7 a4

42 c4!

V.Anand goes along the only path. Deviations from it of the type 42 ♘a3 ♗xc2 43 ♘c5 ♘c3 or 42 ♘c5 ♘b6 43 ♔a3 ♗xc2 44 ♔b4 ♔d4 45 ♔b5 a3, lose.

42...♘b6 43 ♘d6

On 43 ♘c3 could follow 43...a3 44 c5 ♘c4 45 ♔b3 ♘d4 46 ♘d6 ♗c2+.

43...♗d3 44 c5

After 44 ♔a3 ♔d4 45 ♔b4 ♗c2 46 ♘b5+ ♔d3 47 ♘c3 a3 48 ♘a2 ♘xc4, this pawn is lost.

44...♘d5 45 ♔a3 ♗c2

After 45...♔d4 46 ♔xa4 ♔xc5 47 ♘b7+ draw.

46 ♘b5!

White does not allow the black king to come close—after 46 c6 ♘c7 47 ♘c4+ ♔d4 48 ♘b6 ♘b5+ 49 ♔b4 a3, he loses.

46...♘e7 47 ♘a7??

Anand slips at the moment when his heroic resistance could have been rewarded with a draw by the simple 47 ♘c3! ♔d4 48 ♘xa4.

47...♔d4 48 c6 ♘d5

49 ♘b5+

For connoisseurs of beauty, it is worth drawing our attention to the cunning 49 ♔b2! and in the event of 49...♗d1?, as pointed out by S.Shipov, White constructs a beautiful position, 50 ♘b5+ ♔c5 (50...♔c4 51 c7) 51 ♘c3 a3+ 52 ♔a1 ♘xc3 53 c7 ♗g4 54 c8=♕+ ♗xc8 stalemate!! But of course Black is not obliged to take part in this "cooperation". 49...♗f5 might also follow.

49...♔c5 50 c7 ♗f5 and White resigned.

To test the world champion after 51 ♔xa4 ♘b6+ 52 ♔a5 ♘c4+ 53 ♔a6 ♗c8+ 54 ♔a7 ♔xb5 makes no sense.